COVERING MCCARTHYISM

How the *Christian Science Monitor* Handled Joseph R. McCarthy, 1950–1954

Lawrence N. Strout

Contributions to the Study of Mass Media and Communications, Number 58

GREENWOOD PRESS
Westport, Connecticut • London

Library of Congress Cataloging-in-Publication Data

Strout, Lawrence N.
   Covering McCarthyism : how the Christian Science monitor handled Joseph R. McCarthy, 1950–1954 / Lawrence N. Strout.
      p.   cm.—(Contributions to the study of mass media and communications, ISSN 0732–4456 ; no. 58.)
   ISBN 0–313–31091–2 (alk. paper)
   1. McCarthy, Joseph, 1908–1957—Relations with journalists.
   2. Anti-communist movements—United States—Press coverage.
   3. Press and politics—United States—History—20th century.
   4. Christian Science monitor.   I. Title.   II. Series.
   E748.M143S76   1999
   973.921′092—dc21   99–21799

British Library Cataloguing in Publication Data is available.

Copyright © 1999 by Lawrence N. Strout

All rights reserved. No portion of this book may be reproduced, by any process or technique, without the express written consent of the publisher.

Library of Congress Catalog Card Number: 99–21799
ISBN: 0–313–31091–2
ISSN: 0732–4456

First published in 1999

Greenwood Press, 88 Post Road West, Westport, CT 06881
An imprint of Greenwood Publishing Group, Inc.
www.greenwood.com

Printed in the United States of America

The paper used in this book complies with the Permanent Paper Standard issued by the National Information Standards Organization (Z39.48–1984).

10 9 8 7 6 5 4 3 2 1

Copyright Acknowledgments

Materials from *The Christian Science Monitor* and the Church History Department of The First Church of Christ, Scientist, in Boston, Massachusetts, used by permisison of the copyright owner.

DISCARDED

Covering McCarthyism

**Recent Titles in
Contributions to the Study of Mass Media and Communications**

Censorship of Expression in the 1980s: A Statistical Survey
John B. Harer and Steven R. Harris

The U.S. Media and the Middle East: Image and Perception
Yahya R. Kamalipour

Advertising, Alcohol Consumption, and Mortality: An Empirical Investigation
Joseph C. Fisher and Peter A. Cook

The Press in Times of Crisis
Lloyd E. Chiasson, Jr.

Native Americans in the News: Images of Indians in the Twentieth Century Press
Mary Ann Weston

Rights vs. Responsibilities: The Supreme Court and the Media
Elizabeth Blanks Hindman

The Press on Trial: Crimes and Trials as Media Events
Lloyd Chiasson Jr., editor

Personalities and Products: A Historical Perspective on Advertising in America
Edd Applegate

Taking Their Political Place: Journalists and the Making of an Occupation
Patricia L. Dooley

Developing Sanity in Human Affairs
Susan Presby Kodish and Robert P. Holston, editors

The Significance of the Printed Word in Early America: Colonists' Thoughts on the Role of the Press
Julie Hedgepeth Williams

Discovering Journalism
Warren G. Bovée

This book is in memory of my grandfather,
William Lewis Strout

This book is dedicated to my parents,
Donald Leroy Strout and Grace Marion (Lajoie) Strout

Contents

Acknowledgments	ix
Introduction	xi
Joseph R. McCarthy and McCarthyism	xii
Christian Science Monitor	xiii
Richard L. Strout	xvii
1. 1950: McCarthyism Begins	1
Prelude to McCarthyism	1
The *Monitor*'s Pre-McCarthy Cold War Coverage	5
McCarthy's Lincoln Day Speech	7
Tydings' Investigation	9
Reaction to the Tydings Report	18
Amerasia Controversy at the *Monitor*	20
Perspective on the Midterm Elections	22
Communism in America	25
Media Self-Critique	26
2. 1951: McCarthy's Character Assassinations	35
Another Anti-Communism Measure	35
Gillette Subcommittee Investigation	36
Benton Resolution	38
MacArthur, Marshall, Acheson, and Jessup	40

	Republican Party Plans	45
	Rosenberg Case	46
	Media Self-Critique	46
3.	1952: McCarthy in the National Spotlight	53
	Lattimore and the Loyalty Probes	53
	McCarthyism: The Fight for America	57
	1952 Elections	59
	Benton Resolution Resolved	72
	Letters to the *Monitor*	75
	McCarthy's 1953 Strategy	77
	Media Self-Critique	77
4.	1953: McCarthy versus the Press and the Eisenhower Administration	87
	The *Monitor* Pressures Strout	87
	The *Monitor*, McCarthy's Name, and the Term "McCarthyism"	92
	Wechsler Case	92
	Foreign Affairs	96
	The Rosenbergs' Execution	106
	Joseph C. Harsch vs. the Roman Catholic Church	107
	Media Self-Critique	109
5.	1954: McCarthy's Demise	121
	Prelude to Army-McCarthy	121
	Army-McCarthy Hearings	125
	Censure	131
	Postcensure	135
	McCarthy's Death	136
	A Communist at the *Monitor*?	137
6.	The Legacy: The *Christian Science Monitor* and Joseph R. McCarthy	147
Selected Bibliography		157
	Books	157
	Magazines and Newspaper Articles	160
	Scholarly Articles	162
	Dissertations and Master's Theses	163
	Unpublished Letters, Memorandums, and Personal Communications	163
Index		167

Acknowledgments

Countless people should be thanked for having a part in putting this book together. But, I will confine my list to the following individuals.

Special thanks to Dr. Alan Strout who provided me unlimited access to his father's (Richard L. Strout) papers. Also, special thanks to Dr. Marilyn Young and Dr. Neil Jumonville for their feedback while writing the book. Thanks also to Dr. "Ed" Wotring for assisting my acceptance into graduate school; Dr. David Davies for emotional support; Dr. Joseph McKerns for being an inspiration; and Ms. Yvonne C. von Fettweis for assistance in acquiring copyright permission from The First Church of Christ, Scientist, in Boston.

And finally, to my wife, Penny Rodrique, and daughter, Nicole Vincent, thanks for being you.

INTRODUCTION

The *Christian Science Monitor*, particularly during the McCarthy era, was a highly influential newspaper at home and abroad though circulation figures (approximately 167,000 per day) did not match those of other prestige and popular press newspapers, such as the *New York Times* (341,000) and the *Los Angeles Times* (573,000).[1] This book focuses on the *Monitor*'s coverage of Joseph R. McCarthy, from the Senator's famous Lincoln Day speech on February 9, 1950 through his censure by the U.S. Senate on December 2, 1954.[2] It documents the *Monitor*'s coverage of McCarthy and investigates the internal decision-making process that led to the resolution of editorial policy disputes at the newspaper. This reveals how the *Monitor* dealt with the pressures associated with McCarthyism, both editorially and with personnel.

The *Monitor*, in books written during and after the McCarthy era,[3] has been credited as one of the early and consistent critics of the Wisconsin Senator. In fact, after Edward R. Murrow's *See It Now* program about McCarthy on CBS in March 1954, the famous broadcaster conceded that he was now counted among several newspapers, magazines, and broadcast radio and television stations singled out by McCarthy for criticism. The *Monitor* was on the list Murrow read aloud.[4] And, just after the McCarthy era, *Time* magazine wrote that "the *Monitor* was one of the few U.S. dailies that consistently and searchingly matched balancing facts against the Wisconsin Senator's strident fictions."[5] However, one of the most widely quoted books written exclusively about press coverage of McCarthy, *Joe McCarthy and the Press* by Edwin R. Bayley, questioned whether the *Monitor* ever adopted as strong a stance against McCarthy as other newspapers. In addition, the book did not mention the *Monitor*'s coverage following the initial Wheeling, West Virginia speech by McCarthy and the Tydings subcommittee investigation of McCarthy's charges of Communists in the U.S. State Department. Further, Bayley quoted from an interview he conducted with Richard L. Strout of the *Monitor*. Strout told Bayley that the *Monitor* "never did adopt a strong editorial position against McCarthy" and that "the senator or his supporters put a lot of pressure on the paper's board."[6] These conflicting views concerning one of the nation's most respected newspapers led to this book.

Covering McCarthyism: How the Christian Science Monitor *Handled Joseph R. McCarthy, 1950–1954* does for depth what *Joe McCarthy and the Press* did for breadth regarding press coverage of McCarthy. Bayley's work effectively gives the reader a feel for what newspapers, large and small, wrote about McCarthy. However, in such a sweeping study, general conclusions are confined to the press as a whole with little to be learned about the most prestigious newspapers of the time. Conversely, this book looks in-depth at the McCarthy coverage in the *Monitor*, a newspaper with considerable power to influence that was held in high esteem by government officials, businessmen, and readers throughout the world.

Additionally, Bayley relies on anecdotal evidence—interviews with reporters, editors, and the like—in recounting press activities. The interviews were conducted a quarter of a century after the McCarthy era. Memories, as we all know, are fraught with discrepancies over time. This book, on the other hand, relies primarily on written documentation—intra-office memos, letters, and the like—in identifying the effect McCarthyism had on a top-notch newspaper.

Documentation of the *Monitor*'s handling of McCarthyism adds to the understanding of the mass media and its coverage of this controversial Senator. The information may be used by researchers who are continuing to piece together the puzzle of why McCarthyism flourished, and may be used by mass communication and history instructors in helping to explain to students what happened during the McCarthy era. The "small picture" of the *Monitor*'s handling of McCarthyism helps in the creation of the "big picture" regarding the media's coverage of McCarthy. This book illuminates the struggle *Monitor* reporters and editors went through dealing with the newspaper's stance against Communism, and its conservative leanings, and, at the same time, its opposition to McCarthy.

JOSEPH R. MCCARTHY AND MCCARTHYISM

The term "McCarthyism" was derived from the name of Joseph R. McCarthy, a United States Senator from Wisconsin from 1946 till his death,

Introduction

May 2, 1957. There is one generally accepted explanation for the creation of the term "McCarthyism." *Washington Post* satirist/cartoonist Herbert Block (Herblock) is given credit by most people for using the term first. Herblock's cartoon of March 29, 1950 in the *Post* showed the GOP elephant being prodded by right wingers of the party toward a barrel on the top of a stack of tar-dripping buckets. The barrel has the word "McCarthyism" written on it and the elephant asks, "You mean I'm supposed to stand on that?"[7] Dean Walte G. Muelder of the Boston University School of Theology used the term early in more general terms. According to the Associated Press, Muelder described "McCarthyism" as a "spiritual disease" in the country that allowed McCarthy to thrive.[8]

McCarthy was first elected to the Senate in 1946, reelected in 1952, but died before serving out his second term. As mentioned earlier, this book about the *Monitor*'s McCarthy era coverage focuses on the period between McCarthy's famous Lincoln Day speech in February 1950 and his censure by the Senate in December 1954.

CHRISTIAN SCIENCE MONITOR

Understanding the history and purpose behind the creation of the *Monitor* is important when evaluating its editorial policies and practices.

Mary Baker Eddy, head of The First Church of Christ, Scientist, in Boston, Massachusetts, founded the *Christian Science Monitor* in 1908. The publication of the *Monitor* was put under the direction of the Christian Science Publishing Society, which had been created on January 28, 1889.

Archibald McClellan was named the first editor of the *Monitor*. He was a Kent State University law school graduate with newspaper experience who also was one of the Directors of the Mother Church. McClellan indicated from the beginning that the new publication would not be a church newsletter or a propaganda sheet for the church. Rather, the *Monitor* would have its readers as "its only beneficiaries" and would publish "all the news it is worth while reading."[9]

The first issue of the *Christian Science Monitor* was published on November 25, 1908. Mrs. Eddy communicated to the readers of the new newspaper through an editorial:

I have given the name to all the Christian Science periodicals. The first was the *Christian Science Journal*, designed to put on record the divine Science of Truth. The second I entitled *Sentinel*, intended to hold guard over Truth, Life and Love; the third *Der Herald der Christian Science* to proclaim the universal activity and availability of truth; and next I named the *Monitor* to spread undivided the science that operates unspent. The object of the *Monitor* is to injure no man, but to bless all mankind.[10]

These principles laid out by the newspaper's founder, and particularly the final sentence, have been referred to repeatedly over the years as major decisions faced those running the day-to-day operations.

On the day of the first issue in late November 1908, 82,500 copies were printed and circulated. The intent was to get as many issues of the *Monitor* as possible circulated initially, with a printing run of about 38,800 issues for the second day.[11] One year later, on November 24, 1909, 250,000 copies of a 96-page anniversary issue were circulated. In an unsigned article on the front page, the *Monitor* again made it clear that covering spot news and just giving the readers the "facts" were not its intentions: "The *Monitor* not only seeks to keep its readers informed of events all over the world, but to *interpret* [italics added] those events in a way to show their relation to the great movements that are of service to the human race."[12] The newspaper kept its commitment to "interpretive" journalism even as "objectivity" became the ideal in the 1920s and beyond.[13]

Mrs. Eddy passed on December 3, 1910. About ten years later, an event of major significance to the future of the *Monitor* occurred. The controversy involved a power struggle between the Publishing Society's Board of Trustees and the Mother Church's Board of Directors. In March 1919 the Trustees filed suit attempting to prevent the Directors from having the power to remove Trustees. Not long after the suit was filed, the Massachusetts Supreme Judicial Court issued an interim injunction preventing removal of any of the Trustees. This effectively took away power the Directors (and the Mother Church) had over the *Monitor*. According to a book on the history of the *Monitor* by Erwin D. Canham, the *Monitor*'s circulation of 123,080 near the end of World War I fell to 20,939 by the time the suit was settled.[14]

In November 1921, the Massachusetts Supreme Judicial Court upheld the Directors and the (Mother) Church Manual (which had given the ultimate authority over the Trustees and the newspaper to the Directors). It took until the end of January 1922 to clear all the legal formalities, return control to the Directors, and install the founder of the American Society of Newspaper Editors (ASNE), Willis Abbot, as editor.[15] Abbot, perhaps surprisingly, had worked for the Hearst chain (plus many other newspapers and magazines) and resigned from the *Chicago American* staff after the paper reported that the sinking of the *Lusitania* was a legitimate action during war.[16] Abbot rebuilt the staff of the *Monitor*. By 1924, circulation climbed back to 100,000 and by 1930 the newspaper reached about 130,000.[17] In 1927, Abbot was appointed to the governing board of the *Monitor* and was involved in many groups that promoted responsible journalism and peace for the world.[18]

Introduction

xv

Perhaps the most outstanding editor that the *Monitor* has had in its history was Erwin D. Canham. Canham joined the staff in 1925, became a managing editor in 1940 and editor in 1945. As President of ASNE, Canham was also a strong voice in discussions about journalistic problems, and he became regarded as "an influential editor of a great newspaper."[19] Canham summarized the philosophy implemented originally by Dodds and carried forward by subsequent editors and managing editors: "The *Monitor* did not seek to withhold tragic or distasteful news from its readers. It did not suppress news of crime or disaster. It placed such news in perspective, recording such events modestly but factually, without giving them sensational display, and reserving its bigger headlines and larger space for events or situations of long-range importance to humanity."[20]

And, the Board of Directors made it clear to the staff of this daily newspaper that religion need not receive any special attention or be emphasized. Whether religious news (about Christian Scientists or other religions) should be carried would be decided according to the newsworthiness of the event.[21] Further, Canham informed his entire staff that whatever was printed in the *Monitor* (news stories, cartoons, columns, or editorials, etc.) would become directly associated with the paper's mission and goals: "Everything printed in the paper is considered by some readers to express the paper's considered policy, and within reason it does. Hence it must all fall within the range of the *Monitor*'s overall commitment."[22]

Despite the commitment to interpretive journalism identified in the first anniversary issue of the *Monitor*, Canham wrote in his book (after the McCarthy era) that he did not want people to think that interpretation meant "opinion." Canham described the *Monitor* as "profoundly conservative" or subscribing to "liberal humanitarianism" which "stands up very well" over time.[23]

During the McCarthy era, several men played an integral part in the management of the *Monitor*, besides the previously mentioned editor Erwin D. Canham. Roscoe Drummond started as a "cub" reporter with the paper in 1924, and worked his way up to executive editor from 1933 through 1939. From 1940 through 1953 (the later part being critical years during the McCarthy era), Drummond was Washington bureau chief. As bureau chief, he wrote the front-page column "State of the Nation," except for a few interruptions. In 1954, after serving a year as European Director of Information for the Marshall Plan, Drummond left the *Monitor* to become Washington, D.C. bureau chief for the *New York Herald Tribune*.[24] In 1953, William H. Stringer replaced Drummond as Washington bureau chief. Stringer was also a veteran of the *Monitor*. After Harvard Law School, Stringer joined the paper in 1935. He served as London bureau chief on two separate occasions, 1947–1951 and 1965–1967. From 1953 to 1964, he was

Washington bureau chief.[25] Other key personnel during the age of McCarthyism included American news managing editor Saville R. Davis and columnist Joseph C. Harsch. Harsch, early in the McCarthy era, wrote a front-page column (replacing Drummond for a time with the "State of the Nation"). From 1929 to 1943, Harsch was a Washington, D.C. correspondent and despite working for CBS, NBC, and ABC (radio and television networks) at different times for about 30 years, he always contributed to the *Monitor* as a columnist.[26] Harsch also has the distinction of having replaced longtime CBS radio reporter and commentator William Shirer after Shirer was fired by then vice president of CBS News Edward R. Murrow.[27]

Over the years the *Monitor* became one of the most respected newspapers in the country, known for its thoughtful and thought-provoking treatment of the news. The *Monitor*, particularly through the late 1960s and certainly from the 1930s through the 1950s, was consistently cited as one of the nation's best newspapers.

Correspondents surveyed in the 1930s picked the *New York Times*, the *Baltimore Sun*, and the *Christian Science Monitor* as the three most "reliable" and "fair" newspapers in the country.[28] Then in 1952, during the heart of the McCarthy era, Edward Bernays, a New York public relations leader, polled editors and civic leaders (separately) about the top newspapers. Publishers ranked the *Monitor* as the third-best newspaper in the country, just behind the *New York Times* and the *St. Louis Post-Dispatch*, and just ahead of the *Louisville Courier Journal* and the *Kansas City Star*. Opinion leaders were no less kind to the *Monitor*. Again, the *Times* topped the list followed by the *New York Herald*, the *Monitor*, the *Post-Dispatch* and the *Washington Post*.[29] And it should be noted that eight of the top ten on Bernays' list, including the *Monitor*, as well as the *Times*, the *Milwaukee Journal*, and the *Post*, ended up on Senator Joseph R. McCarthy's "left-wing" list.[30]

A poll of the nation's newspaper editors in 1960 placed the *Times*, the *Monitor*, and the *Milwaukee Journal* as the three best newspapers in the country. Still further, three separate polls (editors, publishers, and journalism professors) conducted in 1960 and 1961, rated the top daily newspapers in the country. Only five newspapers appeared in the top ten of each poll: the *Monitor*, the *Times*, the *Journal*, the *Post*, and the *Post-Dispatch*.[31] And finally, in early 1961, the *Saturday Review* commissioned a survey of journalism deans, full professors, and associate professors at 46 schools accredited by the American Council on Education for Journalism. The polling firm hired, Benson and Benson, Inc., of Princeton, New Jersey, asked the educators to identify the top newspapers in the country.[32] The *Times* again captured first, followed by the *Monitor*, the *Wall Street Journal*, the *Post-Dispatch*, and the *Journal*. Those voting for the *Monitor* as the top news-

Introduction

paper particularly appreciated the "absence of hysteria" and the paper's "broader conception of what's important."[33]

The *Monitor*'s standing in the newspaper industry and the respect it received during the McCarthy era are unquestioned and well documented. It is an important source for both mass communication scholars and historians to use in better understanding the media during the Cold War, and specifically during the McCarthy era. Veteran *Monitor* columnist Joseph C. Harsch perhaps stated it best: "My broadcasts on television got me many a flattering glance of recognition on the street and sometimes a sharp word of disapproval from a total stranger, but the opinions I expressed in my columns in the *Monitor* reached the White House and Congress."[34]

RICHARD L. STROUT

The private papers of Richard L. Strout (along with other sources, including the Christian Science Church History Department and individual interviews) provided a window looking into the internal decision-making process of the *Monitor* during the McCarthy era. Strout covered many of McCarthy's committee and subcommittee hearings and was mentioned in McCarthy's book (as a possible Communist sympathizer). After that book, the *Monitor* suspended Strout from covering the Wisconsin Senator, but reassigned him to the story by the time the Army-McCarthy Hearings were held. Strout's assignment covering McCarthy lasted through the censure of the Senator in December 1954.

Strout was a significant journalist in Washington, D.C. at the time of the McCarthy era and for decades before and after. In 1925, with four years of reporting experience in England and the United States and bachelor's and master's degrees from Harvard, he was transferred from Boston to the paper's Washington bureau. From that time until his retirement in 1988, he covered more Presidents than anyone in the history of journalism. He covered many of the most historic events of the century, from the Teapot Dome scandal to D day, the Korean War, the McCarthy hearings (as mentioned earlier), the Watergate scandal, and Reaganomics.

He was a general assignment reporter, Washington correspondent, and columnist for the *Monitor* for about 67 years and the columnist "TRB" for the *New Republic* for nearly 40 years. He coauthored (with E. B. White) *Farewell to the Model T* in 1936, compiled and edited *Maud* (a *New York Times* bestseller in 1939), and a compilation of his columns about the Presidency, *TRB: Views and Perspectives on the Presidency*, was published in 1978. He received the George Polk Award, the Sidney Hillman Foundation Award, and was a recipient of a lifetime achievement special Pulitzer "citation."

Three days after Richard L. Strout died (at age 92), the editor of the *World Monitor*, Earl W. Foell, wrote that Strout was "the preeminent chronicler of the American scene—indeed of the American civilization." Foell further observed that other reporters had covered more parts of the world, or had been more specialized, or covered the White House in more detail, but Strout "covered more of the history of our times, and did so with both intimate, homey detail and historic sweep."[35]

Various publications paid respects to Strout with kind words, hinting at the importance of this man's accomplishments. The *New York Times* stated that Strout's performance "awed his colleagues and enriched his calling";[36] Hendrik Hertzberg, in a special to the *Washington Post*, wrote that Strout showed that "being a journalist need not be incompatible with being a person of dignity." Hertzberg concluded, " . . . we thought he walked on water."[37] The *National Review* represented, on most issues, the viewpoint opposite of Strout's (the *Review* is conservative and Strout, as "TRB," was liberal). But even the *Review* noted the passing of Strout with compliments: "He was a colorful and resourceful writer who could find a different way twenty times a year to damn conservatives, libertarians, free-marketeers, anti-communists, anti-gun-controllers and McCarthyites . . . we extend sympathies to his family; to his successor we tender our heartiest desires for a diminished influence."[38]

Perhaps Strout's legacy was best stated in 1989 by Dwight Jensen. He wrote (before Strout's death) that he "is one of those rare reporters who became idolized by their colleagues during their lifetime."[39]

NOTES

1. Edwin Emery, *The Press and America: An Interpretative History of the Mass Media* (Englewood Cliffs, N.J.; Prentice-Hall, 1972), 623.

2. "Coverage" includes news stories, columns, and editorials.

3. The dates documenting the so-called "McCarthy era" used by scholars have a very wide range, which will be discussed briefly later. For the purposes of this book, the McCarthy era dates from the Senator's Lincoln Day speech until he was censured by the Senate.

4. Edwin R. Bayley, *Joe McCarthy and the Press* (Madison, Wis.: University of Wisconsin Press, 1981), 198.

5. "Newspaper's Newspaperman," *Time*, 27 January 1958, 42.

6. Quoted in Bayley, *Joe McCarthy and the Press*, 148.

7. Thomas Reeves, *The Life and Times of Joe McCarthy: A Biography* (New York: Stein & Day, 1982), 266–267, 714.

8. " 'McCarthyism' Is Excoriated by BU Dean," *Christian Science Monitor*, 17 May 1950, 4.

9. Erwin D. Canham, *Commitment to Freedom: The Story of the Christian Science Monitor* (Boston: Houghton Mifflin, 1958), 74–75.

10. Ibid., 56.

11. Ibid., 109.

Introduction

12. Ibid., 113.
13. Objectivity is the ideal of reporting the "truth" without biases or subjectivity. Over the years it has become clear that not only is the ideal unattainable, it is not even desirable.
14. Canham, *Commitment to Freedom*, 165.
15. Ibid, 176.
16. J. Douglas Tarpley, "John Willis Abbot," *Biographical Dictionary of American Journalists*, ed. Joseph P. McKerns (New York: Greenwood Press, 1989), 3.
17. Canham, *Commitment to Freedom*, 183.
18. Tarpley, *Biographical Dictionary of American Journalists*, 3.
19. Emery, *The Press and America*, 567.
20. Canham, *Commitment to Freedom*, 52.
21. Ibid, 65.
22. Ibid., 373.
23. Ibid., 91.
24. Sam G. Riley, ed. *Biographical Dictionary of American Newspaper Columnists* (Westport, Conn. and London: Greenwood Press, 1995), 75–76.
25. Canham, *Commitment to Freedom*, 207.
26. Riley, *Biographical Dictionary of American Newspaper Columnists*, 124.
27. Stanley Cloud and Lynne Olson, *The Murrow Boys: Pioneers on the Front Lines of Broadcast Journalism* (Boston and New York: Houghton Mifflin Company, 1996), 276.
28. Leo C. Rosten, *The Washington Correspondents* (New York: Harcourt, Brace and Company, 1937), 356. "Reliable" and "fair" were words used by the surveyors to describe how the people perceived the accuracy and consistent quality of the papers.
29. Edward L. Bernays, "Press and Public Agreed on Deviation from Ideals. Appraisal Is Made on the Basis of Pulitzer-Ouchs-Gibson Standards," *Editor and Publisher*, 17 May 1952, 11.
30. Bayley, *Joe McCarthy and the Press*, 127.
31. Emery, *The Press and America*, 654.
32. John Tebbel, "Rating the American Newspaper—Part I," *Saturday Review*, 13 May 1961, 59.
33. Quoted in Tebbel, "Rating the American Newspaper," 60.
34. Joseph C. Harsch. *At the Hinge of History: A Reporter's Story* (Athens and London: University of Georgia Press, 1993), 218.
35. Earl W. Foell, "Harding to Reagan with Dick Strout," *Christian Science Monitor*, 22 August 1990, 19.
36. "Dick Strout's Two Lives," *New York Times*, 22 August 1990, A24.
37. Hendrik Hertzberg, "Columnist with a Conscience: Richard L. Strout, the Journalist Who Found Heart in History," *Washington Post*, 21 August 1990, 1, C1.
38. "Richard L. Strout, RIP," *National Review*, 17 September 1990, 18.
39. Dwight Jensen, "Richard L. Strout," *Biographical Dictionary of American Journalists*, ed. Joseph P. McKerns (Westport, Conn.: Greenwood Press, 1989), 681.

COVERING MCCARTHYISM

1

1950: MCCARTHYISM BEGINS

PRELUDE TO McCARTHYISM

When Joseph R. McCarthy seized the issue of Communists in government as a threat to our national security and foreign policy, he was not the first to capitalize on the nation's fears. As far back as the late 1930s, Democrat Martin Dies of Texas investigated the problem of subversives in government through his House Un-American Activities Committee (HUAC). When McCarthy made famous the idea of "guilt by association," he was merely imitating and refining methods used by Dies and his committee. In fact many of the phrases McCarthy used over the course of his career as a Communist hunter, phrases such as "coddling communists," "soft on communism," and "I hold in my hand . . . ," should be credited to Martin Dies.[1]

The Smith Act of 1940, coming at the beginning of World War II, ushered in an age of intolerance. The Smith Act called for penalties against anyone who advocated the overthrow of the government by force or violence.[2] Then, after World War II (March 12, 1947), President Harry S. Truman issued the so-called "Truman Doctrine." The promise to the United States and the world was that if "aggression" occurred and threatened people's "freedom," then ultimately America's security was involved. That meant the United States must "support free peoples who are resisting attempted subjugation."[3] The "Truman Doctrine" clearly spelled out the United States' view of its role in world peace and freedom—"Calling for economic and military help for people menaced by armed minorities or outside pressures."[4] Truman followed that policy with Executive Order 9835, signed March 27, 1947, setting up a formal federal loyalty program. This was Truman's program for handling the internal Communist threat in the United States. Each federal agency was in charge of screening employees and making a determination of whether they were loyal or not. An accused person, if dismissed, had the right to appeal to the head of his or her agency and the Loyalty Review Board, which had appellate jurisdiction. An accused person also had the right to an attorney when appearing in a formal hearing before the Loyalty Review Board. Under the executive order, dismissal would only be upheld if there were "reasonable grounds" to believe that the employee was disloyal.[5]

Also in 1947, a blacklist of Communists or suspected Communists emerged. Three former FBI agents formed a company called American Business Consultants and published "Counterattack: The Newsletter of Facts on Communism" through a unit of the company specializing in blacklisting. Theodore C. Kirkpatrick, Kenneth M. Bierly and John G. Keenan included in the newsletter names of people in government and business who they claimed had past or present affiliations with Communists. Three years later, "Red Channels: The Report of Communist Influence in Radio and Television" was published to specifically target those broadcasters suspected of having ties with Communists.[6] J. B. Matthews, ex-radical and popular front activist, provided most of the names included in "Red Channels." He compiled the list from letterheads of organizations, Congressional and California Un-American Activities Committee reports, and old issues of the *Daily Worker*.[7] "Red Channels" (the original) listed 151 names and damaging citations in a 213–page pamphlet that was distributed three days before the outbreak of the Korean War.[8]

The legal system also dealt swiftly and severely with suspected Communists. On July 28, 1948, two indictments were handed up against 12 members of the National Board of the Communist Party charging them with conspiracy to advocate the violent overthrow of the government. More than one year later, the members were found guilty and sentenced to five years in prison and a $5,000 fine each (except one war veteran was given a more lenient sentence of three years in prison).[9]

Adding to the fears of Cold War Americans was the September 1949 announcement by President Truman that the Soviet Union had detonated an atomic device. In the United States, Communists had been portrayed as bomb throwing radicals. So, many were shocked at the confirmation that the Soviet Union had tested a bomb similar to the ones the United States dropped on Hiroshima and Nagasaki, Japan. And when a bomb exploded on Wall Street September 16, 1949, killing 30 and injuring hundreds, *Life* magazine captioned a photo of the tragedy "REDS Blamed."[10]

1950: McCarthyism Begins

Civil liberties were not a high priority of many Americans as the 1950s approached. A poll in 1946 found that 69 percent of Americans would deny Communists government jobs and that as many as 57 percent suspected that there were a "great many" Communists in the United States. By 1947, 61 percent of those polled believed that membership in the Communist Party should be outlawed and in 1948 another poll revealed that 77 percent of Americans believed Communists should be required to register with the government.[11] The government responded to those concerns (or perhaps created some of them) by launching a record number of investigations from the end of World War II until the end of "McCarthyism" in 1954. (Four investigations were held in the 1945–46 Congressional sessions, 22 in 1947–48, and 24 in the 1949–50 sessions, just before McCarthy rose to prominence.) But, if there was a worldwide threat of Communism, it certainly did not show up in other countries. For instance, over the same period of the late 1940s, Britain conducted no investigations of government Communism and subversion.[12]

So strong were the feelings of many that despite the numbers, organizations or groups that were not conventional or that criticized the government were immediately categorized as having Communist sympathies or were accused of being "front organizations" for the Communists.[13] One such group that was accused (by some) of having Communist ties was the Americans for Democratic Action (ADA). ADA tried to be an ardent anti-communist organization while at the same time a protector of civil liberties: "It pointed out the real danger of communist subversion, denied that communists had any civil rights, but also raised some minor objections to the procedures though not the spirit of the administration's measures."[14]

But, straddling the fence did not serve the organization well in the eyes of the red-baiters and Communist hunters. Conservative groups quickly labeled the ADA a liberal and Communist-influenced organization, an irony because ADA had warned the country about an international Communist conspiracy. The *Chicago Tribune*, while covering the 1949 political conventions, labeled the ADA politically as the "extreme left-wing of the New Deal." And John Flynn's book, *The Road Ahead*, described the ADA as a "machine of the National Socialist Economic Planners." Further, in February 1950, Indiana Republican Senator Homer Capehart declared that the ADA was involved in an "international conspiracy to socialize America."[15]

By 1948, associating the ADA with Communists led to the decline of the organization in numbers and effectiveness: "In this battle for public opinion, right-wing tactics—some subtle and some not so subtle—were dictated by the overall strategy of attempting to associate and equate American liberalism first with socialism and then with communism." This—the conservative battle against liberalism—can be blamed in part for the decline of the ADA after 1948.[16]

The year 1949 also saw the July 31 launching of a HUAC investigation about espionage that led to the famous Alger Hiss case. On January 21, 1950, Hiss, who had served as an advisor to President Franklin Delano Roosevelt at the Yalta Conference and had held various other positions with the State Department, was convicted on two counts of perjury for lying about his Communist connection in the 1930s. He was sentenced to five years in prison.[17]

McCarthy's actions during a Senate investigation of an incident at Malmédy during World War II involving the Germans taking over Luxembourg and Belgium served as a precursor to the Senator's Communist hunts in the 1950s. The German First SS Panzer Division slaughtered U.S. soldiers and Belgian citizens. In Malmédy, 150 GIs were paraded into a wheat field and shot with machine guns. After the war concluded, 73 SS troopers were convicted by an American War Crimes Court and sentenced to either death or life in prison. Early in 1948, those persons petitioned the government to overturn the convictions on the grounds that they were beaten and forced into giving confessions that were not entirely true.[18]

A Senate subcommittee investigated the prisoners' charges in 1949; though McCarthy was not a member of the subcommittee, he was allowed to sit in on the hearings. Ultimately, he took over the proceedings. McCarthy contended that the United States rounded up German soldiers at random and obtained confessions through force, including breaking teeth and jaws with rifle butts and kicking the soldiers in the groin. McCarthy claimed only "mock" trials were then held, which convicted them.[19] Despite McCarthy's histrionics, the subcommittee report concluded that there had been some cases of improper conduct but that the trials had been conducted fairly and the verdicts should stand.[20] The Armed Services Committee adopted the subcommittee report October 13, 1949.

Popular mythology holds that McCarthy became aware of the value of the "Communists in government" issue at a dinner with friends just prior to his February 1950 Wheeling, West Virginia speech. But the record supports the contention that he used the issue much earlier. For instance, in McCarthy's 1946 Senate campaign, his opponent Howard McMurray was endorsed by the Communist newspaper the *Daily Worker*. McCarthy used that pronouncement to charge that McMurray was a "fellow traveler"[21] even though McMurray denied it.[22] And though McCarthy had relatively few legislative initiatives to be proud of prior to making red-baiting his issue in 1950, he still stood out among senators, for all the wrong reasons:

Where freshman senators usually seek the favor of influential colleagues with gestures of caution and respect, McCarthy took them on in raucous, often insulting public spectacles. Where freshman senators readily accept the ground rules—he

1950: McCarthyism Begins

went it alone, bowing to them when they served his purpose, trampling on them when they did not. Where all senators play up their familial attachments or remain discreet about their private lives, he accentuated his vices in ways that offended some colleagues and certainly baffled the rest.[23]

In his early years in the Senate, McCarthy learned that attacking individuals would garner publicity. Prompted by criticism from the *Wisconsin Capital Times*, McCarthy lambasted the newspaper. That won McCarthy widespread coverage in Wisconsin, and national exposure through an article about the dispute that appeared in *Time*.[24]

THE *MONITOR*'S PRE-MCCARTHY COLD WAR COVERAGE

An incident near the end of World War II became a McCarthy issue both before and during the so-called McCarthy era and contributed to controversy at the *Christian Science Monitor*. It is important in understanding McCarthy's later actions and in illustrating the *Monitor*'s handling of Cold War issues prior to McCarthyism. That incident, along with Cold War–related actions by the *Monitor* and the newspaper industry in general, illustrates the atmosphere in the country prior to 1950.

On March 11, 1945, officials in the Office of Strategic Services (OSS) raided the Manhattan headquarters of the procommunist publication—*Amerasia*—and discovered stolen classified documents. The "seizure" was carried out after a January 26, 1945 article in *Amerasia* that contained information nearly identical to documents from the OSS. Among the six people arrested were the editor of the publication, Philip J. Jaffe, Emmanuel Larsen of the State Department's Far Eastern Division, Lt. Andrew Roth of the Office of Naval Intelligence, and foreign service officer John S. Service. Documents were also seized, but even though some were marked "top secret" they were not of much importance.[25] McCarthy referred to this incident in hearings held in the 1950s. And, Richard L. Strout's commentary about the incident resulted in a threatened malicious libel suit against the *Monitor*.[26]

As the McCarthy era began, the groundwork had been laid legitimizing people's fear of groups, organizations, and businesses thought to be associated with Communists. For example, between 1945 and 1950 the *New York Times Magazine* used specialists with the Institute for Pacific Relations (IPR) to review 22 of 30 books published about China during the time period. But, between 1952 and 1955, when IPR was under scrutiny and criticism from McCarthy and others, not one of the previously used experts was asked to write a single review for the *Times* about books dealing with the issue of China. While *Times* editorials fought McCarthy and his methods, for practical purposes the newspaper caved in to the pressures of McCarthyism and the criticism of IPR.[27]

Despite the pressures of the era, Erwin D. Canham, then president of the American Society of Newspaper Editors (ASNE) and editor of the *Christian Science Monitor*, took a stand for the First Amendment and freedom of the press as infringements by government became too burdensome to bear. Detroit Police Commissioner Harry S. Toy proposed banning Communist and "Communist-tinged" newspapers from covering events. Canham wrote to the chair of the ASNE Committee on Freedom of Information in response to Toy's proposal: "Until Communist newspapers or individuals are banned by Congressional or judicial decision from the status of newspapers, they have the same basic rights of access of public records as all other newspapers. It is unpalatable to have to defend Communists, but I am confident we must unless and until a basic decision is taken to bar them from operation of the Bill of Rights." Canham contended that public officials needed to avoid being hysterical while taking "every conceivable measure which will keep the dangerous information away from communists."[28]

Even prior to 1950, the *Monitor* and its columnists were not altogether uncritical of the government investigative process. In an "Intimate Message"[29] titled "Hollywood Hearings and Headlines," Richard L. Strout took to task a House committee headed by Congressman J. Parnell Thomas, a Republican from New Jersey. Strout wrote that the committee "boggled its vital job . . . after sowing seeds of distrust of a whole industry—one of the three great industries for mass dissemination of ideas in America—the committee suddenly recessed hearings on an inconclusive note, leaving most of the principal charges up in the air."[30]

In another "Intimate Message" prior to 1950 about HUAC, Strout wrote about the differences in the way the Canadian Royal Commission and the U.S. House of Representatives handled its investigations. Strout characterized the Canadian system as "clean, swift and complete" and stated that those investigations "went after the facts, not headlines." On the other hand, according to Strout, the House committees always "put headlines before facts" and "The almost universal feeling here is that it has abused its power."[31]

The five years after the end of World War II set the stage for an increase in the intensity of the Cold War and put Congress on center stage. In fact, from 1950 through 1953, Congress, with investigation after investigation, got much more publicity than the executive branch.[32] In January 1950, Secretary of State Dean Acheson, speaking before the National Press Club in Washington, D.C., defined America's defense perimeter in the Far East as excluding the Republic of Korea and Taiwan. This gave Republicans a point of attack for the next three years—Acheson's "losing" China and then abandoning these other countries.[33]

MCCARTHY'S LINCOLN DAY SPEECH

On February 9, 1950, Lincoln Day, Senator Joseph R. McCarthy spoke to the Ohio County Republican Women's Club in Wheeling, West Virginia. The exact number of Communists he claimed were in the State Department was the subject of great debate for the rest of his speaking tour, as well as during the next four years and beyond. The local newspaper, the *Wheeling Intelligencer*, reported that McCarthy claimed there were 205 Communists in the State Department. The Associated Press picked up the *Intelligencer* story and sent it on the wire; however, the *Chicago Tribune* was one of the few large newspapers in the country to carry details of the McCarthy speech. A speech that is still written about and debated today got very little coverage in the newspapers at the time it was delivered. In fact, the *Christian Science Monitor*'s first mention of the story came on February 11 in a front page article (from the Associated Press) about Dr. Klaus Emil Fuchs, who later was convicted of atomic spying in Britain. The AP story stated that McCarthy's speaking tour left a "trail of accusations related to the State Department's employing Communists."[34] The *New York Times* did not mention the speech until February 12 in a page 2 United Press story emphasizing McCarthy's "open letter" to Harry S. Truman (the junior senator from Wisconsin asked the President to contact Secretary of State Acheson and question him about security risks working in the State Department).[35]

The first *Monitor*-generated story alluding (indirectly) to controversy in the Republican Party appeared on February 14, 1950, and was written by Richard L. Strout. The piece in general concerned the GOP's trying to find "harmony" with a new set of principles and objectives for the party to follow. Further, a one-line comment (on the front page in the news "highlights" box) stated that the State Department had asked McCarthy to turn over the names of the "57 card-carrying communists" he charged were working in the department, and quoted the State Department as declaring the "accusations" were "without foundation."[36] The denial of the accusations came during the State Department's first formal news conference designed to answer McCarthy's charges.[37] A *Milwaukee Journal* editorial printed February 14 stated McCarthy "owed it to the country" to name names without the immunity of the Senate and surmised that the Senator had "done a lot of irresponsible talking in recent months."[38]

While the *Monitor* (and most other newspapers) had not yet provided McCarthy extensive coverage, a February 20 Associated Press story published in the *Monitor* puzzled the paper's editors. The article concerned Marshall Tito and Yugoslavia's attempt to receive aid from the United States (with no strings attached). Tito labeled a number of publications, including the *Monitor*, the *Washington Post*, the *New York Sun*, and the *Dallas News*, as "reactionary" in urging the United States to attach conditions to the aid. *Monitor* Editor Erwin D. Canham noted the "strange bedfellows" Tito created with his attack and stressed that the *Monitor* supported U.S. policy.[39]

Also on February 20, McCarthy spoke before the Senate for six hours explaining the charges he had leveled against the State Department in Wheeling, West Virginia and in subsequent speeches. McCarthy's critics, such as Richard H. Rovere, characterized the presentation as "one of the maddest spectacles in the history of representative government." Rovere wrote that it had been "so disorderly, so jumbled and cluttered and loose-ended, that it was beyond the power of most reporters to organize the mess into a story that would convey to the reader anything beyond the suspicion that the reporter was drunk."[40]

Biographer Thomas C. Reeves simply called it "the most fantastic and supremely dishonest performance ever witnessed on Capital Hill."[41]

Supporters of McCarthy claimed the Democrats repeatedly interrupted, not allowing McCarthy to present his case coherently. William F. Buckley and Brent L. Bozell wrote that Democrats had been clamoring for McCarthy to state his case against the State Department. When he tried to do so, "they made it all but impossible."[42]

Buckley and Bozell also claimed McCarthy had toned down his charges, but no newspapers reported the change. Willard Edwards, of the pro-McCarthy *Chicago Tribune*, wrote that McCarthy was greeted by "scenes of disorder" on the floor of the Senate, but that he presented "evidence that a corps of Communists in the State Department" were of value to the Soviet Union. Throughout Edwards' account of the six-hour session, he referred to "a flow of documented information concerning the communistic records of dozens of State Department officials."[43]

Despite the fact that the speech was "important enough for almost every newspaper in the nation to put it to page one,"[44] the *Monitor* did not cover it with its own reporters and banished the AP story to page 17. The only hint of any disorderliness or cluttering by McCarthy was in the story's description of the Senator "fishing out photographs of records from a large brief case" and a reference to Senator Karl E. Mundt of South Dakota and Senator Homer Ferguson of Michigan, both Republicans, pitching in "frequently" to assist McCarthy.[45]

On February 22, 1950, Senate Democratic Majority Leader Scott Lucus introduced Senate Resolution 231 authorizing a study of whether past or present State Department employees had been or were disloyal to the United States. The resolution resulted in the appointment of a subcommittee of the Senate Foreign Relations Committee to conduct hearings led by Maryland Senator Millard Tydings, a Democrat.[46]

1950: McCarthyism Begins

Even at this point, with formal hearings set for March 8, 1950, the *Monitor* did not deem the story important enough for one of its Washington Bureau reporters to cover. It placed an AP story on page 16 on February 23 to inform people of the upcoming inquiry.[47] Meanwhile, the Fuchs spy case came to a close in England. The *Monitor*'s London Bureau Chief, William H. Stringer, reported that the former mathematical physicist for Adolph Hitler confessed to leaking atomic secrets to the Soviet Union, imperiling "the West's whole nuclear time advantage over Soviet Russia." Fuchs was sentenced to 14 years in prison.[48] And in U.S. Federal Court, Judith Coplon (a former Justice Department Analyst) and Valentin A. Gubitchev (a Russian engineer on the United Nations' staff) were found guilty of conspiracy to commit espionage.[49] As Coplon and Gubitchev faced stiff prison terms and fines, their case, combined with that of Fuchs and others, signaled to many that the Communist threat was greater than ever.

The *Monitor* assigned veteran Washington correspondent Richard L. Strout to cover the Tydings subcommittee inquiry into McCarthy's charges against the State Department. In a page 1 top-of-the-fold story, Strout described the Senate's mood as one of "angry partisanship" and declared that the proceedings "would be one of the bitterest senatorial investigations in years."[50] His story included McCarthy's charge that Dorothy Kenyon had been affiliated with at least 28 Communist front organizations. Kenyon's response describing McCarthy as an "unmitigated liar" provided an immediate balance to McCarthy's statements.[51] Strout further described Tydings as "repeatedly and vainly" seeking to get yes or no answers from McCarthy. Strout reported that Democrats countered evidence in a petition that named Kenyon as a "known communist" by reading other names on the *same* petition, including former Republican Senator Arthur Capper from Kansas, Ernest Hemingway, Senator Claude Pepper, a Democrat from Florida, and Senator Elbert D. Thomas, a Democrat from Utah.[52] The Senate Foreign Relations subcommittee (or what became known as the "Tydings subcommittee") hearings were underway March 8, 1950.

TYDINGS' INVESTIGATION

The Tydings subcommittee consisted of three Democrats, Millard Tydings of Maryland, Brien MacMahon of Connecticut, and Theodore F. Green from Rhode Island, and two Republicans, Henry Cabot Lodge of Massachusetts and Bourke B. Hickenlooper of Iowa. While McCarthy supporters claimed the subcommittee's purpose was to investigate the loyalty of State Department personnel, not "McCarthy's charges,"[53] the actual investigation included three parts: McCarthy's presentation of the names of people associated with the State Department who he claimed were either disloyal or security risks; inquiry into the *Amerasia* affair and the case of

John S. Service; and, specifically, investigations of Philip Jessup and Owen Lattimore.[54]

A *New York Times* editorial prior to the start of the Tydings investigation stated that McCarthy had "been giving a good imitation of a hit-and-run driver in his attacks on the State Department" and that the Wisconsin Senator's effort was a "campaign of indiscriminate character-assassination."[55] The *Monitor* raised questions about McCarthy and his methods about two weeks after the *Times* editorial, and just prior to and after the commencement of the hearings. Joseph C. Harsch, columnist for the Washington News Bureau, tried to ease the "frightened sense that the highest secrets of our diplomacy are falling into unfriendly hands." He consoled *Monitor* readers, explaining that the "security force" already in place was essentially run by Republicans, who would have no incentive in defending Communists or allowing security risks in the State Department.[56] Meanwhile, Strout described the Tydings investigation, after only two days of hearings, as "close to the breaking point" with Tydings and McCarthy clashing over Tydings' desire to see and hear McCarthy's "evidence" case by case, rather than letting McCarthy run through a long list of unsupported charges.[57]

In a column a day later, Harsch welcomed a "new departure" from previous HUAC hearings: "The practice in the previous 'loyalty' investigations and hearings has been to give the accuser a full and free opportunity to pour forth all his accusations without interruption.... The effect has been a longtime lag between presentation of the charges and presentation of the defense, with the later frequently failing to obtain the public attention achieved by the charges."[58]

The *Monitor*'s first editorial stand about McCarthy came March 11, 1950. "Security vs. Smearing" questioned McCarthy's method of crying "wolf" and "recklessly" smearing individuals. The editorial chronicled how two of the accused, Judge Dorothy Kenyon and Mrs. Dean Acheson, by having "an early chance to answer," quickly provided convincing rebuttals to McCarthy's charges. The *Monitor* concluded by suggesting that "smearing will not in the end" be smart politics because "It cannot build loyalty, but rather by injustice undermines allegiance. It cannot foster freedom, but instead develops a police-state atmosphere in which suspicion, intimidation and hate destroy the initiative, mutual trust and effective operation which are the very roots of democratic security."[59]

Just one day earlier a *New York Times* editorial declared "guilt by association repugnant and ridiculous."[60] Two of the nation's prestigious newspapers had, from the start, identified McCarthy and his methods as questionable and, in fact, dangerous.

While many critics of the press who have studied the McCarthy era asserted that McCarthy's charges would make the front page while the denials would not,[61] that simply was not the case with the *Monitor*. On March 12 McCarthy revealed the names of three persons, who along with Kenyon, made a list of four "card-carrying communists" who had been or were now employees of the State Department. Strout's front-page story listed Haldore Hanson, who was helping President Truman with his Point Four Program, Esther C. Brunauer of the UNESCO relations staff, and Dr. Owen Lattimore of Johns Hopkins University as cited by McCarthy. Strout also included a State Department spokesman's statement that Hanson and Mrs. Brunauer had been investigated and cleared for loyalty. Additionally, Hanson was quoted as saying he had been cleared by the FBI, while Miss Kenyon called McCarthy an "unmitigated liar" (previously quoted). The headline on Strout's story was "Denials Rain on McCarthy's Charges."[62] A page 1 story by Strout the next day featured a report about Kenyon's testimony, and described "a scene with few parallels in Senate history" in which she called McCarthy's contention that she had been associated with 28 Communist front groups "outrageous" and "fantastic," citing her long record of opposing Communism.[63]

Editorial page cartoons began appearing in the *Monitor* about McCarthy. For example, the GOP elephant with "Headlines-at-any-cost policy" over its head approached a GOP voter in his living room, and the voter promptly commented, "Can't see that it does much for you."[64] And, in a cartoon titled "Unfairly Matched," a jockey riding "Headlined Disloyalty Charges" streaked ahead of another jockey riding "Less Heralded Exonerations," obviously referring to the claim that McCarthy's charges received more prominent attention than did rebuttals or the evidence (even though the *Monitor* was not guilty of the practice).[65]

Through March, the *Monitor* ran many page 1 stories about the Tydings investigation, while McCarthy started to raise the ire of respected citizens who felt obligated to speak out. Former Secretary of State (under Hoover) and Secretary of War (under FDR) Henry L. Stimson wrote a scathing letter to the *New York Times* about McCarthy's attacks on Secretary of State Dean Acheson. Stimson stated that "ranting and raving" would not ensure the loyalty of government employees and that "personal attacks" on a secretary of state could only come from someone "who seeks political advantage from damage to his country."[66]

By March 30, the *Monitor* was ready for an all-out effort against McCarthy's methods. The paper ran two editorials, an editorial cartoon and an "Intimate Message from Washington" by Strout, in addition to its usual articles about the Tydings investigation. Again, the *Monitor* railed at the smearing techniques used, citing testimony by Mrs. Brunauer about how her life had been adversely affected by the false accusations:

We wish every politician who thinks smearing is a way to gain partisan advantage would take her story home to himself.

We wish every citizen who believes that character assassination is a good way to insure the loyalty of citizens would examine the actual results.

We wish every newspaper publisher who sees in reckless use of reputation-blasting headlines only a boost to circulation would consider how he would like to be on the receiving end.[67]

The *Monitor* added that if Congress failed to "curb McCarthyism" then "the people must apply at the polls an effective penalty for unjust accusation."[68] Strout, who covered the Tydings hearings from the beginning, briefly chronicled McCarthy's actions over the month and a half since the senator's Lincoln Day speech. He wrote that McCarthy's main technique was to leave "one sensation dangling in the air" as he went on to the next one. Strout noted the publicity McCarthy received despite the lack of evidence, and stated that "few men in public life have created a greater stir with the amount of material he has so far disclosed."[69] And finally, the editorial page cartoon titled "Where's the Sportsmanship" showed a large man in complete medieval armor labeled "Congressional Immunity" swordfighting a small man with no outer protection labeled "Investigation Committee Victim."[70]

One of McCarthy's major assaults was on Dr. Owen Lattimore, a professor at Johns Hopkins University identified by the Wisconsin Senator as working for the Russians.[71] McCarthy (while behind closed doors March 20) identified Lattimore as a "top USSR espionage agent." Then, on March 27 Lattimore's name was released to the press and linked to McCarthy's charge.[72] A page 1 story by Strout in the *Monitor* reminded readers that McCarthy had staked his entire case for the presence of Communists in the State Department on the Lattimore charge while at the same time Republicans were plotting a campaign to oust Secretary of State Dean Acheson.[73] President Truman, in a news conference March 30, declared McCarthy "the greatest asset that the Kremlin has" and censured those Republicans who were "trying to dig up that old malodorous dead horse called 'isolationism.'"[74] Nevertheless, McCarthy took center stage before the Tydings' subcommittee and presented "evidence" against Lattimore from 2:00 P.M. till 6:18 P.M.; this, along with the allegation made previously that Lattimore worked for the USSR, caused the university professor to cut short a United Nations mission in Afghanistan to confront his accuser face to face in Washington, D.C.[75]

An editorial in the *Monitor* in early April called for "simple fair play" in legislative inquiry. Contending that McCarthy had abused the immunity from libel granted him as a senator speaking on the Senate floor, the editorial traced the roots of the practice back to its creation by the British Parliament to prevent kings from stifling legislators. The *Monitor* contended that "This privilege, originally demanded as a bulwark against tyrants, is now too often an instrument of tyranny." The newspaper admitted that to "abolish immunity might be dangerous" and called for an "awakened sense of fair play" in recognizing the abuse of the privilege.[76] During this time, the *Monitor* carried a series of United Press stories about Lattimore, with Strout then returning to the "beat" to cover the dramatic testimony of Professor Lattimore. The April 6 story on page 1 detailed Lattimore's refutation of McCarthy's charges. Strout called the testimony "a biting counterattack, winged with satire and barbed with ridicule" and described Lattimore's thesis that McCarthy was acting as "the simple dupe" for a lobbyist of the Nationalist government of China.[77] Further, Lattimore characterized McCarthy's charges as "base and contemptible lies."[78] The *Monitor* coverage not only included the lengthy article by Strout, with many quotations from Lattimore, but also had a page 7 listing of excerpts from Lattimore's testimony.[79] Strout declared that the "virtually unanimous" feeling was that Lattimore's rebuttal, coupled with a statement by Chairman Tydings that the summaries of FBI files did not contain incriminating evidence against the professor, showed that McCarthy had not proved his case: "If Senator McCarthy has any aces left in his hand, it is now time to play them, for the game is coming to an end. Otherwise he must fall back on the excuse that since he does not have confidential FBI files he cannot prove his extraordinary charges."[80]

Strout, in a separate analytical piece, called for a solution to McCarthy's "sensationalism, emotionalism, and diabolism" as simply "quiet thinking."[81] In the same issue, *Monitor* correspondent in the Midwest, Max K. Gilstrap, wrote a lengthy background/psychoanalytical piece informing readers about the junior senator from Wisconsin and what motivated him. Gilstrap noted McCarthy's service record appeared to be "outstanding." However, Gilstrap revealed that evidence existed (from a captain who served with McCarthy in the South Pacific) contradicting the Senator's claim of having been an actual "tail-gunner" in World War II. Gilstrap also chronicled past controversies, such as tax-dodging charges, and McCarthy's disregard for the law in running for the Senate while still a sitting judge in Wisconsin. Gilstrap wrote that both friends and opponents of McCarthy agreed that he was "ambition personified."[82] The *New York Times*, equally troubled by the proceedings, commented about how McCarthyism affected the big picture. The *Times* declared that many government officials "may now deem it no longer prudent to pursue a line of independent thinking" because he or she would "run the risk of being called traitor or spy."[83]

The April 17 testimony of Louis F. Budenz (a former managing editor of the Communist newspaper the *Daily Worker* and frequent former Communist witness) was to be McCarthy's vindication. Six days before the testimony, Strout reported that sources indicated to him that Budenz would testify that Lattimore was a Communist, but that the declaration would be based on second-hand, not first-hand, knowledge.[84] In a page 1 story, "Budenz Accuses Lattimore—In Hearsay Charge," Strout's sources proved correct. Budenz, Strout wrote, admitted that he had never seen or met Lattimore before, but regarded Lattimore as a Communist based on information given to him by others. Strout told the *Monitor* readers in blunt terms that "those who had hoped for decisive and clear-cut evidence to settle the McCarthy charges against Professor Owen Lattimore once and for all were doomed to disappointment in the testimony of Louis F. Budenz, former Communist."[85]

The next day Strout followed his report about the Budenz testimony with a biographical sketch of the witness. Strout's assessment included the conclusion that Budenz had an "authoritarian" personality and saw things in black and white, with no shade of gray. Budenz moved 180 degrees from militant Communist to militant anticommunist. After the sketch, Strout legitimized Lattimore's testimony through Brigadier General Elliot R. Thorpe, who investigated Lattimore three times. Thorpe indicated that the evidence was so strong that Lattimore was loyal that he was given access to top-secret documents.[86] Meanwhile, the *Times*, less vocal against Budenz, simply stated that testimony suggested that "Lattimore's points of view and their expression have been influenced by Soviet machination" and because the professor's "judgments have a bearing on American policy" the charges "should be explored."[87]

Up to this point, the major themes in the news stories, columns (or commentaries), and editorials in the *Monitor* included questioning the value of McCarthy's smear tactics, pointing out the press's weakness for sensationalizing unsubstantiated charges, and evaluating the dangers associated with abuse of congressional immunity. But, another theme emerged after Lattimore's testimony: the *Monitor*'s concern about the effect McCarthyism was having in hampering policymaking at home and hurting the United States' standing abroad. A *Monitor* editorial supporting the path to a continued peace in eastern and western Europe as "strength in the West" declared that "frivolous and reckless indulgence in 'McCarthyism' " had hamstrung American foreign policy. That, along with "political weaknesses in Britain and France," paralyzed diplomacy and "emboldened the totalitarians."[88] Roscoe Drummond, *Monitor* correspondent (who later returned to the position of Washington bureau chief which he previously had held) assessed America's internal battle with Communism. Drummond wrote that "European leaders get cold shivers" at the charges made by McCarthy against the State Department because "they are deeply concerned with the political security of American foreign policy."[89] In a later piece, Drummond noted that McCarthy's attack on the State Department "seriously harms the authority of American foreign policy all over the world."[90]

Meanwhile, Strout, the correspondent observing McCarthy on a near-daily basis, referring to Secretary of State Acheson and President Truman's speeches attacking McCarthy, observed that it was unusual in our country's history for Americans not to unite behind the government's foreign policy.[91] Strout wrote that initially McCarthy's antics were regarded as a "fiasco" but the time had come that "the secondary effects in creating disturbance and bitterness in the domestic and foreign policies" began to outweigh the "primary charges themselves."[92] Additionally, in a page 1 interpretive piece by Strout, the advantages for the coming election Republicans saw in being associated with McCarthyism were balanced against the concern overseas with what was happening in the United States. Strout cited the defeat in a Florida primary of Democrat Claude Pepper after his opponent hammered away that Pepper was a Communist: "Republican strategists believe that Senator McCarthy has raised an emotional issue playing on America's deep sense of insecurity. Whatever its merits, the issue has in it potentialities of millions of votes, it is believed."[93]

Strout noted, however, that a gain by one political party in the next election would come at the expense of respect throughout the world. Strout quoted the *Times* of London, in an article entitled "Calumny in Washington," which said that "the effects of the [McCarthy's] performance are so serious that the secretary of state and his department have been immobilized for many weeks."[94] Privately, Strout referred to the junior senator as "this SOB McCarthy."[95] Clearly in his news stories and analytical pieces, McCarthy's charges were disclosed, but were quickly balanced with denials from the accused, and character assessments from friends and colleagues of the accused.

Finally, on the writing of editorials questioning McCarthy during this early period of McCarthyism, the *Monitor* pointed to "faith" in the "common sense" of the American people. The *Monitor* noted the weight of evidence contradicting McCarthy's charges—evidence from the FBI files. FBI Director J. Edgar Hoover's report stated there was nothing to support McCarthy's contentions. To the contrary, the FBI files supported Republican Seth W. Richardson, head of the Loyalty Review Board, who said, in reviewing 10,000 cases, "not a single spy" was found and "on the record so far we've had more than enough evidence to choose between faith in our fellow Americans and the unsupported suspicions of McCarthyism. And we submit that faithlessness against such evidence and in a time like this is most dangerous folly—a folly that must be highly pleasing to Moscow."[96]

Meanwhile, in the Lattimore case, evidence mounted each day corroborating the professor's contention that he was not and had never been a Communist. The *Monitor* reported that former Communist Dr. Bella V. Dodd testified that Lattimore was not a Communist, former American Communist Party chief Earl Browder testified that there were no Communists in the State Department and that he did not know Lattimore, and Frederick Vanderbilt Field denied that he ever labeled Lattimore a Communist as Budenz had contended.[97] Historians and media critics contended that the denials rarely got the same front-page play as McCarthy's charges.[98] Clearly, these page 1 denials, coupled with previously mentioned efforts by Strout to include denials and counter evidence to McCarthy's charges within the initial stories, suggest that the *Monitor* was one newspaper making an effort to be fair to the accused, and it was succeeding.

On May 2 the *Monitor* focused a page 1 story on a 62–page rebuttal to McCarthy's charges that Lattimore issued to the press (at the same time he was testifying before the Tydings subcommittee). Lattimore claimed, and Strout reported, that McCarthy had "criminally libeled" him "from a foxhole of immunity on the Senate floor."[99] A lengthy *Monitor* article the next day summed up the document, frequently using direct quotations from Lattimore. Republican Senator Bourke B. Hickenlooper, a staunch McCarthy supporter, grilled Lattimore about his political beliefs and past affiliations. The *Monitor* summed up Lattimore's case and asked a rhetorical question: "What it seemed to boil down to was that Dr. Lattimore, like any journalist, had met some communists and communist sympathizers in his time, had gone on trips with them, had interviewed them. Does this prove he was influenced by them?"[100]

And Strout, in commentary and analysis appearing on the editorial page, revisited the original McCarthy charges to bring context to the story—something that had been lost in a barrage of new accusations. Strout wrote that McCarthy had not kept his pledge to repeat elsewhere without the protection of immunity anything he said on the Senate floor. McCarthy failed to provide information on the "205, the 81, the 57 cases" against the State Department. The actual evidence indicated these were previously investigated cases with "two years' dust" on them. Further, since Dr. Lattimore never worked for the State Department and McCarthy's charge that the professor was the "principal architect" for U.S. China policy had not even been supported by McCarthy's own witness (Louis Budenz), the Senator's statement that he would "stand or fall" with this single case meant he fell.[101] Despite the fact that many of the nation's newspapers reported that none of McCarthy's charges against Lattimore and others were proved, polls showed that those who followed the story (70 percent of the people) sided with McCarthy by a margin of four to three.[102]

1950: McCarthyism Begins

On May 27, 1950, Strout wrote "Ordeal by Publicity," an analysis of the McCarthy proceedings that has been quoted widely as a thorough and thoughtful account of the shortcomings of press practices in the early 1950s. Though (as already pointed out) Strout took great care to include the rebuttal as well as the charges in each of his stories, he lamented the lack of interpretive reporting by most newspapers covering McCarthy:

> Now in this turmoil of give and take the charge always has the head start. The business of "straight reporting," in any case, never gives the reader much time to catch up. If the reporter had been permitted the freedom of interpretive reporting customarily followed by the great dailies abroad he could have commented as well as reported. He would have been a historian as well as photographer with words. But this would have violated one of the dearest rules of American journalism.[103]

Strout contended that McCarthy used this convention of "straight reporting" as a "shrewd device" keeping "one sensation ahead of his trackers" and hiding behind "fresh attacks." Strout suggested that McCarthy's charges, although none had been proved, left a "cloud of anxiety, suspicion and fear over Washington and the nation," and that it would be difficult for Tydings' subcommittee report to "dissipate this mood."[104]

By June 1, 1950, the "schism" developing in the Republican Party became apparent as Maine Senator Margaret Chase Smith, troubled by McCarthy and his methods, delivered a "declaration of conscience" address to the Senate. While the speech did not mention McCarthy by name, Mrs. Smith repudiated the tactics of the junior senator while he sat "barely three feet behind her," face white and voice silent.[105] Strout reported the speech as a "serious revolt" among Republicans that "caused glee among Democrats" by revealing the lack of solidarity in the GOP.[106] And the *Monitor* viewed the speech as having such importance that it printed the *entire* text. A *Monitor* editorial lauded Mrs. Smith and the senators who signed the "declaration" for putting "patriotism above politics"; the editorial eloquently declared how "character assassination" endangered the "basic principals of Americanism," among them "the right to criticize, the right to hold unpopular beliefs, the right to protest, and the right of independent thought." The newspaper specifically stated its opposition to McCarthyism, citing first the use of immunity from libel suits on the floor of the Senate: "It is this injustice, plus the dangers of intimidating free opinion by loose charges of communism, plus the damage to America's diplomatic front against Moscow, that causes this newspaper to oppose McCarthyism. We want no whitewashing of the guilty. We insist that Reds be rooted out, but by more efficient, professional methods."[107]

Clearly, Chase's speech called for a more thoughtful and dignified approach to Senate investigations and thus won the approval of the *Monitor*. It backed fair play, and by not naming McCarthy nor viciously attacking him, it even followed Mrs. Eddy's tenant to "injure no man." The *Milwaukee Journal* also gleefully supported the Maine Republican's action. An editorial declared that "All things that needed so terribly to be said about Senator McCarthy and his witch hunt" were expressed in Smith's speech.[108] And just a few days later, the *Journal* suggested that Senator Smith would make a fine vice presidential candidate, given "her speech of recent date on the evils of McCarthyism, plus her feminine charms."[109] The *Times* wrote that Senator Smith made "it incisively clear what a disgraceful thing it is that certain Republicans to whom the public has a right to look for responsible leadership" had actually "abetted" McCarthy in his "character assassination behind the cloak of senatorial immunity."[110]

REACTION TO THE TYDINGS REPORT

In mid-June, the Korean War began and stole the front page away from McCarthy. The *Monitor* used many of its resources to cover the war and limited stories about McCarthy to wire service accounts buried in the inside pages. However, when the Tydings subcommittee report was released on July 17, McCarthy was back in the limelight in the *Monitor* as well as in newspapers across the country.

The Tydings report, which was 347 pages in length and contained more than 300,000 words, split along party lines, both at the subcommittee level and in the full Senate. On the Tydings subcommittee the three Democrats approved it, and the two Republicans issued separate statements about the investigation in what amounted to the "minority" opinion. Similarly, the full Senate vote was 45 Democrats in favor and 37 Republicans against.[111]

Strout's article quoted the report's characterization of McCarthy's charges as a "fraud and a hoax" perpetrated upon the Senate and the American people. The report stated that McCarthy had "no evidence" supporting his claims against either the State Department or individuals; that he kept the "affair" alive by "additional charges based on heresay, rumor"; and that he had kept the "whole nation in a ferment" while doing the "divisive work of the Communists" in creating dissension in the United States. Only a brief statement by McCarthy was included in the page 1 story: the Senator contended that the report signaled to subversives that the Communists in government have "no fear of exposure by this administration."[112] Strout, who by this time had covered Washington for more than 25 years, placed the Tydings report in historical context: "Not before in this century have fellow senators denounced a colleague in such searing terms, and the question is raised whether expulsion action will be attempted."[113]

Joseph C. Harsch, in his front page *Monitor* column "State of the Nation," contended there were few Republicans who really believed any of McCarthy's charges and that the entire affair was an embarrassment to most in the GOP:

Senator McCarthy has, beyond question, employed tactics which are unfair and contrary to Anglo-Saxon principles of justice. He has tried to establish the doctrine of "guilt by association" which is medievalism revived in our times by communism. He has undermined public confidence in a branch of the federal government which Republicans would command were they to win the next general election.[114]

While both Strout and Harsch noted the "fiery language" of the report, a *Monitor* editorial took a moderate approach.[115] While conceding that the majority report could not be "free from political motivation," it stated that "fair-minded" people would be convinced that McCarthy failed to prove any of his charges—as pointed out in the Tydings report. Further, the *Monitor* summarized Senator Henry Cabot Lodge's separate "minority" report stating there were "positive reasons to believe" that persons working in the State Department who were accused of Communist connections were loyal and that there was "no positive evidence that it is infiltrated by subversives." The *Monitor* supported the study of the question of government security, but, like Lodge, wanted a "nonpartisan commission of distinguished citizens appointed jointly by the President and Congress" to carry out future investigations.[116]

The *New York Times* published extensive segments of the Tydings report, and included a separate story with the verbatim response by McCarthy. A *Times* editorial, much in the same tone as the *Monitor*, noted that the subcommittee was divided along party lines but stated that the majority conclusion would also "have been reached by all fair-minded readers of the reported evidence." The newspaper stated that McCarthy's allegations that Dr. Owen Lattimore and other prominent persons in and out of government were or had been Communists were "accusations" that were made "recklessly."[117] The *Milwaukee Journal* not only strongly supported the findings, but went to the trouble and expense of "printing thousands of words" from the lengthy majority report.[118] The *San Francisco Examiner* and the *Chicago Tribune* saw the Tydings report in a totally different light. The *Examiner* called the majority report "the most disgracefully partisan document ever to emanate from the Congress of the United States." The *Examiner* concluded that given the "perilous times" in our country, the report "verges upon DISLOYALTY."[119] The *Tribune* called Tydings' findings "The Report Nobody Believes," declaring the majority report a "large bucket of whitewash" from the "party of lies."[120] In similar fashion, editorials in all the major newspapers sought to put the report and the proceedings in perspective, with many taking strong positions for or against.

AMERASIA CONTROVERSY AT THE *MONITOR*

The Tydings subcommittee work included investigating the five-year-old *Amerasia* case. The case (mentioned briefly earlier in this chapter) involved the Office of Strategic Services (OSS), which discovered 1,700 government documents, copies of government documents, and newspaper clippings at the Manhattan headquarters of the procommunist publication *Amerasia*. Initially, six persons were arrested. In June 1945, editor Philip Jaffe and Emanuel Larsen of the State Department's Far Eastern Division were indicted and prosecuted, with Jaffe receiving a fine of $2,500 on his guilty plea and Larsen pleading nolo contendere and being fined $500. Another indicted person, Lt. Andrew Roth of the Office of Naval Intelligence, was not prosecuted (due to lack of evidence); John S. Service, a foreign service officer, Kate Mitchell, a coeditor of *Amerasia*, and a writer for *Collier's*, Mark Gayn, were initially arrested but not indicted.[121]

With the Cold War "heating up," the penalties in retrospect seemed lenient. In addition to the Tydings subcommittee revisiting the case, 21 Republicans asked for a separate Congressional inquiry specifically investigating how the Justice Department handled the prosecutions. A federal grand jury in New York investigated the matter,[122] though it returned no new indictments after concluding its probe. The *Monitor* reported that the grand jury blamed the lack of prosecution on espionage laws that were weak at the time, and loose security regulations. The panel recommended that it would be prudent for the Justice Department to release details about how it handled the case.[123]

The *Amerasia* case connected to McCarthy in a couple of ways. First, it was taken up as part of the Tydings subcommittee investigation of McCarthy's charges against the State Department. Second, once it became clear that McCarthy's charges against Professor Lattimore had not been proved, the junior senator shifted his focus on *Amerasia*.[124]

Richard L. Strout's column about the *Amerasia* affair gave the *Monitor* its first libel scare of the McCarthy era. In a July 21 analysis appearing on the editorial page, Strout made several errors that led to the threat of a lawsuit by Isaac Don Levine, a co-editor of the magazine *Plain Talk*—a publication with ties to an importer named Alfred Kohlberg. A letter from Levine's lawyers to Richard L. Strout contended that inaccuracies in Strout's piece were written with "actual malice" with a "culpable disregard of the facts and of Mr. Levine's rights" and "can not be regarded as inadvertent."[125]

The letter did not stop with general statements, but rather cited specific instances where the "libel" occurred. Strout wrote (largely lifting from the language of the Tydings report) that the New York importer Kohlberg financed *Plain Talk* and that Kohlberg's wealth appeared to have come from "contracts" with the Chinese National Government.[126] Levine's lawyers

1950: McCarthyism Begins

wrote that Kohlberg never had "contracts" with the Chinese National Government. He had "contacts" as stated in the Tydings report. They contended that the implications toward their client's ties to China were magnified with the change of "contacts" to "contracts" in Strout's analysis.[127] A second example of "libel" given by Levine's attorneys was the omission of the words "If true" in quoting this passage from the Tydings report: " 'One of the most despicable instances of a deliberate effort to deceive and hoodwink the American people in our history,' the Tydings majority report calls the episode."[128]

After citing a couple of other mistakes in Strout's piece, Levine's lawyers issued a final threat: "Always having had a high regard for your distinguished and influential newspaper, Mr. Levine and we await prompt word from you as to what you propose to do with respect to this seriously injurious malicious libel."[129]

The *Monitor* quickly reacted on two fronts. First, a correction appeared on the editorial page. The correction admitted the "inaccuracies" of the *Amerasia* piece, but cautioned that the errors made were "entirely the result of inadvertence, and were intended to inflict no malice toward any person mentioned in the article." The *Monitor* stated not only its "deep regret" for the mistakes, but recognized "the services of Isaac Don Levine in uncovering subversive activities in the United States."[130] Second, *Monitor* editor Erwin D. Canham informed Strout by letter of the charge of libel and admonished him to be more careful with delicate subjects. Canham wrote that the number of inaccuracies in the piece "placed us in a seriously embarrassing position" and with editors not having access to lengthy government reports and therefore not able to catch errors of fact, Canham explained that he expected "an extra measure of care" by correspondents in the field in handling such stories.[131]

Upon returning from vacation, a humbled Strout responded to the Canham letter and expressed regret for "letting my team down" and "having embarrassed" the *Monitor* with "carelessness." However, while admitting the "most unfortunate" error was the omission of the words "If true," Strout contended that the errors made in the article, while inexcusable, could hardly be considered the basis for a "genuine libel suit" especially a "clerical slip" such as changing "contacts" to "contracts."[132] A return letter from Canham (11 days later) to Strout stated that *Monitor* management "quite possibly misjudged the libel hazard" but that other actions of the newspaper, including accepting materials years ago from Gunther Stein for publication (he fled the country after the War Department issued espionage charges against him), caused the newspaper to feel "to some degree vulnerable."[133]

In September 1950, on the heels of the McCarthy/Tydings controversy, after the start of the Korean War, and just before the fall midterm elections,

Editor Erwin D. Canham issued a memo to the entire staff about the obligation of reporters, writers, editors, and columnists to make the *Monitor* unique. The Board of Directors asked him to pass on the advice that writers should not forget that the paper was published by Christian Scientists and (particularly) editorials and columns (or commentaries) should be written from that "viewpoint.... This is a rigorous test. It should not lead us into doctrinal writing or any kind of mysticism or obscurity. The *Monitor* must be intelligible to all mankind. But we have the responsibility of doing a totally special job." Canham continued that "There is a tendency for worldly thinking and loose expressions to get in the paper" and that "we can do far better than that."[134] This suggested that the *Monitor* editor was not only worried about its admonition from its founder "to injure no man, but to bless all mankind," but also about the uniqueness of the newspaper's calling being lost in the mainstream day-to-day operations of a newspaper.[135] Communication between the Mother Church and Canham did not end with Canham passing on these policy reminders to the staff. A November 16 communication from the Board of Directors to Canham reiterated that the *Monitor* "must be against evil wherever it appears, and likewise quick in its recognition of good in any quarter" and that the newspaper "should miss no opportunity to aid in upholding or elevating ethical standards in government."[136]

While the *Monitor* renewed its effort to ensure the paper's uniqueness, recognizing "good" while not ignoring "evil," interpretive reporting (in general) won the plaudits of some in New England. In a speech to the New England Associated Press News Executives Association in Osterville, Massachusetts, the publisher of the *New Bedford Standard-Times*, Basil Brewer, conceded importance, accuracy, and timeliness as critical in news production, but hailed the AP as adding "color" to the previous three elements. Brewer stated that "flavor, heart and soul" may be added to the story without disturbing the other three elements.[137] The *Monitor* had sought to do that since its inception. The newspaper industry debate about the strengths and weaknesses of current-day journalistic practices (as Strout noted in his May 27, 1950 piece) increased as the threat from McCarthyism pressured the industry.

PERSPECTIVE ON THE MIDTERM ELECTIONS

For a number of reasons, there was great anticipation leading up to the November 1950 midterm elections. For instance, there were upsets in the primaries, such as incumbent Democrat Senator Claude Pepper of Florida losing after his opponent accused him of being a Communist. Strout wrote that "nobody seems to be safe anymore ... as the situation stands, a reporter asking a departing congressman about the election is almost certain to

1950: McCarthyism Begins 23

evoke a counter-question... what the reporter thinks?"[138] Strout and others at the *Monitor* wrote stories prior to the election assessing the national picture and trying to identify key races. In order to gain control of the Senate and the House, Republicans would have had to capture 7 seats held by the Democratic Party in the Senate and 47 in the House. Strout listed Democrats Millard Tydings of Maryland, Pat McCarran of Nevada, and Warren G. Magnuson of Washington State as probable winners along with Republicans Bourke B. Hickenlooper of Iowa, Charles W. Tobey from New Hampshire, and Alexander Wiley from Wisconsin.[139] He also, in excruciating detail, described the "real contests" in the House and Senate while lamenting the mean spirit and lack of substance in many of the campaigns: "The first party that discovers the voters' yearning for high-caliber candidates who stress modern programs rather than mud-slinging, it frequently is added among newspapermen, will sweep any election."[140]

In general terms, *Monitor* columnist Joseph C. Harsch predicted the upcoming election would result in the status quo, writing that the Democratic Party was "likely to come through Election Day with its grip on the federal government almost undisturbed" and urged Republicans to "redouble" their efforts and not become "confident that it's in the bag."[141] *Monitor* editorials, which rarely endorsed U.S. House and Senate candidates, were designed to shed "all possible light on the issues and the records of candidates concerned with them." However, the *Monitor* all but endorsed Senator Robert A. Taft of Ohio because he had provided an "important balance between liberal and ultraconservative wings of the Republican party." In addition, for various reasons, the *Monitor* showed support for Republican Colorado Senator Eugene D. Millikin, Democratic Representative A. S. "Mike" Monroney of Oklahoma and Democratic Senator Millard Tydings of Maryland. The influence that McCarthy might have on the elections was *not* mentioned by the *Monitor* except to say that some supporters of Tydings' opponent were out to make the Senator "pay for his recent fight against the methods of Senator McCarthy."[142]

While the Democrats held onto the majority in the Senate and the House, Congress was far from the "status quo" that Harsch predicted. Republicans gained 30 seats in the House and 5 in the Senate, but sheer numbers did not tell the whole story. Strout wrote of the "spectacular defeat" of Tydings, and of the victories by Richard M. Nixon in California, Taft in Ohio, and Millikin in Colorado—as well as other Republicans—as possibly McCarthy-related: "Many reporters feel that the strength of Senator McCarthy was underrated in earlier estimates of the political situation. Charges of 'softness toward communism' were an important or major issue."[143]

Strout concluded that the Communism issue influenced the victories of Republicans Richard M. Nixon, Everett Dirksen, Bourke B. Hickenlooper,

John M. Butler, and Alexander Wiley. And with Republicans making significant gains, Strout saw a different kind of Congress taking office in 1951: "For the next two years Congress will be Democratic, but it will be anti-administration. Real legislative control will rest in a conservative coalition of southern Democrats and Republicans. Republicans will be in a strong position to block administration measures without assuming responsibility."[144]

While the *Monitor* headlines on news stories included phrases such as "Stunning GOP Gains" and "Republican Surge Batters Truman Policies,"[145] just one day later an editorial page cartoon illustrated less dramatically that the Democrats had lost ground, but still controlled the Senate. The cartoon, titled "Thrown for a loss but still holding the ball," used a football scene to show the Democrat symbol of the donkey holding the ball at the bottom of a pile of GOP elephants.[146] Meanwhile, the *Monitor* editorial sizing up the midterm elections stated that it was "a swing, not a sweep" with "no clear mandate" to be implied from the Republican gains. The surprise, according to the *Monitor*, was the defeat of four-term Senator Millard Tydings of Maryland, largely blamed on his opposition to McCarthy.[147]

Perhaps *Monitor* columnist Joseph C. Harsch placed the midterm elections in the best historical and least alarmist context. He admitted that in times of prosperity incumbents generally win, and that did not happen universally in 1950. However, he noted the old rule that in a midterm election the opposition party (to the President) is likely to "pick up about five seats in the Senate and about 25 in the House" and observed that was "almost precisely what the Republicans gained." According to Harsch, taking that into account helped in truly assessing the meaning of the election: "The Republicans achieved what is 'normal' for a midterm election, no more, and no less."[148] Further, the *Monitor*, in its "Washington Letter" insiders' column, declared that the election "shattered one myth, namely a big vote means a Democratic victory"; the best examples were the states of Ohio and Illinois, where "Republicans picked up the largest majorities."[149]

While it is clear that the *Monitor* acknowledged the possible influence of McCarthy in the elections, many other newspapers and columnists were much more vociferous in their belief that McCarthy was the reason many Republicans won. Williams S. White wrote in the *New York Times* that the consensus around the Senate was that McCarthy beat Tydings and that Tydings' defeat was a direct message from the people expressing their dismay about his subcommittee's investigation.[150] Marquis Childs of the *St. Louis Post-Dispatch* went so far as to declare that in every "major" contest nationwide, "McCarthyism won."[151] Willard Edwards in the *Chicago Tribune* wrote that in every case, "apologists for State Secretary Acheson went down to defeat" and the candidates who emphasized their dedication to "an exhaustive inquiry into communism at Washington were triumphant."[152] A *Tribune* editorial bluntly stated that the results of the election demanded "the removal of Acheson" and a "wholesale revision of our foreign policy."[153] And a second editorial (in the same issue) declared that the *Tribune*'s purchase of the *Washington Times-Herald* was intended to take "Americanism to Washington because Washington wouldn't come to America." It offered proof of "attaining" its objective in the defeat of Millard Tydings in Maryland.[154] The *San Francisco Examiner* interpreted the election results much the same as the *Tribune*. An editorial stated that Americans did not vote Republican, they "VOTED AMERICAN." The *Examiner* linked the Republican gains to a repudiation of the Truman administration's "ARROGANT DISREGARD OF OUR MOST VITAL NATIONAL INTERESTS IN ITS CODDLING AND SHELTERING OF COMMUNISTS." [155]

While Tydings' 40,000-vote loss to Butler was largely blamed on the people's repudiation of the Senator's opposition to McCarthy (as well as the voters' dissatisfaction with Democratic President Truman), many historians believe that was a simplistic explanation. Many other issues surrounding Tydings entered into the results, such as:

Tydings' support of the Taft-Hartley Act, which alienated labor votes; his chairmanship of the Senate Armed Services Committee, which focused on himself some popular resentments against theUnited States involvement in the Korean War; his heavy official duties in Washington, which made it impossible for him to conduct a sustained personal campaign in Maryland; a split in the Maryland Democratic Party, which affected his political forces.[156]

The Tydings/Butler Senate race controversy continued into 1951 when a formal investigation was conducted. In December, Butler campaign manager Jon M. Jonkel assumed responsibility for a tabloid showing Tydings smiling and enjoying the company of former American Communist Party leader Earl Browder. The photo was a composite, which Tydings described as "totally false and fraudulent."[157] The admission of the composite photo and other details about McCarthy's part in the Butler victory prompted some Democrats to consider contesting the race, but a formal challenge to seating Butler did not occur.[158]

COMMUNISM IN AMERICA

By 1950, the Communist Party was already dwindling in numbers in the United States despite all the talk of Communists in government. The *Monitor*, in its effort to provide more than "just the facts," conveyed that to the public. Estimates of Communist Party membership ranged from 60,000 to 80,000 people at the beginning of World War II, but that number dropped to 43,000 by 1950. A major reason for the drop was the disillusionment that many party members felt, caused, in part, by the brief alliance in 1939 between Joseph Stalin and Adolf Hitler.[159] A "Washington Letter" piece explained that the height of popularity of the Communist Party in this country was in the early 1930s when about 100,000 persons were members and about ten times that number were sympathizers. Early in 1950, the "FBI estimated that the Communist Party membership was down to about 50,000, half of whom were in New York State and 7,000 in California."[160] However, those statistics had little effect on the Communist scare—the age of McCarthyism had begun.

MEDIA SELF-CRITIQUE

Although for months during 1950 Senator Joseph R. McCarthy and his accusations were front-page news, other issues overshadowed the year in the eyes of the men and women covering the events. A poll of International News Service editors rated the Korean War as the most important story of 1950, followed by the U.S. mobilization for war. The issue of Red espionage, including the Hiss, Fuchs, and Coplon trials, ranked fourth, but had no direct relationship to McCarthy and his allegations. A similar poll of United Press editors rated the Korean War as the number 1 story followed by the attempt by Puerto Rican assassins to murder President Truman at Blair House. The Alger Hiss conviction for perjury, which again had no direct link to McCarthy's assertions, was rated eighth.[161] So, at least in two news service polls, McCarthy's actions and the subsequent Tydings investigation did not make the 1950 top-ten list of important news stories.

Pro- and anti-McCarthy newspapers debated McCarthy's real intentions, his shrewd use of the press, and the manner in which newspapers handled the continuing story. Wallace Odell of Westchester County Publishers contended that, in at least one speech McCarthy delivered, reporters overemphasized McCarthy's response to a question about the competence of Secretary of State General George C. Marshall, while ignoring the thrust of the entire speech. On the other hand, Robert N. Caldwell of the *Bayonne Times* defended newspapers' treatment of the story, stating that "McCarthy's intention was to indicate that General Marshall was incompetent as Secretary of State, and that deserved the head [headline and emphasis] it got."[162] The debate raged on at a meeting of the Associated Press Managing Editors (APME). Carl Hazen, of the *Shreveport Louisiana Times*, presented the editors with a 66-page report documenting 58 cases of "left-wing bias" in AP news reports, most of which involved McCarthy. The editor and publisher of the Wisconsin *Capital Times*, William T. Evjue, filed his own letter of protest to the AP complaining of right-wing bias and claiming the AP portrayed McCarthy as "a present day Horatio Alger of the United States Sen-

1950: McCarthyism Begins

ate." The AP Board of Directors reported the results of its investigation into the point-by-point charges of Hazen; no bias was found.[163]

Meanwhile, in *Editor and Publisher*, Louis Lyons was quoted as saying that it was "probably no accident that the papers I can think of which have no columnists outside their own staff writers are three of our strongest newspapers."[164] The three newspapers that Lyons referred to were the *New York Times*, the *Milwaukee Journal*, and the *Christian Science Monitor*.[165]

NOTES

1. Robert Griffith, *The Politics of Fear: Joseph McCarthy and the Senate*, 2d ed. (Amherst: University of Massachusetts Press, 1987), 32.

2. Alan Barth, *Government by Investigation* (New York: Viking Press, 1955), 140.

3. Quoted in David Caute, *The Great Fear: The Anti-Communist Purge under Truman and Eisenhower* (New York: Simon & Schuster, 1978), 30.

4. Charles Sellers and Henry May, *A Synopsis of American History* (Chicago: Rand McNally & Company, 1969), 387.

5. Richard M. Fried, *Nightmare in Red* (New York: Oxford University Press, 1990), 68.

6. Thomas Rosteck, *See It Now Confronts McCarthyism: Television Documentary and the Politics of Representation* (Tuscaloosa, Ala. and London: University of Alabama Press, 1994), 15.

7. Ellen Schrecker, *The Age of McCarthyism: A Brief History with Documents* (Boston and New York: St. Martin's Press, 1994), 80. Note: Matthews later briefly served as an investigator and aide to McCarthy.

8. Caute, *The Great Fear*, 523.

9. Ibid., 187–188.

10. James Aronson, *Press and the Cold War* (Indianapolis and New York: Bobbs-Merrill Company, 1970), 57.

11. Fried, *Nightmare in Red*, 60.

12. Caute, *The Great Fear*, 85.

13. A "front organization," as defined by Ellen Schrecker in *The Age of McCarthyism: A Brief History with Documents*: "An organization associated with the Communist Party. Often, but not always, established to carry out a program that promoted causes the party supported, from groups often attracting liberals and other non-communists," 248.

14. Steven M. Gillon, *Politics and Vision: The ADA and American Liberalism, 1947–1985* (New York and Oxford: Oxford University Press, 1987), 74.

15. Quoted in Gillon, *Politics and Vision*, 77.

16. Clifton Brock, *Americans for Democratic Action*, (Westport, Conn.: Greenwood Press, 1985), 132.

17. Caute, *The Great Fear*, 58, 61.

18. Griffith, *The Politics of Fear*, 20–21.

19. David M. Oshinsky, *A Conspiracy So Immense: The World of Joe McCarthy* (New York: The Free Press, 1983), 77.

20. Griffith, *The Politics of Fear*, 25.

21. A "fellow traveler," as defined by Ellen Schrecker in *The Age of McCarthyism: A Brief History with Documents*: "A person who did not actually belong to the Communist Party but who worked closely with it and supported its policies. During the McCarthy period, anti-communist investigators made few distinctions between fellow travelers and party members," 248.

22. Oshinsky, *A Conspiracy So Immense*, 50, 51.

23. Ibid., 71.

24. Thomas C. Reeves, *The Life and Times of Joe McCarthy* (New York: Stein & Day, 1982), 192.

25. Oshinsky, *A Conspiracy So Immense*, 95–96, 128.

26. The *Amerasia* controversy at the *Monitor* will be detailed later in this chapter.

27. Aronson, *Press and the Cold War*, 21.

28. Quoted in *Editor and Publisher*, 19 March 1949, 45.

29. An "Intimate Message" was a column in the *Monitor* where reporters and/or correspondents were allowed to analyze and express their opinions about politic, social, and societal issues. It appeared on the editorial page.

30. Richard L. Strout, "Hollywood Hearings and Headlines: An Intimate Message from Washington," *Christian Science Monitor*, November 1947, ed. page.

31. Richard L. Strout, "House Un-American Activities Committee: An Intimate Message from Washington," *Christian Science Monitor*, 31 December 1948, ed. page.

32. Douglass Cater, *The Fourth Branch of Government* (New York: Houghton Mifflin Company, 1959), 7.

33. Richard M. Fried, *Men against McCarthy* (New York: Columbia University Press, 1976), 13.

34. "Fuchs Case Intensifies Security Drive in Britain; U.S. Waits Extent of 'Leaks': Soviet Agents Names Asked," *Christian Science Monitor*, 11 February 1950, 1.

35. Richard H. Rovere, *Senator Joe McCarthy* (New York: Harper & Row, 1959), 126. "McCarthy Hits 'Reds' in Office," *New York Times*, 12 February 1950, 2.

36. At this point, McCarthy had settled on the figure of 57, not 205 as had been originally alleged.

37. Richard L. Strout, "GOP Diners Find 'Harmony' Elusive; Democratic Test Set," *Christian Science Monitor*, 14 February 1950, 1.

38. Editorial, " 'Jumping' Joe McCarthy," *Milwaukee Journal*, 14 February 1950, 18.

39. "Tito Assured by U.S. Envoy of No Internal Interference," *Christian Science Monitor*, 20 February 1950, 8.

40. Rovere, *Senator Joe McCarthy*, 131, 137.

41. Reeves, *The Life and Times*, 242.

42. William F. Buckley, Jr. and Brent L. Bozell, *McCarthy and His Enemies: The Record and Its Meaning* (Chicago: Henry Regnery Company, 1954), 54–55.

43. Willard Edwards, "3 Lead Reds in State Dept., M'Carthy Says: Contact with Soviet Agents Charged," *Chicago Tribune*, 21 February 1950, 1.

44. Aronson, *Press and the Cold War*, 73.

45. "Senate Democrats to Sift Spy Charges," *Christian Science Monitor*, 21 February 1950, 17.

46. Earl Latham, ed. *The Communist Controversy in Washington: From the New Deal to McCarthy* (Cambridge, Mass.: Harvard University Press, 1966), 270.

47. "Senate Broadens Probe of Communist Charges," *Christian Science Monitor*, 23 February 1950, 16.

48. William H. Stringer, "Fuchs Sentenced to 14-Year Term for Atomic Leak," *Christian Science Monitor*, 1 March 1950, 1.

49. "National's Espionage Trial Ends in New York," *Christian Science Monitor*, 7 March 1950, 1.

50. Richard L. Strout, "Senators Clash on How to Stage Communist Hunt," *Christian Science Monitor*, 8 March 1950, 1.

51. Quoted in Strout, "Senators Clash," 1.

52. Strout, "Senators Clash," 1.

53. Buckley and Bozell, *McCarthy and His Enemies*, 67.

54. Latham, *The Communist Controversy in Washington*, 272.

55. Editorial, "Mr. McCarthy's Campaign," *New York Times*, 22 February 1950, 28.

56. Joseph C. Harsch, "State of the Nation: Sharp Eyes Curb Communist Spy Peril in the U.S.," *Christian Science Monitor*, 7 March 1950, 1.

57. Richard L. Strout, "Communist Probe Hits New Snags," *Christian Science Monitor*, 9 March 1950, 1.

58. Joseph C. Harsch, "State of the Nation: Loyalty Quiz Airs New Partisan Twist," *Christian Science Monitor*, 10 March 1950, 1.

59. Editorial, "Security vs. Smearing," *Christian Science Monitor*, 11 March 1950, 18.

60. Editorial, "The Right to Join," *New York Times*, 10 March 1950, 26.

61. Fred J. Cook, *The Nightmare Decade: The Life and Times of Joe McCarthy* (New York: Random House, 1971), 178.

62. Richard L. Strout, "Denials Rain on McCarthy Charges," *Christian Science Monitor*, 13 March 1950, 1.

63. Quoted in Richard L. Strout, "Miss Kenyon Flays McCarthy," *Christian Science Monitor*, 14 March 1950, 1.

64. Editorial Cartoon, "Spring Bonnet," *Christian Science Monitor*, 16 March 1950, 20.

65. Editorial Cartoon, "Unfairly Matched," *Christian Science Monitor*, 18 March 1950, 18.

66. Henry L. Stimson, to editor, "Loyalty in Washington," *New York Times*, 27 March 1950, 22.

67. Editorial, "How You Would Feel," *Christian Science Monitor*, 30 March 1950, 24.

68. Ibid.

69. Richard L. Strout, "The McCarthy Molehill: An Intimate Message from Washington," *Christian Science Monitor*, 30 March 1950, 24.

70. Editorial Cartoon, "Where's the Sportsmanship?" *Christian Science Monitor*, 30 March 1950, 24.

71. Oshinsky, *A Conspiracy So Immense*, 136.

72. Latham, *The Communist Controversy in Washington*, 275.

73. Richard L. Strout, "McCarthy Nears Climax in Hunt for Communists," *Christian Science Monitor*, 27 March 1950, 1.

74. Quoted in Fried, *Men against McCarthy*, 69.

75. Oshinsky, *A Conspiracy So Immense*, 144.

76. Editorial, "Simple Fair Play," *Christian Science Monitor*, 5 April 1950, 21.

77. Richard L. Strout, "Lattimore Terms McCarthy Charge Contemptible Lie," *Christian Science Monitor*, 6 April 1950, 1.

78. Quoted in Strout, "Lattimore Terms McCarthy Charge Contemptible Lie," 1.

79. "Excerpts from Lattimore's Statements," *Christian Science Monitor*, 6 April 1950, 76.

80. Richard L. Strout, "McCarthy: Has He Witnesses?" *Christian Science Monitor*, 7 April 1950, 1.

81. Richard L. Strout, "Policy vs. Passion and Prejudice: An Intimate Message from Washington," *Christian Science Monitor*, 7 April 1950, 20.

82. Max K. Gilstrap, "McCarthy Unfolds Career of Charm Matched with Intense Ambition: Audacious Tactics Spur Meteoric Rise," *Christian Science Monitor*, 7 April 1950, 7.

83. Editorial, "The Menace of 'McCarthyism,' " *New York Times*, 8 April 1950, 12.

84. Richard L. Strout, "Budenz Key to M'Carthy Accusations," *Christian Science Monitor*, 11 April 1950, 1.

85. Richard L. Strout, "Budenz Accuses Lattimore—In Hearsay Charge," *Christian Science Monitor*, 20 April 1950, 1.

86. Richard L. Strout, "Budenz Accusations of Lattimore Sifted; Thorpe Aids Defense," *Christian Science Monitor*, 21 April 1950, 1.

87. Editorial, "The Budenz Testimony," *New York Times*, 21 April 1950, 22.

88. Editorial, "High Command for Peace," *Christian Science Monitor*, 18 April 1950, 18.

89. Roscoe Drummond, "The State of Europe: Overheated McCarthy Drive Stirs Shivers Abroad," *Christian Science Monitor*, 22 April 1950, 1.

90. Roscoe Drummond, "State of the Nation: McCarthy Shots Heard Round the World," *Christian Science Monitor*, 6 May 1950, 1.

91. Richard L. Strout, "McCarthy Attack Forces Administration Rebuttal," *Christian Science Monitor*, 24 April 1950, 1.

92. Richard L. Strout. "McCarthy Blasts Set Off Internal Political Crisis," *Christian Science Monitor*, 31 May 1950, 1.

93. Richard L. Strout, "McCarthy Tactics Seen Blow to U.S. Abroad," *Christian Science Monitor*, 12 May 1950, 1.

94. Quoted in Strout, "McCarthy Tactics," 1.

95. Richard L. Strout to Mother, Alan, Phyliss, and Nancy, 23 April 1950, Richard L. Strout Papers, Weston, Mass.

96. Editorial, "The Case for Faith," *Christian Science Monitor*, 8 April 1950, 16.

1950: McCarthyism Begins

97. Richard L. Strout, "McCarthy Fires News Blast 'Gags' Hostile Evidence; Russia Seen Spy-Ridden: Witness Reappears," *Christian Science Monitor*, 26 April 1950, 1. "Browder: No Communists in U.S. State Department," *Christian Science Monitor*, 27 April 1950, 1. "Field Denies Mentioning Lattimore," *Christian Science Monitor*, 28 April 1950, 1.

98. The veracity of this statement is documented earlier in this book.

99. Quoted in Richard L. Strout, "Lattimore Turns Guns on Accuser," *Christian Science Monitor*, 2 May 1950, 1.

100. "Hickenlooper Grills Lattimore," *Christian Science Monitor*, 3 May 1950, 1.

101. Richard L. Strout, "When Charges Turn to Chaff: An Intimate Message from Washington," *Christian Science Monitor*, 5 May 1950, 22.

102. Fried, *Nightmare in Red*, 127.

103. Richard L. Strout, "Ordeal by Publicity: The McCarthy Hearings Prove Once More the Distorting Effects of 'Straight Reporting,' " *Christian Science Monitor Magazine*, 27 May 1950, 5.

104. Ibid, 15.

105. Cook, *The Nightmare Decade*, 261.

106. Richard L. Strout, "Eight Republican Senators Repudiate 'McCarthyism': Mrs. Smith Leads 'Bolt,' " *Christian Science Monitor*, 2 June 1950, 1.

107. Editorial, "A Call to Conscience," *Christian Science Monitor*, 3 June 1950, 18.

108. Editorial, "A Declaration of Conscience against 'McCarthyism,' " *Milwaukee Journal*, 2 June 1950, 20.

109. Editorial, "Mrs. Smith for Veep," *Milwaukee Journal*, 8 June 1950, 24M.

110. Editorial, "Mrs. Smith's Conscience," *New York Times*, 3 June 1950, 14.

111. "The World's Day," *Christian Science Monitor*, 20 July 1950, 1. Editorial, " 'A Fraud and a Hoax,' " *Milwaukee Journal*, 18 July 1950, 18.

112. Quoted in Richard L. Strout, "McCarthy Charges Denounced as Hoax in Tydings Report," *Christian Science Monitor*, 18 July 1950, 1.

113. Strout, "McCarthy Charges Denounced," 1.

114. Joseph C. Harsch, "State of the Nation: McCarthy Ordeal Jars Both Sides," *Christian Science Monitor*, 21 July 1950, 1.

115. Reeves, *The Life and Times*, 304.

116. Editorial, "Report on Loyalty," *Christian Science Monitor*, 19 July 1950, 20.

117. Editorial, "The M'Carthy Charges," *New York Times*, 18 July 1950, 28L.

118. " 'A Fraud and a Hoax,' " *Milwaukee Journal*, 18.

119. Editorial, "A Shameful Performance," *San Francisco Examiner*, 19 July 1950, 18.

120. Editorial, "The Report Nobody Believes," *Chicago Tribune*, 19 June 1950, 20.

121. Griffith, *The Politics of Fear*, 35–37. Oshinsky, *A Conspiracy So Immense*, 95–96. Reeves, *The Life and Times*, 290–293.

122. "Tydings Vow 'Full Story' about '45 *Amerasia* Case," *Christian Science Monitor*, 23 May 1950, 13. "Probe of *Amerasia* Case Urged by GOP Senators," *Christian Science Monitor*, 13 June 1950, 7. "*Amerasia* Case Kindles Partisanship," *Christian Science Monitor*, 14 June 1950, 10.

123. "Grand Jury Clears U.S. in *Amerasia*," *Christian Science Monitor*, 15 June 1950, 1.

124. Richard L. Strout, "Korea, McCarthy, and Lattimore: An Intimate Message from Washington," *Christian Science Monitor*, 30 June 1950, 20.

125. Gale, Bernays, Falk, and Eisner to Richard L. Strout, 15 August 1950, Richard L. Strout Papers, Weston, Mass., 1.

126. Richard L. Strout, "*Amerasia*: So That's What Happened: An Intimate Message from Washington," *Christian Science Monitor*, 21 July 1950, 20.

127. Gale, Bernays, Falk, and Eisner letter, 2.

128. Strout, "*Amerasia*," 20.

129. Gale, Bernays, Falk, and Eisner letter, 2.

130. Editorial, "Inaccuracies in *Amerasia* Article," *Christian Science Monitor*, 18 August 1950, 18.

131. Erwin D. Canham to Richard L. Strout, 18 August 1950, Richard L. Strout Papers, Weston, Mass.

132. Richard L. Strout to Erwin D. Canham, 4 September 1950, Richard L. Strout Papers, Weston, Mass.

133. Erwin D. Canham to Richard L. Strout, 15 September 1950, Richard L. Strout Papers, Weston, Mass.

134. Erwin D. Canham to Staff, September 1950, Richard L. Strout Papers, Weston, Mass.

135. This may have been particularly true at this time because of the trouble created in covering McCarthy.

136. Christian Science Board of Directors to Mr. Erwin D. Canham, 16 November 1950, 1–4. Church History Department, The First Church of Christ, Scientist, Boston, Mass.

137. "Associated Press Chief Hailed for Liberating New Writing," *Christian Science Monitor*, 27 September 1950, 5.

138. Richard L. Strout, "Republicans Turn Campaign Sights on Capturing Congress," *Christian Science Monitor*, 28 September 1950, 1.

139. Richard L. Strout, "Senate Race Stiff Test for Republicans to Gain 7 Seats," *Christian Science Monitor*, 20 October 1950, 3.

140. Richard L. Strout, "Strategy of Both Parties Cuts Choice for Voters: Smear Campaigns Hit," *Christian Science Monitor*, 3 November 1950, 1.

141. Joseph C. Harsch, "State of the Nation: Election Preview," *Christian Science Monitor*, 23 October 1950, 1.

142. Editorial, "National Leadership and the Midterm Elections," *Christian Science Monitor*, 24 October 1950, 18.

143. Richard L. Strout, "Republican Surge Batters Truman Policies; Democrats Control Senate by Close Margin: Trend Set by McCarthy," *Christian Science Monitor*, 8 November 1950, 1.

144. Richard L. Strout, "Congressional Gains of Republicans Pose Major Problems for President; Early Call of Congress, Acheson Fate Weighed," *Christian Science Monitor*, 9 November 1950, 1.

145. "Stunning GOP Gains Leave Democrats in Shaky Control of Congress," *Christian Science Monitor*, 8 November 1950, 11. Strout, "Republican Surge Batters Truman Policies," 1.

1950: McCarthyism Begins   33

146. Editorial Cartoon, "Thrown for a loss but still holding the ball," *Christian Science Monitor*, 8 November 1950, 24.

147. Editorial, "Reading the Returns," *Christian Science Monitor*, 8 November 1950, 24.

148. Joseph C. Harsch, "State of the Nation: The Midterm Election," *Christian Science Monitor*, 9 November 1950, 1.

149. "Washington Letter," *Christian Science Monitor*, 18 November 1950, M2.

150. William S. White, "McCarthy's Influence Is Greater in the 82D," *New York Times*, 7 January 1951, E7.

151. Marquis Childs, "GOP Victories Threaten Foreign Policy," *St. Louis Post-Dispatch*, 10 November 1950, 3E.

152. Willard Edwards, "Blame Commie Whitewash for Tydings Defeat," *Chicago Tribune*, 9 November 1950, 8.

153. Editorial, "A Victory for America," *Chicago Tribune*, 9 November 1950, 16H.

154. Editorial, "Americanism Reaches Washington," *Chicago Tribune*, 9 November 1950, 16H.

155. Editorial, "An American Victory," *San Francisco Examiner*, 10 November 1950, 26.

156. Reeves, *The Life and Times*, 286.

157. Quoted in "Butler Aide Assumes Blame for Tabloid," *Christian Science Monitor*, 21 December 1950, 16.

158. "Democrats Ponder Protest over Butler Taking Senate Seat," *Christian Science Monitor*, 29 December 1950, 6.

159. Caute, *The Great Fear*, 185.

160. "Washington Letter," *Christian Science Monitor*, 30 December 1950, M2.

161. "INS Editors and Publishers Compile 'Big 10' Stories of '50," *Editor and Publisher*, 6 January 1951, 60.

162. Quoted in "Are Our Headlines Fair?," *Bulletin of the American Society of Newspaper Editors*, no. 320, 1 May 1950, 8. Quoted in "The McCarthy Headlines," *Bulletin of the American Society of Newspaper Editors*, no. 321, 1 June 1950, 3.

163. "The Hazen Report," *APME Red Book 1950*, 65, 69–70.

164. Quoted in Robert U. Brown, "Shop Talk at Thirty," *Editor and Publisher*, 18 November 1950, 72.

165. Brown, "Shop Talk at Thirty," 72.

2
1951: McCarthy's Character Assassinations

ANOTHER ANTI-COMMUNISM MEASURE

As the actual threat of domestic Communism decreased, the need felt by politicians to appear tough on Communism increased. This was largely due to the publicity surrounding government investigations of Communism, and an interpretation of the 1950 midterm elections that the winning formula included being tough on Communism or claiming your opponent was not. The Communist Party *Daily Worker* felt the effects of a shrinking membership: It issued a warning to its readers that if circulation figures did not increase, the publication would have to cease operations. The newspaper reported in January 1951 that circulation had dropped to 14,000 with fewer than 50,000 subscribing to the Sunday edition. And, with 28,000 subscriptions expiring in the coming months, the paper claimed its existence was threatened.[1] A midyear "retrenchment" effort by the newspaper guaranteed its survival; the paper was reduced from 12 to 8 pages and the price was raised from five to ten cents per issue.[2] Although the newspaper survived, there were only 50,000 registered Communists in the United States.[3]

Congressmen, Senators, and some citizens knew of the dwindling numbers of Communists, yet at the beginning of 1951, there were no fewer than six government agencies designed to fight the "menace" of Communism at home. They were the House Un-American Activities Committee (HUAC), the McCarran subcommittee of the Senate Judiciary Committee, the Federal Loyalty Review Board (FLRB), the Subversive Activities Control Board (SACB), the Federal Bureau of Investigation (FBI), and a newly appointed

President's Commission on Internal Security and Individual Rights. On January 23, President Truman named Admiral Chester W. Nimitz as chair of the new civilian commission. The Nimitz Commission's charge was to figure out how to test the loyalty of people.[4]

The *Monitor*'s Richard L. Strout wrote a couple of interpretive pieces about the Nimitz Commission. He stated that "it can be argued that they [members of the Truman administration] are creating civil division and nationwide fears out of proportion to their size" in creating another investigative body, but Strout conceded that "it is recognized that atomic secrets make the situation serious out of proportion to alleged membership."[5] So, although the threat from Communism was "smaller in the United States than in any other country" in numbers, Strout nevertheless saw the wisdom of such a commission.[6] A *Monitor* editorial likened the new commission to "British royal commissions," which had "been urged by this newspaper off and on since early 1947." The newspaper declared that "only a commission towering above partisanship can lift the nation out of this sorry mess of charges, innuendo, and suspicions," replacing congressional inquiries that "split along party lines" and "neither clear the innocent nor expose the guilty before the bar of public opinion."[7] While the idea of creating an independent commission circulated, a Congressional subcommittee began investigating charges of improprieties in the 1950 Senate campaign in Maryland.

GILLETTE SUBCOMMITTEE INVESTIGATION

The Senate Rules Committee's Privileges and Elections subcommittee reviewed the campaign practices of Republican John M. Butler in defeating incumbent Democrat Senator Millard Tydings. Tydings filed a complaint, alleging, among other things, that campaign literature from Butler showed a misleading composite photograph of Tydings enjoying the company of former Communist Party leader Earl Browder. This and other "unadorned lies" were outlined in Tydings' 9,000-word statement to the subcommittee, which was chaired by Guy M. Gillette, a Democrat from Iowa, and included two other Democrats and two Republicans.[8] Pro-McCarthy *San Francisco Examiner* columnist George Rothwell Brown observed that the word "liar" had never been used as often in describing a political opponent as in Tydings' description of Butler. Brown called Butler's alleged improper campaign methods "Sunday school variety as compared with the tactics of the labor bosses and their Democratic stooges in the unsuccessful campaign of vilification to defeat Taft in Ohio."[9] Other newspapers, including the *Monitor*, chose to wait for the subcommittee investigation before editorializing.

Bizarre stories emerged from the hearings. One concerned Baltimore printer William H. Fedder who claimed he was taken on a late night ride and roughed up by Butler's people, who demanded he return a letter from the campaign that guaranteed Fedder $12,000 for printing campaign literature. McCarthy investigator Don Surine labeled Fedder's story a "fantastic fabrication" and said that Fedder falsely claimed to have stamped and addressed 50,000 postcards.[10] Using stories written by Strout, along with Associated Press dispatches, the *Monitor* gave its readers the essence of the charges and countercharges. Strout also brought context to the proceedings by discussing the possible outcome and subsequent consequences. He wrote that many people believed "McCarthy-type campaigns featuring the 'communist' issue could be a major feature of the 1952 elections," and Strout suggested that if the label of Communist "could be made to stick . . . against a conservative like Mr. Tydings" that "it could be made to stick against most candidates."[11] Eventually, Butler campaign manager Jon M. Jonkel took responsibility for the tabloid composite photograph, but not before suggesting that McCarthy and others urged its use. In fact, McCarthy and other outsiders acting in McCarthy's behalf played an integral part in Butler's campaign.[12]

The hearings lasted until August, when the subcommittee issued its *unanimous* opinion.[13] The Gillette subcommittee stated in part that "Senator McCarthy deliberately set out to thwart any investigation of him by refusing to testify," but it made no recommendation of action against McCarthy.[14] The subcommittee further stated that the tactics used by the Butler campaign were "despicable," and there were irregularities in the campaign's financing, improper outside influences, and defamation of character.[15] The report clearly identified a "front and back street" campaign by non-Maryland people, and urged the Senate Rules Committee to set formal procedures for contesting elections and disciplining senators for conduct unfit for high office. The report did not recommend unseating Butler and was considered by many as merely a slap on the wrist for both Butler and McCarthy.[16]

However, Strout considered the action important—it "unreservedly denounces, condemns and censures" Butler's campaign practices. He described the subcommittee report as "one of the strongest denunciations of election tactics in many years." Strout noted the unanimous nature of the vote and stated that the subcommittee "warned the nation of the danger of a political smear campaign based on the effort to throw doubt on a rival candidate's loyalty and patriotism."[17] A *Monitor* editorial stated that the "most vital task before the American people today is the raising of fundamental moral standards." It stated that even after the subcommittee report's criticism of the Maryland election campaign of Senator Butler, some discounted it under the premise that all elections were corrupt. The *Monitor* did not support that thinking. It expressed remorse at the subcommittee's declaration that since "no standards for the proper conduct of campaigns exist," this meant that Butler went unpunished, and "as the reward for a campaign such as this" he was elected to the U.S. Senate. The newspaper concluded that a proposal to set up rules and standards for election behavior was a good idea, but stressed that change would "be carried out only if the public shows that it is aroused enough to demand moral standards for elections."[18]

A *New York Times* editorial stated that "evidence is too clear that a smear campaign against Senator Tydings" occurred and that Tydings was unfortunately punished by the voters for refusing "to convict accused persons on insufficient evidence."[19] Not surprisingly, the most vociferous response came from the *Milwaukee Journal*. An editorial declared the campaign by Butler—greatly aided by McCarthy's office—a "national disgrace" and flatly called for the "ouster" of Butler, contending that Congress needed to develop "enough intestinal fortitude to punish the beneficiary of such frauds" or nothing would change in the future.[20] Just as vehement on the other side, George Rothwell Brown, columnist for the *San Francisco Examiner*, called the report a "whitewash of the whitewashers," "lopsided and manifestly unfair" to McCarthy and Butler in many of its particulars. Brown surmised that the reason the report did not recommend expelling Butler from his Senate seat was that "the full committee would REPUDIATE THE RECOMMENDATION" or that the entire senate "would overwhelmingly sustain Senator Butler's right to his seat."[21]

Meanwhile, McCarthy responded to the subcommittee's report, claiming he did not misrepresent the facts in urging the use of the composite photo of Tydings and Browder (because it represented a true relationship between the men's ideas, according to the Senator) and vowed to file a "one-man" minority report.[22]

BENTON RESOLUTION

Not long after the Gillette subcommittee issued its opinion about the 1950 Butler Senate campaign, Democrat Senator William Benton of Connecticut asked the Senate to pursue expulsion hearings or request that Senator McCarthy resign. Benton saw this as the only way to "make amends" to Wisconsin and the Senate for McCarthy's improper actions during the Maryland election. McCarthy countered by labeling Benton a "hero" to every Communist and crook "in and out of government."[23] Despite the less than enthusiastic vocal support for the ouster of McCarthy, Benton's resolution was referred to the Senate Rules Committee, which voted September 24 to hold hearings, again tabbing the Gillette subcommittee to investigate the matter.

Joseph C. Harsch, *Monitor* columnist, wrote that Benton's call for expulsion or resignation was an "extraordinary incident" that "challenged the dark-

1951: McCarthy's Character Assassinations

jowled man from Wisconsin who has come to be feared by his colleagues more than Huey Long ever was." Harsch stated that anyone who had "tangled" with McCarthy "regretted it," and likened the Benton-McCarthy battle to David versus Goliath, only "this David doesn't have a slingshot." Harsch saw the odds as "99 to one on the slugger from Wisconsin."[24]

Benton submitted a 59-page Bill of Particulars citing ten specific cases of "amoral" conduct. Benton claimed that McCarthy lied in denying he said there were "205 card-carrying communists in the State Department" at his original Lincoln Day speech; that McCarthy accepted $10,000 of "influence money" from Lustron Corporation; and that McCarthy lied in declaring he had seen a confidential FBI chart about Communists, a chart FBI Director J. Edgar Hoover identified as a "hoax." [25] Benton's long list of McCarthy's alleged improprieties attempted to establish a pattern of conduct that was unbecoming a senator.[26]

The *Monitor* wrote that it was doubtful that McCarthy would be ousted from the Senate, but that McCarthy for the first time was put on the "defensive." The newspaper made it clear that, along with Republicans (and most of the rest of McCarthy's colleagues in the Senate), the *Monitor* wanted "as strongly as anyone to root out communism," but stated it "could be done without resorting to smearing and intimidation of opponents." The editorial reiterated its support for a nonpartisan commission of distinguished citizens to be appointed to investigate charges of Communism in government, which would "curb smearing" and "more than that, it could enlist the confidence of the nation behind its judgments."[27]

A September 29 edition of the *New York Times* devoted nearly an entire page (starting on the front page and covering nearly all of page 6) to Benton's ten specific charges of "misconduct" by McCarthy.[28] While the *Times* listed each of the ten accusations, it also carried a short story quoting McCarthy as calling Benton an "old little mental midget."[29] Hearst columnist Fulton Lewis, Jr. called the Senator "Wee Willie" Benton, and concluded that the expulsion attempt would fail. Lewis criticized Benton's record as showing no urgency "when it came to the matter of cleaning Commies and Pinkos out of the State Department" and suggested that perhaps McCarthy's charges had "touched home" with Benton.[30] The *Chicago Tribune* was not immune to name calling itself. Describing Benton as a "blowhard," an editorial criticized him for labeling McCarthy's "efforts to expose Communists and drive them out of the administration" as conduct "unbecoming" a senator. While discounting the possibility of expulsion for McCarthy, the *Tribune* stated that a censure vote was possible, and if carried out, those senators opposing McCarthy would be identified, offering "the opportunity at the coming elections of sending un-American senators out of Washington along with the Reds."[31]

Before Benton's resolution against McCarthy was acted on (which was not until 1952), Benton tried to force McCarthy to give federal prosecutors any "evidence" of Communists in the State Department. Meanwhile, when Gillette resigned as subcommittee chair, Democrat Senator Thomas C. Hennings, Jr. of Missouri took over. McCarthy immediately requested that Hennings "disqualify" himself from the hearings.[32] According to Strout, McCarthy claimed that Hennings' law firm represented people opposing the Senator's anticommunism effort, and that Hennings' firm was retained by the *St. Louis Post-Dispatch*, a newspaper on record opposing McCarthy. Hennings took exception to McCarthy's charges and called the Senator's argument against him a "misrepresentation" of the facts.[33] The charges contained in the Benton resolution surfaced and resurfaced during 1952, a Presidential election year, and Hennings' subcommittee report was not completed until early January 1953.[34]

Clearly the *Monitor* took a stand against McCarthy, and proposed solutions to his method of smearing individuals. And just as clearly, the *Monitor's* credo "to injure no man, but to bless all mankind" precluded it from name calling and other crude methods of offering its opinions, unlike the *Examiner* and the *Tribune*, but not unlike the *New York Times*.

MACARTHUR, MARSHALL, ACHESON, AND JESSUP

Meanwhile, from April through December 1951, various prominent Americans felt the wrath of McCarthy. President Harry S. Truman was the first, as a war of words between the President and General Douglas MacArthur eventually led to the dismissal of MacArthur from his command in the Far East. The *Monitor's* Joseph C. Harsch speculated two days before the President's actions that MacArthur might be on the way out. Harsch cited MacArthur's refusal to obey a December 5, 1950 order for field commanders to cease making comments about high policy. MacArthur stated that if he had permission to carry the war to China (bomb bases in Manchuria), he could win in Korea. This was expressly contrary to State Department, Defense Department, and United Nations' policy in the region.[35]

When MacArthur officially was ordered to give up his duties in the Far East and return to the United States, the events dominated the *Monitor's* pages (and most newspapers) with 11 stories and commentaries in the April 11 issue. A *Monitor* editorial, published that day, failed to take a hard stand about MacArthur's dismissal, yet leaned toward supporting Truman. It pointed out the need to assess the situation cautiously. The *Monitor* contrasted MacArthur's view that conquering Asia was important with Truman's belief that Europe's interests were more important. It stated that MacArthur believed in military solutions while Truman believed advancing the concept of freedom was the best weapon against Communism's expansion. Finally, the *Monitor* found fault with MacArthur for failing to follow the chain of command by disobeying the President's and State Department's policy.[36]

The *New York Times*, after reviewing the events that led to MacArthur's dismissal, stated in an editorial that "we do not see how it is possible to question the correctness of the President's decision."[37] The careful and thoughtful approach to MacArthur's firing was countered by a front-page editorial in the *San Francisco Examiner* calling for Truman's impeachment. The editorial bluntly stated that "President Truman must be impeached and convicted" and that every day Truman "remains in office menaces the safety of the United States." But the newspaper did not stop there. It called Truman a "fool" and predicted that the country "will demand" impeachment because of MacArthur's firing.[38]

Later in 1951, Major General Charles A. Willoughby, former Chief of Intelligence for General MacArthur, accused six newsmen of biases and inaccuracies that brought aid and comfort to the enemy in Korea. Willoughby also blamed newsmen for the ultimate dismissal of MacArthur. Among those listed by him were syndicated columnists Joseph Alsop and Drew Pearson and *New York Times* correspondent Hanson Baldwin.[39] Though the *Monitor* was not implicated by Willoughby, it labeled the charges unfounded. An editorial declared that blaming the firing of MacArthur on the newspapers was "like saying that President Truman and the Joint Chiefs of Staff based their decision on what they read in the newspaper when they had before them continually secret information."[40]

On June 14, 1951, Joseph R. McCarthy delivered his "most famous"[41] speech, but you would not have known that by the coverage given to it by the *Monitor*, or even the most adamant pro-McCarthy papers, such as the *San Francisco Examiner*. Actually, only about 20,000 words of the 60,000-word speech were read on the floor of the Senate; the rest was submitted for the record unread. McCarthy probably did not even write the speech, which may have been the "most daring and seditious" of his career.[42] He claimed that General George Catlett Marshall, secretary of defense (and a true American hero), had participated in failed China policy, stood by Stalin in war and peace, and was "with" Roosevelt when "Poland was delivered to the Reds."[43] There were no banner headline stories in the *Monitor* about McCarthy's outrageous charges; in fact the first mention of the speech came buried in a page 3 story two days later. A short editorial appearing the same day questioned McCarthy's logic in making the charges, and asked questions: "Is Senator McCarthy helping to clear the air and to unify the American people against their common enemy, Russian communistic imperialism? Or is he doing that which sows suspicion, undermines confidence, and sets good Americans against each other, while the Kremlin looks on and laughs?"[44]

While MacArthur's dismissal received heavy coverage in the *Monitor*, no spot news story and only one short editorial was born out of McCarthy's blast against Marshall. The researcher was not able to determine whether the *Monitor* tired of the Senator's continual charges and downplayed them on purpose, or misread the "newsworthiness" of the event—which emerged with the passing of time.[45] The *Milwaukee Journal* stated in an editorial that McCarthy's latest outburst was an attempt to return to the front pages with "his exclusive brand of misstatements, misquotations and vilification." As one of the Senator's most vocal critics, the *Journal* declared that "there is no such quality as decency in McCarthy" and the "depravity" of the man had "shamed" the people of Wisconsin.[46] The *Examiner* ran a lengthy story about the speech, highlighting 13 different points made by McCarthy. Yet, the story was buried on page 6.[47] Meanwhile, the *Chicago Tribune* carried a front-page story, but without any banner headlines to call attention to it. Reporter Willard Edwards' story described McCarthy speaking to "galleries packed with spectators" and declared that the junior senator "did not disappoint his listeners."[48] While many Americans did not believe McCarthy's charges against Marshall, in December, McCarthy—apparently undaunted—published a 187-page revised version of his June 14 speech called "America's Retreat from Victory, the Story of George Catlett Marshall."[49]

Secretary of State Dean Acheson was another of McCarthy's early and consistent targets. McCarthy claimed that Acheson was "soft" on Communism, severely lambasting the secretary when Acheson declared that he wouldn't turn his back on Alger Hiss (prior to the Hiss guilty verdict on perjury).[50]

Richard L. Strout wrote about the McCarthy-Acheson battle in a February "Intimate Message." Strout saw the appointment of McCarthy to the Senate appropriations subcommittee as indicating that the "dominant congressional Republican wing" supported McCarthy and planned to "use him in the 1952 election." He reported that the "bumping" of Senator Margaret Chase Smith of Maine from the expenditures investigating subcommittee, apparently in connection with her "declaration of conscience" speech against McCarthy, caused "some resentment." But Strout saw McCarthy—by virtue of his position on the appropriations' subcommittee which oversees money for the State Department—as dangerous to American foreign policy. Strout contended that McCarthy so much as called Acheson a "traitor," claiming the secretary worked "against his country's good." With McCarthy's Senate immunity, Acheson simply had no "legal recourse" against the attacks. McCarthy's subcommittee, appointment would put

1951: McCarthy's Character Assassinations 43

Acheson "face to face with his tormentor." Strout asked, "Who would like to be in Mr. Acheson's shoes?," with McCarthy having "opposed mild approaches to Russia" and the "eventual issue" being "war or peace" with the use of atomic weapons.[51] But, before this "face to face" encounter between Acheson and McCarthy occurred, the Senator was removed from the appropriations subcommittee.

In April, Joseph C. Harsch, Chief of the *Monitor's* Washington Bureau, saw an opportunity for President Truman to replace Acheson without losing face. After reporting that dismissing Acheson would just deliver his replacement into the same firestorm (because Truman contended the criticism of Acheson was actually a result of disgruntlement at the administration's policies, and was not aimed at Acheson personally), Harsch contended that Senate Republicans had "laid off" Acheson for a time, so his dismissal would not look as if Truman were buckling to pressure. Additionally, Harsch observed a lull between McCarthy being removed from the appropriations subcommittee and the Wisconsin senator positioning himself to resume his attacks on the State Department, a time Truman could have taken advantage of by asking Acheson to step down. Finally, Harsch claimed that MacArthur's return to the United States "created a new bond" between the White House and the Republican leadership in Congress, a bond that could lead to more bipartisan agreement on foreign policy, which was desperately needed and could be further promoted with the removal of Acheson.[52]

In the summer of 1951, Roscoe Drummond replaced Harsch as the Washington News Bureau's front-page "State of the Nation" columnist. Drummond wrote about the nomination of Phillip C. Jessup (a McCarthy foe) as a delegate to the United Nations. Drummond predicted that the decision by some Republicans to fight Jessup's nomination, and Truman's pledge that Acheson would remain Secretary of State, certainly would be in the news for "some time," perhaps even as part of the rhetoric of the 1952 election.[53] Drummond was correct, and McCarthy challenged Truman's nomination of Jessup to the UN, citing the ambassador's affiliation with organizations on a "left wing list."[54] McCarthy's strongest charges against the Ambassador-at-Large came during the Senator's naming of 26 State Department employees whose loyalty was under investigation. McCarthy claimed that Jessup was "the prize of them all" and had strong connections and sympathies with the Kremlin.[55] Strout, in a front-page *Monitor* story about the controversy, hinted that General Dwight D. Eisenhower's name might surface in the confirmation fight because Jessup was a professor at Columbia University and Eisenhower, on leave as President of Columbia, had "warmly declared his belief" in the "loyalty and patriotism" of Jessup. Strout also wrote that the latest charges by McCarthy came immediately under attack by New Deal Senate Democrats.[56] Clearly, Strout's story focused less on the latest McCarthy charges and more on the Senate's reaction to those charges.

A *Monitor* editorial attempted to evaluate the legitimate arguments for and against Jessup's confirmation, but took no strong position. The newspaper stated that McCarthy's charges had "largely collapsed of their own inaccuracy and exaggeration." The *Monitor* contended that the allegation that the State Department (Acheson) and Jessup advocated "recognition of Communist China" apparently was overstated; the evidence pointed only to consideration of such a measure. This consideration, the *Monitor* continued, must also be taken in the context of the time, which was before the Korean War. In short, the *Monitor* urged a balanced approach regarding Jessup's appointment, using a "rounded evaluation of his total record and of his present usefulness."[57]

During the Jessup confirmation hearings, many clashes between McCarthy and other senators were about the issue of "guilt by association." For instance, Strout's October 2 story detailed the give-and-take between McCarthy and Democrat Senator J. William Fulbright of Arkansas. Fulbright asked McCarthy if Fulbright's wife had an "affinity" for Communism because she was an active member of the American Red Cross, of which George Catlett Marshall was chairman.[58] Strout again was careful not to give McCarthy's charges more prominence than the rebuttals. In contrast, the *Milwaukee Journal*'s coverage went into great detail about Jessup's background, paragraph by paragraph, painting a picture of a distinguished diplomat. The *Journal*'s chief rationale for supporting Jessup was that, other than McCarthy, no one hated Jessup more than "Soviet spokesmen—Vishinsky, Gromyko, Tass and Pravda" because he "thwarted them so frequently and so successfully."[59]

Nevertheless, the Senate Foreign Relations subcommittee defeated Jessup's nomination by a three-to-two vote claiming Jessup was a "symbol of Far Eastern policy," not disloyal. Then Truman, clearly sidestepping the vote of the subcommittee, avoided another confrontation with McCarthy and the Senate by naming Jessup to an "interim" post in which he would still represent the United States at a UN meeting in Paris.[60]

Given the extent of the controversy surrounding the Jessup nomination, it was somewhat surprising that the *Monitor* used an Associated Press dispatch for its story about the subcommittee rejection vote. And, though the committee's rejection of Jessup's nomination was portrayed by many in the press as a victory for McCarthy and a defeat for Truman,[61] the *Monitor* did not subscribe to that theory. An editorial stated that McCarthy's charges against the diplomat had broken down "badly," yet even Democrat Guy M. Gillette joined the two Republicans on the committee in rejecting Jessup.

Gillette did not give validity to any of McCarthy's charges, but rather voted against the nomination because he sensed that the American public had lost confidence in the diplomat. The *Monitor* concluded that this lack of confidence may have been due to some unsubstantiated charges against Jessup, so the "proven usefulness" of his negotiating ability was outweighed by the public perception of the man who became a "scapegoat."[62] There never was a declaration in a *Monitor* editorial, in any news stories, or in any columns, that the rejection of Jessup was interpreted as a victory for McCarthy. Not so for the *Chicago Tribune*, whose editorial was titled "McCarthy Sustained." The *Tribune* argued that "because of communist attachments and poor judgment" Jessup was "unfit" to serve in the United Nations representing the United States, and that McCarthy's position had "been borne out."[63]

REPUBLICAN PARTY PLANS

McCarthy's repeated attacks against individuals in 1951 prompted speculation about the Republican Party's 1952 election strategy, as it related to the junior senator. *Monitor* editorials and columns dealt with the issue.

On June 20, 1951, Joseph C. Harsch declared the 1952 presidential campaign open. Harsch wrote that the first effort to draft Ohio Senator Robert A. Taft had begun and that an August clambake in Maine would be the place where Taft would formally announce his intentions. Harsch contended that there already existed "well developed cleavage in the Republican Party" between the Taft Midwest and Taft "seaboard" supporters. The "international-progressive segment of the GOP" did not support the "McCarthy attacks on the State Department and the MacArthur campaign for expanding war against China." Harsch referred also to a pro-Eisenhower movement slowly emerging with backers claiming "that they already have pledges from enough delegates to prevent a Taft nomination."[64]

Strout reported that the "demoralization of the Democratic Party" made conditions ripe for Republicans to take over the White House in 1952. He contended President Truman's 1948 victory was more a rejection of Republican leadership in Washington than a Truman win. Strout stated Republicans were divided into factions about foreign affairs and the "difference of feeling about the role of Senator McCarthy" in the Party. On the one hand, at various times Taft had condoned McCarthy's methods, though he did not publicly support the Wisconsin Senator's attack on General George C. Marshall. Another faction of the Republican Party, including Senator Margaret Chase Smith of Maine, denounced McCarthy's techniques, particularly the practice of hiding behind congressional immunity while assassinating the character of innocent people. Despite the split within the Republican Party, Strout surmised that "the Republicans should win in

1952."[65] In a *Monitor* editorial lamenting how early the 1952 political campaign season started and how long it would be, the newspaper urged President Truman not to step out of "his role as representative of all the people" a year before the election and consider instead the "larger obligations of the Chief Executive." A year of political partisanship would open the country to "sniping that can destroy many elements of mutual trust and national unity," so the *Monitor* urged the politicians to "halt thought killing smears and to encourage debate that will be informative and clarifying."[66]

ROSENBERG CASE

While continuing to defend individuals against McCarthy's attacks, the *Monitor* displayed a hard-line Cold War position in connection with the Rosenberg spy case. Julius and Ethel Rosenberg, charged and found guilty of conspiracy to commit espionage for passing secrets to the Russians during World War II, were sentenced to death April 5, 1951. The *Monitor* wrote in an editorial that Judge Kaufman "apparently hopes to shock other would-be traitors into awareness of the seriousness of that crime" with a punishment that was "the severest ever applied for treason by a civil court in America." However, the *Monitor* expressed its belief that punishment was not the greatest deterrent to treason—that fostering loyalty was.[67] James Aronson's 1970 book, *The Press and the Cold War*, took the Monitor to task for the editorial because of what Aronson considered a major factual error. Aronson wrote that referring to the Rosenbergs as committing "treason," when it actually was conspiracy to commit espionage (a much lesser charge), showed the callousness of the press.[68] At the time, no one wrote or requested that the *Monitor* "correct" its wording.[69] The *Monitor*'s position on the Rosenberg sentence again displayed the conservative nature of the publication overall, despite its anti-McCarthy stance. Of course, the *Chicago Tribune* soundly endorsed the sentences, describing the crime as "atrocious ... for which no punishment could be too severe." The editorial even took a swipe at President Franklin Delano Roosevelt for "repeatedly ridiculing the efforts of the Dies committee and its successor," and criticized President Truman for dismissing the threat of Communism in this country as a "red herring."[70]

MEDIA SELF-CRITIQUE

McCarthyism became a growing concern. By midyear 1951, serious discussions occurred within most of the organizations and associations representing newspaper editors and reporters.

An editorial writer for the *Washington Post*, Robert H. Estabrook, noted that newspapers were doing a fine job in analyzing McCarthy and his tactics on the editorial pages, but "their news pages have contributed at the same time to the very things they were deploring editorially." Estabrook credited McCarthy with being "astute enough to play on a deeply ingrained suspicion that all is not right in Washington, that somebody is to blame for the totalitarian menace we face."[71]

Columnist Marquis Childs, in a piece published in Harvard's *Nieman Reports*, expressed concern about McCarthy's proposal that citizens and merchants of Milwaukee boycott the *Milwaukee Journal* because of its opposition to the Senator. However, Childs happily reported that McCarthy did not succeed in his boycott effort, and that the *Journal* had since gone on to new heights.[72]

The Chief of the American Society of Newspaper Editors (ASNE), Dwight E. Young, who was also editor and publisher of the *Journal-Herald* in Dayton, Ohio, warned of possible "encroachments" on the traditional freedom of the press. He lamented the rapidly growing tendency of public officials to suppress information, and expressed anxiety about the possibility of censorship for those covering the Korean War. Meanwhile, the Committee on Freedom of Information of ASNE, without specifically naming McCarthy, issued a statement that it was "beginning to suspect that the biggest uncovered story of our time is the insidious seizure of news prerogatives by public officials."[73]

The *Monitor* struck back against an unnamed "extreme right wing columnist" who suggested that the death penalty would be appropriate for all Communists "and some flagrant accomplices." The *Monitor* described how scary it was to espouse such harsh and unreasonable actions in the name of "Americanism:" The paper wrote that "to indulge the growing tendency to speak of political opponents as though they were traitors is in itself to be a 'flagrant accomplice' of the most irresponsible sort of thinking—the sort that is nothing less then tyranny in democracy's clothing, communism's identical twin."[74]

During the summer of 1951, *Editor and Publisher* polled some of its membership about the indictment of 21 Communist leaders. The respondents reacted to the fact that the indictment mentioned newspapers, magazines, and books circulated as part of the conspiracy to promote the violent overthrow of the government. *E&P* asked if this reference threatened the First Amendment or in any way violated the free press guarantee. While 3 of the 12 people polled, including Irving Dilliard of the *St. Louis Post-Dispatch*, believed there was an implied threat to freedom of the press, 9 others, including the editor of the *Monitor*, Erwin D. Canham, saw *no* long-term threat.[75] Canham wrote that he was "not disturbed at these indictments . . . even though some of them were newspaper men." He wrote that it was possible for "an arbitrary government to use this same technique against legitimate newspapermen," but argued that "our government is not going to do that as long as we remain vigilant."[76]

The stir that McCarthy and others made during congressional inquiries started to become more prominent in the eyes of many in the press. The top story for 1951, as voted by the Associated Press editors, was the dismissal of General Douglas MacArthur by President Truman and the General's subsequent trip back to the United States. The Korean War was chosen as the second most important story of the year. The Kefauver crime hearings in Congress, along with the many other investigations (including those related to alleged Communists in government), were voted collectively the third most important story of the year.[77]

NOTES

1. "Daily Worker Says It May Have to Quit," *Christian Science Monitor*, 20 January 1951, 3.
2. "Daily Worker Launches Retrenchment Policy," *Christian Science Monitor*, 26 June 1951, 13.
3. Richard L. Strout, "Nimitz Heads New Agency to Tackle Loyalty Cases," *Christian Science Monitor*, 24 January 1951, 3.
4. Richard L. Strout, "Six U.S. Probe Agencies Follow Communist Trail," *Christian Science Monitor*, 26 January 1951, 12.
5. Richard L. Strout, "Nimitz Heads New Agency," 3. Richard L. Strout, "Six U.S. Probe Agencies," 3.
6. Strout, "Six U.S. Probe Agencies," 12.
7. Editorial, "To Balance Security and Freedom," *Christian Science Monitor*, 25 January 1951, 20.
8. Quoted in "Tydings' Charges of 'Lies' Weighed," *Christian Science Monitor*, 21 February 1951, 24.
9. George Rothwell Brown, "Political Parade: McCarthy Issue in Senate Quiz," *San Francisco Examiner*, 23 February 1951, 23.
10. Richard L. Strout, "McCarthy Aide Named in Maryland Voting Probe," *Christian Science Monitor*, 27 February 1951, 1. Quoted in "McCarthy Brands Story of Printer as 'Fantastic,' " *Christian Science Monitor*, 28 February 1951, 14.
11. Strout, "McCarthy Aide Named," 1.
12. "McCarthy Linked to Tabloid Used to Defeat Tydings," *Christian Science Monitor*, 7 March 1951, 3.
13. Even the two Republicans on the committee, Robert C. Hendrickson of New Jersey and Margaret Chase Smith of Maine, voted with the Democratic majority.
14. Quoted in David M. Oshinsky, *A Conspiracy So Immense: The World of Joe McCarthy* (New York: The Free Press, 1983), 249.
15. Quoted in Richard L. Strout, "Senate Subcommittee Blasts Tactics Used to Defeat Tydings in Maryland," *Christian Science Monitor*, 3 August 1951, 1.

16. Robert Griffith, *The Politics of Fear: Joseph R. McCarthy and the Senate* (Amherst, Mass.: University of Massachusetts Press, 1987), 153. Richard M. Fried, *Men against McCarthy* (New York: Columbia University Press, 1976), 149.

17. Strout, "Senate Subcommittee Blasts Tactics," 1.

18. Editorial, "Moral Standards for Elections," *Christian Science Monitor*, 8 August 1951, 18.

19. Editorial, "The Butler-Tydings Report," *New York Times*, 5 August 1951, 8E.

20. Editorial, "Butler Should Be Ousted," *Milwaukee Journal*, 8 August 1951, 24.

21. George Rothwell Brown, "Political Parade: Timid Report on Tydings' Defeat," *San Francisco Examiner*, 9 August 1951, 23.

22. Quoted in "McCarthy Defends Activity in Maryland," *Christian Science Monitor*, 21 August 1951, 7.

23. Quoted in Harlan Trott, "Benton Appeals to Senate to Remove McCarthy," *Christian Science Monitor*, 7 August 1951, 3.

24. Joseph C. Harsch, "State of the Nation: David, or Babe in the Wood?," *Christian Science Monitor*, 9 August 1951, 1.

25. Quoted in Richard L. Strout, "Benton Presses Action against McCarthy," *Christian Science Monitor*, 28 September 1951, 12.

26. Griffith, *The Politics of Fear*, 163.

27. Editorial, "Better Than Smearing," *Christian Science Monitor*, 2 October 1951, 18.

28. William S. White, "Benton Gives Senate 10-Case Brief on McCarthy 'Lies' and 'Deceits,' " *New York Times*, 29 September 1951, 1, 6.

29. Quoted in "McCarthy Won't Answer 'Old Mental Midget,' " *New York Times*, 29 September 1951, 6.

30. Fulton Lewis, Jr., "Washington Report: McCarthy vs. Benton Issue," *San Francisco Examiner*, 28 September 1951, 21.

31. Editorial, "McCarthy's Enemies," *Chicago Tribune*, 29 September 1951, 8.

32. Richard L. Strout, "New Blasts by McCarthy Irk Senate," *Christian Science Monitor*, 22 September 1951, 1.

33. Quoted in Strout, "New Blasts by McCarthy," 1.

34. Chapter 5 covers the controversial nature of Hennings' report.

35. Joseph C. Harsch, "State of the Nation: MacArthur Crosses Line on Military Policy," *Christian Science Monitor*, 9 April 1951, 1.

36. Editorial, "Quietly Assess Situation," *Christian Science Monitor*, 11 April 1951, 24.

37. Editorial, "Truman and M'Arthur," *New York Times*, 12 April 1951, 32.

38. Editorial, "Impeach Truman," *San Francisco Examiner*, 12 April 1951, 1.

39. "MacArthur Aide & Six Newsmen Argue Factors behind Yalu Retreat," *Christian Science Monitor*, 28 November 1951, 9.

40. Editorial, "Responsible Reporters," *Christian Science Monitor*, 29 November 1951, 24.

41. Richard H. Rovere, *Senator Joe McCarthy* (New York: Harper & Row, 1959), 175.

42. Oshinsky, *A Conspiracy So Immense*, 200.

43. Quoted in Oshinsky, *A Conspiracy So Immense*, 200.

44. Editorial, "The Marshall Record," *Christian Science Monitor*, 16 June 1951, 20.

45. There were no interoffice memos in Strout's papers or available in the *Monitor* archives to explain this editorial decision.

46. Editorial, "Wisconsin's Shame," *Milwaukee Journal*, 15 June 1951, 20.

47. Sam Fogg, "Marshall Sided with Stalin, Caused 'High Level Blunder,' M'Carthy Says," *San Francisco Examiner*, 15 June 1951, 6.

48. Willard Edwards, "M'Carthy Rips Marshall for Aid to Russia," *Chicago Tribune*, 15 June 1951, 1.

49. "McCarthy Book Repeats Attack upon Marshall," *Christian Science Monitor*, 31 December 1951, 3.

50. The U.S. Supreme Court refused to review Hiss's perjury conviction March 12, 1951, and Acheson's only comment was that the Supreme Court's action "disposes of the matter." Quoted in "Acheson's View on Hiss Verdict," *Christian Science Monitor*, 13 March 1951, 18.

51. Richard L. Strout, "McCarthy and Acheson: An Intimate Message from Washington," *Christian Science Monitor*, 9 February 1951, 20.

52. Joseph C, Harsch, "State of the Nation: A Doorway Out for Acheson," *Christian Science Monitor*, 27 April 1951, 1.

53. Roscoe Drummond, "State of the Nation: Communist Issue Faces Showdown," *Christian Science Monitor*, 19 September 1951, 1.

54. Quoted in Strout, "New Blasts by McCarthy," 1.

55. Quoted in Harlan Trott, " 'Smear Tactics' Hit by State Department in Blast by McCarthy," *Christian Science Monitor*, 10 August 1951, 1.

56. Strout, "New Blasts by McCarthy," 1.

57. Editorial, "The Case of Dr. Jessup," *Christian Science Monitor*, 11 October 1951, 24.

58. Quoted in Richard L. Strout, "McCarthy Clashes with Fullbright at Hearing on Jessup," *Christian Science Monitor*, 2 October 1951, 1.

59. Editorial, "About Philip Jessup," *Milwaukee Journal*, 4 October 1951, 24.

60. Richard L. Strout, notes on confirmation hearings of Jessup-Stassen, Richard L. Strout Papers, Weston, Mass., 2 October–9 November 1951, 4.

61. Oshinsky, *A Conspiracy So Immense*, 217.

62. Editorial, "The Jessup Decision," *Christian Science Monitor*, 20 October 1951, 18.

63. Editorial, "McCarthy Sustained," *Chicago Tribune*, 22 October 1951, 26.

64. Joseph C. Harsch, "State of the Nation: Presidential Campaign Opens," *Christian Science Monitor*, 20 June 1951, 1.

65. Richard L. Strout, "A Challenge for the GOP: An Intimate Message from Washington," *Christian Science Monitor*, 22 June 1951, 22.

66. Editorial, "Too Long an Open Season," *Christian Science Monitor*, 23 November 1951, 22.

67. Editorial, "To Prevent Treason," *Christian Science Monitor*, 7 April 1951, 22.

68. James Aronson, *The Press and the Cold War* (Indianapolis and New York: Bobbs-Merrill Company, 1970), 58.

1951: McCarthy's Character Assassinations

69. Aronson's complaint did not come until 1970, which would have been a little late for the *Monitor* to correct a story published in 1951!

70. Editorial, "Traitor's End," *Chicago Tribune,* 8 April 1951, 24F.

71. Robert H. Estabrook, speech "The Free Man's Color," reprinted *Nieman Reports* 5/2 April 1951, 24.

72. Marquis Childs, "What Signs Threaten Free Press?" *Nieman Reports*, 5/3 July 1951, 88.

73. Quoted in "ASNE Chief Warns U.S. Press of Encroachments on Freedom," *Christian Science Monitor*, 9 March 1951, 14.

74. Editorial, "Flagrant Accomplices," *Christian Science Monitor*, 29 June 1951, 20.

75. Robert U. Brown, "Editors See No Press Threat in Communist Indictments," *Editor and Publisher*, 1 September 1951, 7.

76. Quoted in Brown, "Editors See No Press Threat," 54.

77. "Top '51 Story: MacArthur's Return to U.S.," *Christian Science Monitor*, 31 December 1951, 6.

3

1952: McCarthy in the National Spotlight

LATTIMORE AND THE LOYALTY PROBES

Johns Hopkins University Professor Owen Lattimore was repeatedly investigated during the McCarthy era, starting with McCarthy's astonishing charge in 1950 that Lattimore was a "top Russian espionage agent." Lattimore's ordeal did not end until five years later.[1] But 1952 marked a year in which Lattimore was continually in the newspapers appearing in hearings and constantly defending his record, his beliefs and his honor.

Richard L. Strout wrote a piece in the *Monitor* largely based on a Duke University professor's scholarly study of McCarthy's many charges over the previous two years. The charge against Lattimore was completely false according to the study. Sociology Professor Hornell Hart concluded that McCarthy's actions had "contributed little or nothing to discovering or weeding out communists from our government."[2] According to Strout, McCarthy reportedly contacted Duke University and threatened to hold the school liable for any false statements in Dr. Hart's study.[3]

This was one of the few Lattimore-related stories that Strout covered in 1952. Neal Stanford and Roland Sawyer, also Washington correspondents for the *Monitor*, wrote the bulk of the stories with Washington Bureau Chief Roscoe Drummond occasionally writing commentary about Lattimore.

In early February, reacting to McCarthy's renewed attack on Lattimore and the State Department, General Conrad E. Snow, Chief of the State Department's Loyalty Security Board, spoke about the allegation of Communists in the State Department. Snow contended McCarthy was deliberately trying to make people think the State Department was "infested with communists or communist sympathizers." According to Snow, there was no truth behind any charge that any Communist remained in the State Department.[4] Stanford's story largely centered on Snow's comments, while, for instance, a story in the pro-McCarthy *Chicago Tribune* devoted more space to McCarthy's rebuttal than to the General's comments. McCarthy called Snow "completely incompetent" and claimed the General did not have the "faintest conception of what a communist" was.[5]

Strout wrote the opening story about a brand-new probe of Lattimore, not by McCarthy and company, but by Senator Pat McCarran's Senate Judiciary Interior Security subcommittee. Strout surmised that "next to the Alger Hiss case itself probably no other subject of charges and countercharges has caused such a storm."[6] Lattimore started the hearings with a formal 50-page statement, and as Roland Sawyer wrote, under brutal questioning, Lattimore refused "to be cowed, intimidated, or shouted down, whether he is out of order or not."[7] Lattimore testified that he was not a Communist nor a Communist sympathizer, and under cross-examination claimed that former Communist Louis Budenz perjured himself in making the charge. A *Monitor* editorial fully supported a suggestion (being discussed by various politicians in Washington) that the Justice Department investigate and find out which person was lying. The newspaper explained that what the country needed were the facts to be considered "objectively free from the poisonous miasma of suspicion, the prejudgments, the politics, the personal rancor" that "too often" had been part of the McCarran subcommittee hearings.[8]

More than a week later, the *Monitor*, apparently tired of the charge that Lattimore was responsible for the United States' failed policies in the Far East, made it clear that "for better or for worse" Secretary of State Dean Acheson was "the chief architect of foreign policy" and judgment about Acheson will "rest less on his choice of advisors than on his choice of policies." The *Monitor* concluded that the "final responsibility" for policy rests with the State Department, so whatever Lattimore may or may not have told officials, Secretary Acheson was responsible.[9]

The *Monitor*, and Sawyer in particular, received critical letters charging that the newspaper favored Owen Lattimore in its news stories about the McCarran proceedings. Sawyer answered the criticism in an "Intimate Message from Washington," writing about the problems associated with covering such an event. He contended that even with balanced stories, many partisans on both sides were dissatisfied. Sawyer told the readers that the consensus among reporters, both supporters and opponents of McCarthy and McCarran, was that it was impossible for the professor to receive a "fair hearing in the judicial sense."[10]

In concluding the lengthy questioning of Lattimore, Senator McCarran, in a 2,300-word statement, denounced Lattimore for lying under oath. Surprisingly, the *Monitor* ran an Associated Press story instead of having a reporter present for the close of the professor's testimony. The *New York Times* characterized the McCarran denouncement of Lattimore as a "tongue-lashing," as did the *Chicago Tribune*, which added that the subcommittee had to put up with Lattimore's "consistently evasive, contentious and belligerent attitude."[11]

Meanwhile, *Monitor* editorials continued to attack the "guilt by association" atmosphere that prevailed under the aura of McCarthyism. For example, Harvard Professor John K. Fairbank was accused of Communist affiliations; Fairbank had expressed sympathy for the Chinese Communists, the *Monitor* wrote, but that was a very different statement than saying he was a Communist or had Communist sympathies in general. The newspaper agreed with the contention by Fairbank that effective American China specialists "must depend in part upon freedom of contact—now imperiled by the doctrine of guilt by association." The *Monitor* contended that "experts of all varieties of opinion" were needed for consultation in order for the government to decide what the U.S. foreign policy should be.[12]

During the summer of 1952, a story surfaced that the State Department had received a tip from an informant that Lattimore was arranging a trip behind the Iron Curtain and had been denied a passport by the U.S. Customs Service.[13] After the State Department confirmed the story, the *actual* truth unraveled. Neal Stanford reported that a Seattle travel agent admitted passing along the false information to the CIA, who gave it to the FBI, who passed it on to the State Department. Stanford rhetorically asked, "Is it a plot to discredit Lattimore or the work of a creative nut?"[14] A "Washington Letter" column (which was written jointly by all the reporters and editors in the *Monitor*'s Washington Bureau) called the entire affair a "fiasco" and surmised that the CIA, FBI, and State Department were now all trying to prove they were not inept. The column also ended with a similar question to the one previously posed by Stanford: "Did this CIA tipster dream up this charge by himself or did he get help from some source out to discredit the administration or Professor Lattimore?"[15]

Eventually the State Department apologized to Lattimore for confirming the false information, the Seattle travel agent was indicted for giving false information, and Lattimore urged that steps be taken to prevent such an incident in the future.[16] The apology came on June 30; one day later the McCarran subcommittee recommended the Justice Department pursue perjury charges against Lattimore by submitting evidence (not related to the passport "fiasco") to a grand jury. An Associated Press (page 11) story told *Monitor* readers about the latest development;[17] on the other hand, the

New York Times, the *Chicago Tribune,* and the *San Francisco Examiner* all ran front-page stories about the McCarran recommendation. The 226–page report, which was the culmination of an 18-month investigation into the Institute of Pacific Relations (IPR), charged (among other things) that Lattimore and John Carter Vincent "were influential in bringing about a change in United States policy in 1945 favorable to the Chinese Communists."[18] The news story in the *Chicago Tribune* declared that McCarthy was "vindicated." An editorial stated that the "notorious administration whitewash" carried out by Tydings' subcommittee in 1950 was intended to make the term " 'McCarthyism' a term of opprobrium" but that the Senate Judiciary Committee, made up of seven Democrats and six Republicans, voted approval of the subcommittee's report. This action would quiet those who derided "the accusers" and sanctified "the accused" in the case of the original McCarthy charges.[19]

On December 19, Owen Lattimore's predicament went from bad to worse as an indictment was handed up for seven counts of perjury. It was a front-page story in nearly all the newspapers in the country. All listed the charges against Lattimore, which included asserting falsely that he had not published any articles written by Communists in a magazine sponsored by the IPR, and denying he knew that a writer named Asiaticus was a Communist. Roscoe Drummond assured the *Monitor's* readers that whatever the status of Lattimore, over the last 10 to 15 years the Communist "conspiracy has been stopped in its tracks" in this country, and though "we most certainly cannot afford to drop our guard, there is no need to be hysterical." Drummond explained that Lattimore was not indicted for his views about Communism or the Chinese Communists; he was indicted for allegedly failing to tell the truth to a Senate committee. Drummond demanded that the job of locating and removing Communists from government should not restrict freedoms inherent in being American: "The destruction of freedom by those trying to ferret out subversives needs to be avoided as much as the destruction of freedom from failing to deal with subversives."[20]

Monitor columnist Joseph C. Harsch wrote about the declining status of the State Department in the United States and around the world. The decline had been linked by most to the Lattimore case and charges brought over the previous couple of years by McCarthy. But, Harsch claimed the decline started well before McCarthy leveled any charges in 1950—it started before Franklin Delano Roosevelt became President in the early 1930s. Harsch contended that if the State Department had been held in high regard prior to McCarthy's charges, the Senator's attacks would have been treated as "mere annoyances."[21]

Meanwhile, the *Chicago Tribune* and *San Francisco Examiner* reveled in the indictment against Lattimore. The *Tribune* admonished the "McLiberals" who "blubbered over Hiss" and talked about witch-hunts by McCarthy. The paper declared that those who "always insist on the rights of Communists and fellow travelers" should take note that a grand jury said McCarthy and McCarran were right.[22] The *Examiner* hailed the indictment as news that was "hot and good" forcing a showdown in open court "where it should have been long ago." The newspaper described Lattimore's appearance before the McCarran subcommittee as "twelve days of snarling, sneering testimony."[23]

The seven-count perjury indictment was not fully disposed of until 1955. On December 19, 1952 Lattimore pleaded not guilty to all seven counts. On May 2, 1953 the first four counts were dismissed, but on August 24, 1953 the government asked the court to restore all four counts. On July 8, 1954 the Federal Court of Appeals restored two of the four counts leaving five counts of perjury remaining. And finally, on June 28, 1955 the U.S. Attorney General ordered all charges against Lattimore dismissed.[24] Dr. Owen Lattimore was just one of many individuals whose loyalty was questioned by McCarthy in a book the Senator wrote, which was released in midyear 1952.

MCCARTHYISM: THE FIGHT FOR AMERICA

In many circles, Joseph R. McCarthy's book *McCarthyism: The Fight for America* was not thought of as an important work. The *New York Times* and most other newspapers did not write formal reviews, perhaps because the book was seen as largely a rehash of McCarthy's speeches and "evidence" he felt he had of Communists in government.

McCarthy did not hesitate to name names in the book, including Richard L. Strout's. Strout's name appeared early in the book (page 5), even before McCarthy started "documenting" the "facts" regarding his 1950 speech in Wheeling, West Virginia.[25] It is clear what McCarthy intended to accomplish by mentioning Strout and the *Monitor*: While the *Monitor* had published no name-calling, "blasts," or personal attacks against McCarthy, and had stressed the importance of ridding the government of dangerous Communists, it had explicitly condemned the "smear" methods of McCarthy and others (such as Democrat Senator Pat McCarran of Nevada). In the space of just three paragraphs, McCarthy intended to impugn the integrity of the *Monitor* through questioning the motives of Strout and a former contributor to the newspaper, Gunther Stein. McCarthy claimed that he heard a "slight commotion" during the Tydings subcommittee hearings and witnessed Strout shaking the hand of (Communist) *Daily Worker* newspaper reporter Rob Hall. McCarthy stated that he had always thought of the *Monitor* as "a respected paper" especially for its coverage of foreign news. But McCarthy concluded that after seeing Strout and Hall in a "comradely" handshake he experienced a flashback of the story of Gunther Stein, who had been the *Christian Science Monitor's* correspondent in China. General MacArthur's intelligence headquarters had exposed the fact that Gunther Stein was a Communist and an "indispensable and important member" of the famous Sorge Communist spy ring. Within 24 hours after the War Department released a report on the activities of this Communist spy ring, Gunther Stein disappeared.[26]

McCarthy wrote that he believed at the time that Stein had "cleverly deceived" the *Monitor* and that the newspaper was unaware of the fact that Stein was a traitor. However, after witnessing Strout and Hall "cheek by jowl" at the Tydings hearings and then reading "the venomous distorted parallel stories which they both wrote," he concluded that "if a columnist for a paper like the *Christian Science Monitor* could so closely follow the Communist line, no publication and no institution in the entire country could be secure from Communist infiltration."[27]

The *Monitor* now joined the increasing list of newspapers across the country accused of Communist connections because of criticizing McCarthy's methods. And Strout also was added to the list of journalists, which included Marquis Childs of the *New York Post* and ABC Radio broadcaster Elmer Davis, who criticized McCarthy and, though no legitimate evidence was uncovered, were labeled by the Wisconsin Senator as having Communist sympathies or the like.[28]

Strout wrote the initial story in the *Monitor* that mentioned McCarthy's book. The July 16 story talked about views opposing McCarthy that were available in "The McCarthy Record" compiled and published by the Wisconsin Citizens Committee. Strout wrote that many discrepancies occurred between the facts in "The McCarthy Record" and *McCarthyism: The Fight for America*. For instance McCarthy claimed he had said in his Wheeling speech that he had names of 57 people in the State Department who were Communists or loyal to the Communist Party. "The McCarthy Record" quoted two employees of radio station WWVA who covered the speech and remembered that McCarthy did claim there were 205 Communists in the State Department.[29]

Strout wrote that McCarthy attacked a "respectable" group of media outlets, including *Time*, the *New York Times*, the *St. Louis Post-Dispatch*, the *Milwaukee Journal*, and the *Monitor*, not to mention many others. Strout told readers that while McCarthy's book retold many of the Senator's "famous attacks" on Dean Acheson, Philip C. Jessup, Dr. Owen Lattimore, and others, the anti-McCarthy publication reviewed McCarthy's tax difficulties in Wisconsin and with the Wisconsin State Supreme Court, and the $10,000 fee he accepted from Lustron Corporation for writing an article for a pamphlet about public housing. The *Monitor's* news story also mentioned McCarthy's claim that Strout had shaken hands with Rob Hall and in parentheses (apparently added by a *Monitor* editor to Strout's story) stated bluntly, "Whatever the truth of Senator McCarthy's other charges this one is a fabrication, for Richard L. Strout never shook hands with Rob Hall in his life."[30]

This statement was the only mention in the *Monitor* about the incident until it published a book review about *McCarthyism: The Fight for America* on September 3, 1952. Editor Erwin D. Canham titled the book review "McCarthyism: A Question of Fact." Canham stated that the McCarthy publication "appears to add little or no new information to that which he has made public already." Canham conceded that as of the writing of his review "we have not had a truly judicial weighing of this evidence" and went on to say that the book review was not the "place to review the evidence or present a considered judgment." The rest of the review set the record straight about the *Monitor*, Gunther Stein, and Richard L. Strout. Canham stated that Stein was never on the *Monitor* "staff," rather he was hired at the "recommendation" of William Henry Chamberlin, "a distinguished anti-communist writer." Stein wrote dispatches from China as a "special" correspondent. Canham wrote further that long before spy charges were levied against Stein, the *Monitor* had "ceased this relationship." Canham claimed that when Stein was writing for the *Monitor* he was highly regarded and "enjoyed the confidence of the National Government of China."[31]

On the issue of Strout shaking the hand of Rob Hall, Canham contended (as in the earlier Strout article) that Strout did not know Hall and had never shaken his hand. Canham wrote that the incident "never took place, and must be the result of some kind of mistaken identity." He also made it clear that the stories Strout wrote bore "no resemblance" to those written in the *Daily Worker* by Hall. This was a softer refutation than Strout's July denial, which described McCarthy's account as a "fabrication."[32] Canham ended the review making the *Monitor*'s position on Communism clear: "Needless to say, The *Christian Science Monitor* never knowingly follows a Communist line, and it eagerly supports the exposure of any subversive activity. It believes, however, that the facts must be judicially and honestly established in any given case."[33]

While it appeared that the refutation was the end of McCarthy versus Strout and the *Monitor* controversy, by late 1952 and early 1953, pressure had increased on the paper, and action taken was not easily detectable to the readers of the *Monitor*. (That action, suspending Strout's coverage of McCarthy, will be discussed in detail in Chapter 4.[34])

1952 ELECTIONS

Throughout the many controversies concerning Senator McCarthy during 1952, major analytical stories about the General Election appeared in the *Monitor*—starting as early as January and continuing through the national conventions, the primaries, and the November election.

Strout identified the major campaign issues facing congressmen as they opened their election-year session. He wrote that cutting government expenses at home and abroad was on the minds of voters and therefore subject to Congressional action. With a seemingly isolationist attitude among Americans, Strout speculated that there would be a drive to cut foreign aid immediately. Further, Strout thought that Congress would be pressured to enact some sort of Cold War universal military training for all of the young men in America, and approve a pay increase of about 10 percent for those in the service.[35]

The election campaigns in Wisconsin were followed closely by the *Monitor*. While Strout traveled with each of the Democrat and Republican Presidential hopefuls, Max K. Gilstrap, as head of the *Monitor*'s Midwest Bureau, wrote extensively about Senator McCarthy and Wisconsin. Gilstrap wrote in January that Senator Robert A. Taft, candidate for the Republican Presidential nomination, had campaigned in Wisconsin and heaped praise upon McCarthy. Taft stated that the junior senator was "fully justified" in his Communists-in-government investigations.[36] One day later, Gilstrap reported that a Democrat who was an attorney from Milwaukee (Henry S. Reuss) planned an aggressive campaign to unseat McCarthy. Reuss was an unknown to politics in Wisconsin, and Gilstrap did not speculate about McCarthy's chances of being beaten in the fall.[37]

Going into the summer and the national conventions, the *Monitor* focused heavily on the split among Republicans, and ultimately the GOP nominee's strategy in dealing with the right wing of the party. Strout wrote that the "liberal wing has been virtually ostracized from the guest speaker's list at the Republican National Convention." He implied that the forces surrounding Senator Taft's bid for the Presidency controlled the convention, and those forces included some of the worst-rated senators in the country, including Styles Bridges of New Hampshire, Harry P. Cain of Washington, and Joseph R. McCarthy of Wisconsin. Meanwhile, Strout reported that the "Eisenhower wing" was "all but excluded" and that Senator Margaret Chase Smith of Maine, who rose to prominence with her "Declaration of Conscience" speech criticizing McCarthy and his methods, was not even invited to speak.[38] However, since Eisenhower gained the nomination, Strout clearly misread how most Republicans were leaning.

After the national conventions, a *Monitor* editorial explored the degree to which the Republican and Democrat candidates for President were held "captive" to small pockets of radicals within each party. The editorial concluded that Eisenhower seemed to be in the best position to handle the "deeply disappointed wing of his party" but faced the difficult task of avoiding embracement of the "splinter which has tarred itself with what has come to be known as 'McCarthyism.' " The *Monitor* implied that Stevenson would not be in as good a position to get the country off to a new start, rhetorically *asking* whether the Democrat nominee would be "as free to clean out the accumulated dry rot of 20 years as could the General?"[39]

As the campaign moved closer to the primaries, however, what dominated the *Monitor* and many other newspapers was not the battle between Stevenson and Eisenhower; it was what Eisenhower was going to do with the right wing of the party, and specifically McCarthy. The *Milwaukee Journal*, in the home state of the junior senator, certainly analyzed and editorialized on the issue more than most, but the *Monitor* also repeatedly commented about the so-called "endorsement" of McCarthy by the General. The *Journal* wrote as early as August that because of McCarthy's harsh criticism of General George C. Marshall, among other things, reports were that Eisenhower would "brush-off" McCarthy. The *Journal* contended that such an action would "take rare political courage" by Eisenhower but suggested that if there was still "such a thing as political morality," something close to a brush-off was "certainly called for."[40] True to form, the *Monitor* published less frequent and definitive comments about Eisenhower and McCarthy, perhaps being cautious not to place any burden on Eisenhower while readying itself to endorse "Ike" in the general election. One editorial asked the Democrat and Republican parties to place a lesser emphasis on "hatchet men." The *Monitor* wrote that "evidence that both Democratic and Republican high commands plan to subordinate demagoguery is a compliment to the electorate" and that without name-calling and the like voters could assess their positions on the candidate, issues, and party and decide who "will best serve the nation at this time."[41] The *Monitor*, through the interpretive reporting of Max K. Gilstrap, published many stories about McCarthy's opponent in the primary election, Leonard F. Schmitt, and Schmitt's radio "talk-a-thon's." At one point, Schmitt was on the air for 22 consecutive hours. Gilstrap conceded that few Wisconsinites believed Schmitt would defeat McCarthy, but "some believe possible inroads on the McCarthy vote made by Mr. Schmitt may make it possible for the Democratic nominee to beat him in the general election."[42] The *Milwaukee Journal* wrote that if nominated, Schmitt would be "a positive asset and a strong campaigner."[43]

Just three days before the primary election, *Editor and Publisher* released the results of a poll about the Presidential race conducted through questionnaires sent to newspapers across the country. Fifty-two percent of the dailies returned their questionnaires and a whopping 75 percent favored Eisenhower with just 15 percent for Stevenson. *Editor and Publisher* reported that the overwhelming support for Eisenhower was the greatest for a Republican candidate for President in recent years.[44]

Meanwhile, Gilstrap, continuing to follow the McCarthy renomination bid, highlighted the divided public opinion about McCarthy in Wisconsin. Gilstrap wrote that one faction in support of McCarthy believed that the threat from Communism in this country was real and that McCarthy had alerted people to the danger. Another faction believed that the McCarthy method of rooting out Communism in government was a "form of demagoguery," which threatened individual liberties guaranteed by the Constitution.[45] In an Election Day story, Gilstrap explained that Schmitt's only hope was to get Democrats to cross over and vote in the Republican primary in order to defeat McCarthy. Gilstrap, in stating the slim hopes Schmitt had for an upset, wrote that Schmitt had a better chance of defeating McCarthy in the primary than a Democrat challenger would have in the November election.[46]

A staunch McCarthy supporter, the *Chicago Tribune* declared that a "smear" campaign against McCarthy had "boomeranged" and that everyone predicted an easy renomination in the primary. The *Tribune* called Schmitt a participant in the smear campaign and questioned the party loyalty of a man who had stated that if defeated, he would vote for the Democrat nominee.[47] Meanwhile, George Rothwell Brown in the *San Francisco Examiner* wrote that he was confident Wisconsin voters would not fall prey to the "distortion" of "left wing dupes" trying to "destroy Joe McCarthy." Brown wrote that McCarthy had done a "grand job for America" and that he had been singled out for "smearing" as part of the "Communist technique to concentrate on one point of attack at a time."[48]

"McCarthy Wins Smashing Victory" was the headline on the *Monitor's* page 1 Associated Press story after the primary election. McCarthy declared that the 431,422 to 173,701 victory was the voters' endorsement of his Communists-in-government hunt.[49] The day after the election, Gilstrap also wrote a detailed story about the results. Gilstrap quoted McCarthy as pledging his full support to Republican Presidential nominee Dwight D. Eisenhower, and quoted Schmitt warning Wisconsin voters that in the future they would be ashamed of returning McCarthy to office.[50] The *Milwaukee Journal* bluntly described for the voters of Wisconsin the "man they nominated," listing all the irregularities and extremes of McCarthy's career and declaring, "This is not only appalling—it is frightening."[51] While the *New York Times* described McCarthy's victory as the voters refusing to "repudiate" the Wisconsin senator,[52] a *Times* editorial described the McCarthy victory as "overwhelming as it is depressing" and that the "entire nation has a vital stake in a Democratic victory in the Wisconsin senatorial election in November."[53] The *Chicago Tribune* wrote that the McCarthy win was "vindication of which few politicians have ever received" and that while some thought McCarthy would have to "ride the coattails" of Eisenhower

1952: McCarthy in the National Spotlight 63

in the general election, most now believed that to win in Wisconsin, Eisenhower would have to ride McCarthy's coattails, and the coattails of other "stalwart" Republicans.[54]

After the initial story documenting the McCarthy victory, Gilstrap looked into the obvious and not so obvious reasons for the lopsided victory. Gilstrap noted that some people believed that McCarthyism had started to show results in uncovering Communists in government and some believed that McCarthy had been unfairly attacked for his methods. Under the surface, Gilstrap disclosed, Republicans and some Democrats were "alarmed" over the evidence of Communist sympathizers in the federal government, and many had been disappointed in the lack of an effective method of dealing with the problem. So, despite reservations about the methods McCarthy employed, many felt that his work was alerting the people to a legitimate danger.[55] On the same day as Gilstrap's piece, Strout had a front-page story about what the Democrats planned to do in the general election. Strout wrote that Democrat nominee Adlai Stevenson planned to ask Eisenhower to address the issue of supporting right-wing senators such as McCarthy. McCarthy's big victory in the primary clearly elevated the issue of the Communist threat at home, and left unanswered the question of how Eisenhower was going to deal with it.[56] Two days later, the *Monitor* agreed with Strout's assessment that McCarthy's big primary victory showed the public's concern about Communism, so something responsible needed to be done to deal with the problem fairly. The *Monitor* reiterated the paper's position that rooting out Communists in government was important, but that McCarthy's methods certainly were not the way to accomplish the goal. Again, as the *Monitor* wrote repeatedly during the McCarthy era, the newspaper called for an independent commission, nonpartisan and named by the President and Congress, to get the "business" of dealing with Communists "out of politics."[57]

The *Times* contended, in a story several days after the election, that overall there was a "minimum of trends on how the Presidential and Congressional contests in November might work out" but conceded the "big surprise" was the margin of victory McCarthy enjoyed over his opponent because of making Communists in the State Department and other government agencies the central issue of the campaign.[58]

With the climax to the 1952 election campaign fast approaching, on October 27, McCarthy, speaking from the Palmer House in Chicago, addressed the nation about the candidacy of Adlai Stevenson for President. Prior to the broadcast, the *Monitor* hinted that the speech intended to show Stevenson surrounded by left-wing advisers and soft on Communism for his position relative to Alger Hiss.[59] Strout wrote that the McCarthy speech was independent of Eisenhower's campaign and that it was "a major test of whether Senator McCarthy can translate his power in state politics into the national sphere."[60] Strout was correct about the "independence" of the speech. The nationwide address cost $18,000 and was paid for largely by the Chairman of the Board of Sears-Roebuck and Company, Robert E. Wood.[61] The day of the scheduled McCarthy speech, the *Monitor* carried three different stories about the Presidential race, two of which specifically dealt with McCarthy. A *Monitor* staff report indicated that the Eisenhower campaign discreetly informed the press that part of an Eisenhower speech (already delivered) repudiated what McCarthy was going to say about the proper method of dealing with Communists in the government. Eisenhower was quoted as saying, "We have to destroy the reputation of no innocent man. We can do it and we must do it [remove Communists from government] . . . but in the American way."[62] Another story detailed how Stevenson had set a "backfire" in dealing with the forthcoming McCarthy address. Stevenson predicted that the people would hear a "magnificent smear" out of the mouth of McCarthy, designed, according to Stevenson, to "save the Republican Party."[63] However, Stevenson was not reaching the same number of people as the Republicans. His speech, designed to counter McCarthy's, was during a campaign stop in New England and it was attended by about 2,500 people, about 5,000 fewer than Vice Presidential candidate Richard M. Nixon addressed a few weeks earlier at the same location.[64]

Strout's story claimed that Eisenhower's visit to Korea and McCarthy's speech about Stevenson were key issues in the campaign. Strout wrote that the race for President mav be the "closest . . . in 36 years" but that the "vague feeling" by reporters was that Eisenhower was in the lead. Strout boldly asserted that McCarthy's speech could affect the Presidential race: "If his speech is successful, he will be raised to new and striking political importance; and many believe that in the nice balance now obtaining a characteristic McCarthy speech could conceivably spell Eisenhower victory." Strout observed that while Eisenhower might be distancing himself from the speech, his campaign workers had indicated back on September 17 that Eisenhower intended to use McCarthy in the campaign.[65]

The speech aired on both network radio and television. McCarthy ran through a long list of what he maintained was incriminating evidence that the Americans for Democratic Action (ADA) were Communist sympathizers (included were the ADA's support for repeal of the Smith Act, its opposition to government security procedures, its opposition to the House Un-American Activities Committee, and its support for recognition of Red China); McCarthy went on to claim that Stevenson was an ADA member. In many newspapers, McCarthy's charges appeared on page 1, while the rebuttal(s) from the Stevenson campaign and the ADA appeared inside.[66] The *Monitor* was not one of those papers. In fact, the newspaper went out of its way to balance McCarthy's attack with the response of those involved, along with commentary from politicians of both parties. A page 1 story (credited to the *Monitor* staff) reported that McCarthy had charged that Stevenson had left-wing advisers and "implied that the Democratic candidate is pro-communist." It included a quotation from Democratic Vice Presidential candidate Senator John J. Sparkman, who characterized the entire speech as a "pathetic smear."[67]

In a page 2 story about Stevenson's response, Strout wrote that Stevenson had given 11 speeches in New England before going to New York City, pounding home a couple of themes. First, Stevenson repeatedly relayed his scorn for McCarthy and his methods. Second, Stevenson charged that Eisenhower was playing politics with the Korean War. These themes were established before McCarthy's speech and continued after, according to Strout. Besides the stories, the *Monitor* published extensive quotations from McCarthy's speech and many rebuttals on pages 15 and 16.[68]

One day later, the *Monitor* wrote a lengthy and thoughtful editorial about the McCarthy speech, quoting Eisenhower extensively (from speeches given previously) in rebutting McCarthy's attack on Stevenson and the Democrats. It noted that Eisenhower attempted to dissociate himself from the Wisconsin senator prior to the speech by stating in part that "one of America's freedoms is the freedom from guilt, freedom from being damaged by false charges."[69] The *Monitor* warned readers that the "very mildness of the McCarthy television manner covered the violence with which statements were wrenched out of context and given sinister meanings." It also admonished the media, though indirectly, by stating that many people would never have access to the "denials and refutations" of those McCarthy attacked. But the newspaper did not simply criticize McCarthy for being irresponsible, it suggested a right way to deal with "rooting out Communists" while still preserving freedom: "We believe the key is to build on the islands of public trust that remain in the spreading swamps of suspicion. They are to be found in the popular regard for unofficial, distinguished Americans whose integrity and loyalty is unquestioned." To do that the *Monitor* again recommended, as it had in the past, a nonpartisan commission of outstanding citizens to do the "deep-digging, clean job." The *Monitor*, again in citing the words of General Eisenhower, added that "every effective" instrument already being used—such as the FBI and the courts—must continue to be utilized.[70]

The *New York Times*, after running a front-page story (which included rebuttals on the jump page) about the McCarthy speech, also ran an editorial. The *Times* declared that McCarthy had won "national fame" for "wild charges, gross distortions and assorted forms of demagoguery" and his speech did nothing to "change this estimate of him." The newspaper added that it wished the speech was McCarthy's "swan song" but that indications in Wisconsin were that he would be reelected.[71] The *Milwaukee Journal* editorialized that McCarthy "turned his evil genius" against Governor Stevenson as he had against Eisenhower (before he was a candidate) and General George C. Marshall. The *Journal* reminded readers that the text of the speech was available for them to read, and if they read it and were open-minded and reasonable, they would see how the "character assassination" was "unjustified."[72] The *Chicago Tribune* made no attempt at balance in covering McCarthy's speech. Two front-page stories contained no rebuttals: One was the entire text of the speech (which continued to page 4) and the second story was filled largely with quotations from McCarthy and his "documentation" that Stevenson aided Communists.[73] In fact, the *Tribune* saw the speech "primarily directed at Democrats" rather than at Stevenson in particular. The *Tribune* found the "most impressive quality" of the presentation was McCarthy's meticulousness in documenting "almost every statement he made."[74] The *San Francisco Examiner* ran the story on page 2, but also failed to seek out and report any direct rebuttals to McCarthy's charges.[75] The *Examiner* stated that McCarthy provided a "devastating recital of the record" about how Stevenson had been two different candidates—first calling the Communist hunt a look for "phantoms" and then describing the "communist peril" as a "hard and dangerous reality." The *Examiner* applauded McCarthy for naming names "down the line" of Stevenson associates who were soft on Communism, painting a "very disturbing picture" of this man who wanted to be President.[76]

Historian Richard Fried characterized the McCarthy speech in very critical terms. Fried wrote that McCarthy "droned" 40 minutes beyond his allotted half-hour time block and that sponsors of the event described the speech as a "bust" and a "waste of money."[77] The *Monitor* and many other newspapers were extremely critical of the content of the address but never mentioned any regret by its sponsors. And the pro-McCarthy newspapers (including the McCormick and Hearst chains) hailed the speech as the documented truth, never hinting at any dissatisfaction by the backers of the speech.

Strout, in the months leading up to the national conventions and ultimately to the primary and general elections, traveled with each Presidential hopeful and could make a first-hand assessment of the candidates. Immediately after the primary election, knowing the *Monitor's* history of supporting Republicans (even during the popularity of FDR) and the clear favoritism shown toward Eisenhower in editorials to that point, Strout lobbied heavily for the newspaper not to endorse Eisenhower. Personal messages between Strout and American News Editor Saville R. Davis revealed differences between the *Monitor* staff (including reporters, editors, and editorial writers) and the Mother Church Board of Directors that amounted to a huge chasm.

Strout told Davis that "it would be folly for the *Monitor* to come out for Ike." Strout called Stevenson the "ideal *Monitor* candidate" because he was "Christian, idealistic, literate, articulate and conservative . . . more conservative than Ike in some ways." Strout noted that he was "incredulous" at times over some editorials leaning toward Eisenhower and stated it was interesting that a majority of the Washington press, made up largely of old conservative correspondents, endorsed Stevenson for President.[78]

Davis's response described a troubled *Monitor* editorial staff. He wrote to Strout that the Directors were "Republican through and through—the sort of attitude that no amount of Stevenson exposure would change." He called the mental state of chief editorial writer Don Richardson "grim" because of the circumstances. Davis complained that articles strongly critical of McCarthy had been altered. He explained that with any piece written complimentary to Stevenson "the Directors yell you can't do that that will give the wrong impression to our readers of where we stand." Davis suggested that the fight waged over the years by editor Erwin D. Canham against the Directors endorsing only Republicans might pay off. He raised the possibility that Eisenhower would not be endorsed. However, in an odd twist, Davis revealed that if the paper did not support Eisenhower, it would be despite the fact that Canham and Richardson requested permission to endorse the General because they knew of no other alternative given the pressure from the Directors. Additionally, Davis asked Strout who he thought would win the Presidential election; but Strout refused to predict, at least to Davis.[79] A communication from Erwin D. Canham to the Mother Church Board of Directors confirmed that as far back as August, Canham leaned toward endorsing Eisenhower. Canham wrote, "Considering the candidates as individuals, and without disparagement to Stevenson, General Eisenhower is a trustworthy and statesmanlike leader." Canham proposed that the *Monitor* publish the endorsement no sooner than October 1, and no later than October 15.[80]

Meanwhile, not knowing the decision to support Eisenhower had nearly been finalized, Strout wrote to his family that the polls indicated the General was leading, but that he thought Stevenson would win because "he impresses me greatly as a sensitive, intelligent, whimsical, highminded person: in fact I think I never found a presidential candidate more attractive."[81] This was a remarkable statement from a man who had covered presidents from the time of Harding, and idolized FDR. Strout wrote that he was "disappointed at the moral compromises Ike has been willing to make," referring to endorsements of Senators Jenner, McCarthy, and Taft, and the naming of Richard M. Nixon as his running mate.[82]

Less than a week later, Strout traveled to Wisconsin to cover Eisenhower's campaign swing through McCarthy's home state. Prior to Eisenhower's speech, Strout wrote that Eisenhower "will put party unity before private feelings and will support 'all' Republican candidates." Strout indicated that Eisenhower's "managers" had recognized the "substantial political value" of McCarthy and asked the junior senator to campaign for Ike outside Wisconsin.[83] The General had been persuaded by his staff to delete a strong paragraph supporting General George C. Marshall, and apparently Strout either sensed or had found out through sources in the Eisenhower campaign that the speech had been softened for the sake of party unity.[84] The next day, in a story about Eisenhower's endorsement of the GOP in Wisconsin, Strout exclaimed that Ike welcomed McCarthy to the "team" and was willing to exploit the issue of Communists in government by charging that executive departments were "infested with communism." Strout surmised that Eisenhower "wished to identify himself with the McCarthy crusade and to associate himself with the man who instituted it."[85]

Five days later, Saville R. Davis's original inclination that the *Monitor* would refrain from endorsing a Presidential candidate proved wrong. In true *Monitor* fashion of criticizing not too harshly and endorsing not too boldly, on October 9, the newspaper labeled the Democrats effort in running the country filled with "good intentions" but charged them with being "extremely careless of individual and state's rights to say nothing of taxpayer's money." The paper further alleged that the Democrats' methods had "produced paternalism, mushrooming bureaucracy, regimented statism, and deficit financing." The *Monitor* admitted that it was "deeply concerned about certain reactionary isolationist and witchhunting elements in the Republican Party" but also indicated that having a Republican in the White House for a change might allay some of the fears about Communism in government. Specifically, the *Monitor* supported Dwight David Eisenhower: "Coupled with his proven capacity for dealing with broad problems, both military and civilian, by getting people to work together, this quality gives promise that he would provide the leadership so imperative at this extraordinary time." With respect to Stevenson, while admitting he was an honorable man, the editorial argued that the "mess in Washington," supposedly created by the Democrats, was his great handicap.[86] This was a clear endorsement of Eisenhower for President, absent any great character flaws in Stevenson. The *Monitor* again would "injure no man."

In mid-October, Strout wrote an extensive article about the vast difference between newspapers supporting Eisenhower and reporters supporting Stevenson. Strout found the "degree and extent of this endorsement" of Eisenhower in editorial pages "one of the social phenomena of the era."[87] An Associated Press story carried by the *Monitor* (quoting a survey) indicated that Ike had the support of 80 percent of the newspaper circulation in the country, or more than 67 percent of all the newspapers. This compared to 1948 when Dewey received the support of 65 percent of all the newspapers with Truman receiving just 15 percent.[88] On the other hand, of the 37 correspondents traveling with Eisenhower, 24 favored Stevenson, 7 wanted Eisenhower, and 6 were undecided. Of the 35 correspondents covering Stevenson, 19 favored Stevenson, 9 Eisenhower, and 7 were undecided.[89] The differences between newspaper management and reporters clearly coincided with the differences at the *Monitor*, where reporters, editors, and even the chief editorial writer favored Stevenson (or at least did not want to endorse Eisenhower) yet the newspaper's management (the Directors of the Mother Church) demanded endorsement of Eisenhower.

The *Monitor* did not repeatedly push for Eisenhower to be the next President, but reminded voters of its position a couple of weeks before the election. In "Reasons for Our Confidence," the newspaper cautioned that some of the General's followers were threatening to "desert him" because of Eisenhower's efforts to unify the Republican Party by not distancing himself from McCarthy and other right-wing elements of the party. The *Monitor* cited major reasons to vote for Eisenhower, including; to "revive the two-party system"; to obtain a "thorough housecleaning in Washington"; to "check the drive toward centralization and socialization"; and to provide a "fresher more imaginative approach" to dealing with foreign affairs. The *Monitor* closed by stating it respected the right of all people to make their own evaluation and choice, but that Eisenhower "requires continued clear-sighted, steadfast support" in helping America toward attainment of its goals.[90]

Some historians have a strong view of how the press covered the election and, more important, how the press misinterpreted the results. The press was accused of playing up the assets of McCarthy's Republican primary opponent Len Schmitt and overlooking "his liabilities, which were substantial." The "liberal press" pretended that Schmitt was a legitimate threat to McCarthy although "Schmitt never posed a serious threat." The primary election results, and then Eisenhower's subsequent victory, were portrayed as a McCarthy victory, though among Republican statewide candidates in Wisconsin, McCarthy got the lowest vote total.[91] But, Edwin Bayley, in *Joe McCarthy and the Press*, revealed, "there were so many McCarthy news stories, pro and con, available" that a news editor could pick and choose to suit his newspaper's politics."[92]

The *Monitor* cannot be counted among those in the press who were negligent in putting McCarthy's victory into proper perspective. One editorial stated that the main developments from the election were that General Eisenhower would have "almost unprecedented power and freedom from obligations" as he entered office; that Eisenhower received "a massive mandate for fresh, strong and imaginative leadership"; and that the shift in party control really was a mandate for "the continuing support for it [Republican Party] overspread party lines." The editorial repeatedly stated the "tremendous popular endorsement of the general" but also mentioned McCarthy and other right-wing Republicans. The *Monitor* did not credit McCarthy with the entire Republican election victory, rather it theorized that the coattails of Eisenhower helped many Republican candidates and those candidates thought to oppose the General within his own party failed reelection or still won because of the "Eisenhower wave." The newspaper noted the exceptions, Senators McCarthy and Jenner, but quickly pointed out that each "ran behind their state leaders" in the vote count. In other words, there was no evidence that McCarthy led the Republican Party to victory. He had a low vote total among Republicans in Wisconsin although he defeated Democrat Thomas E. Fairchild. Finally, the *Monitor* declared that Eisenhower would bring "unifying leadership" to the country and not be involved in "petty politics and the old-line politicians."[93]

The *Monitor* later wrote that Republicans may have gained votes because of concern about Communism, but that McCarthy actually received 100,000 fewer votes than he had in 1946, 150,000 fewer than Eisenhower received in Wisconsin, and a whopping 250,000 fewer than Wisconsin Governor Kohler did in his reelection. And, Secretary of State Fred R. Zimmerman received the highest vote total of any Republican in Wisconsin though he had been "denied the Republican Party endorsement because he had denounced Senator McCarthy." Expanding on that theme, the *Monitor* explained that McCarthy carried no one to victory. It anticipated (as did many other newspapers and Republican leaders) that with Eisenhower as President, the Communists-in-government issue would not be a fight between the executive and legislative branches of government, but a cooperative effort.[94]

The *New York Times* also was among those newspapers writing that McCarthy and the issue of Communists in government were not responsible for the Republican Party victory. The *Times* wrote that Wisconsin did vote for Republicans for only the third time in a national election since 1920; however, achieving the lowest vote total among the Republicans was a "rebuke" of McCarthy's methods in rooting out Communists in government and how "leisurely" the Senator had treated his campaign.[95] The weak vote total among Republicans in the state, according to the *Times*, "proved one of the unexpected features of the election" in Wisconsin and additionally showed that McCarthy had not "proved as much of a political asset to the Republican ticket as some party officials had expected."[96] The *Monitor* and the *Times* clearly showed the context of the McCarthy win in relation to

1952: McCarthy in the National Spotlight 71

other candidates, particularly Eisenhower and the Republican Party. Certainly these two prestige newspapers were not negligent in analyzing the election results, contrary to the blanket claim of many historians.

The *Chicago Tribune* and *San Francisco Examiner*, strong McCarthy supporters and Republican papers, rejoiced at the Eisenhower victory. The *Tribune* contended that "McCarthy's magnificent victory" in the Wisconsin primary had suggested the landslide that was to follow for the General.[97] The *Examiner* surmised that Stevenson tried to make a major campaign issue out of "McCarthyism," a strategy that boomeranged in states such as Connecticut, Illinois, and New York.[98] Writing in the *Examiner*, Fulton Lewis, Jr. contended President Truman's "final act of vindictiveness before retiring" was to instruct "political henchmen" to ruin McCarthy and what he stood for, and "he [Truman] and his assistants have set about to destroy every other man or woman who has publicly fought against communists in Government."[99]

At the *Monitor*, Strout analyzed the possible dynamics between "Ike" and the Congress, and considered the U.S. position in the world. He wrote that McCarthy's win meant that Eisenhower would have to deal with a troublemaker within his own party. Strout added a European perspective, quoting the *Manchester Guardian* to the effect that as long as the "worrying crudities of a McCarthy pass with little challenge in a great party" the "influence [of America] must be weakened" in the world.[100] The British treated McCarthyism as an "obsession" and saw the Senator as a "Frankenstein monster leading the American people down the road to fascism."[101]

Because of the large number of newspapers that editorially supported Eisenhower, charges of bias in the media surfaced before and after the election. Adlai Stevenson complained of a "one party press" and the Sigma Delta Chi press organization proposed a "sweeping study" of 1952 campaign coverage.[102] A *Monitor* editorial discussed a proposal by one representative to limit the amount of editorial space given to support a candidate—the idea was dismissed by the newspaper and it was not taken seriously by virtually anyone. On the other hand, the newspaper supported the proposed Sigma Delta Chi study, stating that out of it may come the "further crystallization of the ethics of newspaperdom" providing the public a "clearer understanding" of what it "can properly demand" from the press.[103]

Historians have documented some favoritism for Eisenhower and some problems in the coverage of Stevenson. For instance, McCarthy told the Associated Press that in a speech he would "show" connections between Stevenson and known Communists and Communist causes. But when delivered, the speech mentioned nothing of the sort and the AP did not point this out.[104] On the other hand, one study found that in 26 pro-

Eisenhower newspapers, 11 gave the Democrats more front-page coverage, 15 gave the Republicans more, while 7 pro-Stevenson newspapers all gave the Democrats more front-page coverage.[105]

BENTON RESOLUTION RESOLVED

As the 1952 Presidential election came and went, the unsettled controversy over the 1950 Senate campaign in Maryland dragged on. The Benton Resolution called for the expulsion of Joseph R. McCarthy from the Senate for improper involvement in the campaign to defeat Senator Millard Tydings of Maryland, and other "amoral" acts. The Senate Privileges and Elections subcommittee, which investigated Benton's charges, was originally headed by Senator Guy M. Gillette; Gillette eventually resigned as subcommittee chair and Democrat Senator Thomas Hennings, Jr. of Missouri took over. From about the time he started investigating Lattimore through the fall elections, McCarthy fought any effort by Congress to question him; simultaneously, the junior senator continued his verbal jousts with Benton.[106]

In January 1952, a former assistant counsel, Daniel Buckley, made a scathing attack against the subcommittee. Buckley said he thought he had been hired by the Senate panel to find out the truth about whether McCarthy had perjured himself in testimony about his original Wheeling, West Virginia speech. But, Buckley reported, seven of eight witnesses he talked to upheld McCarthy's figure of 57 Communists (instead of the 205), and he had learned that the State Department had prepared statements by two radio station employees who said that the figure was 205. Buckley claimed he was fired for uncovering that the truth was McCarthy's version of the story, while the subcommittee wanted to carry out the wishes of Benton and find evidence to expel McCarthy.[107] Meanwhile, McCarthy accused the subcommittee of "picking the pockets" of the taxpayers in service of the Democratic National Committee during an election year.[108]

Following an appearance by McCarthy on Edward R. Murrow's CBS television show, Strout used an "Intimate Message from Washington" to set the record straight about some of the Senator's comments. McCarthy claimed during the television broadcast that Benton was a hypocrite for charging McCarthy with using Congressional immunity from libel suits to hide behind false accusations. McCarthy claimed that a 30,000 word statement read to the Senate by Benton was released to the press with a warning not to use it until "it becomes immune as I testified."[109] This was effectively the same thing Benton had charged against McCarthy, according to the junior senator. Biographer Thomas C. Reeves wrote that "reporters knew instantly that McCarthy had twisted a standard press release statement for his own purpose" but "only a few newspapers . . . called it to the public attention."[110] The *Monitor*'s Richard L. Strout corrected McCarthy by quoting from the statement Benton had given to the press. The document never mentioned immunity and merely asked the press to hold for release until after the speech was delivered, which was a common "embargo" practice of the press. Strout observed that the problem with McCarthy had grown "more acute" since the ten charges of alleged fraud and deceit were issued by Benton (during an ouster motion seven months previously). McCarthy demonstrated not only a lack of cooperation, but disdain for the investigating subcommittee. Strout wrote that while the subcommittee still had not finished its work, McCarthy was busy attacking publications that had been critical of him, asking advertisers to boycott the newspapers and magazines.[111] According to Strout, "twisted evidence" delivered to an "unsuspecting American television public on a reputable TV show," coupled with some members of Congress who were either afraid of McCarthy or holding back criticism for political purposes, added up to a troubling situation.[112]

To prove he was not hiding behind Senate immunity, Benton announced that he would waive his Senate privilege for his statement that McCarthy committed perjury, fraud, and calculated deceit on the American people. That immediately prompted McCarthy to file a two-million-dollar lawsuit against Benton for "libel, slander and conspiracy" in pushing for the expulsion.[113] Benton challenged McCarthy to push the suit to court before the November election so that he could "prove in court the truth of my carefully documented charges."[114]

The *Monitor*, in an editorial, welcomed the chance for a federal court to determine the truth or falsity of the charges and countercharges made by Benton and McCarthy, arguing that a federal court even "with all its faults" was "not a political forum" and that the "rules of evidence it applies are considerably more stringent than the rules—if any—followed by some congressional committees and observed in some speeches on the Senate floor." The newspaper questioned whether McCarthy would allow matters to be cleared up in the courts (he had not done so to date) prior to his reelection bid. The *Monitor* concluded, "It would be a pity to have an untried libel suit adding its miasma to an atmosphere already badly fogged."[115]

Meanwhile, Strout watched Republican Senator Margaret Chase Smith of Maine "bawl out Senator McCarthy on the Senate floor" during an April 10 speech and he "wrote an emotional piece about it for the *Monitor*—that was fun."[116] In this essay, Strout recounted the electricity in the air when reporters learned that Smith was going to speak, admitting a "prejudiced audience" in the press corps; correspondents had repeatedly voted McCarthy the worst senator in the country. But, the article largely focused on Smith's stand against McCarthy and McCarthy's methods of investigation. Strout's well-known talent for descriptive writing showed:

Senator Smith is not a tall woman, but to some admirers who watched her in this scene she seemed to tower. Her accent is not musical but it has in it some of the strength of the Maine hills and the surge of the Maine waters. Her voice is not the bull like roar of some of her male colleagues, but like the still small voice of conscience it could be heard through the chamber all the more so because there was absolute silence.[117]

What did Senator Smith actually say? In part, she charged that McCarthy had made false accusations which he could not and had not had the courage to back up with proof.[118] Smith obviously pushed for the subcommittee to continue its work.

A Senate vote of confidence for the work of the investigating subcommittee was 60–0 and not one senator rose to support McCarthy's charges that the subcommittee was prejudiced and wasting money. The *Milwaukee Journal* called the vote of confidence "the most damaging blow that McCarthy has suffered to date."[119] The *Chicago Tribune* story did not interpret the 60–0 vote as a defeat for McCarthy and a vote of confidence for the subcommittee. Rather, a page 1 article focused on McCarthy's countercharge that Benton protected Communists and Communist sympathizers while assistant secretary of state. It was not until the last line of the story that the vote against discharging the subcommittee was mentioned.

In May, the probe into McCarthy's activities turned toward his finances. Strout wrote that a $10,000 fee paid by Lustron Corporation to the Senator for writing a pamphlet about housing came during the company's "most critical days when it was kept alive by loans from the Reconstruction Finance Corporation and when Senator McCarthy was a key figure in the investigation of the matter."[120] Benton charged that this action broke "every known" code of ethics. This charge and others, once Benton withdrew Senate immunity, prompted the previously mentioned federal lawsuit by McCarthy.[121] Years later, Reeves contended that the article that eventually appeared in the Lustron Corporation publication actually had been written for educational purposes and submitted to *Life*, *Collier's*, and the *Saturday Evening Post*—and was rejected by each—prior to being sold to Lustron.[122]

While Strout continued to cover the Senate probe, the *Monitor* relied on dispatches from the Associated Press to report on the pretrial maneuvering in the McCarthy-Benton lawsuit. The hearings were suspended at one point when McCarthy pushed to have a judge force Benton to answer some of his questions.[123] The feud between McCarthy and Benton lingered throughout the year. At one point McCarthy stated that Benton was worth "100 million dollars to the Kremlin on the floor of the U.S. Senate" because Communist front sympathizers were at least indirectly in Benton's employ.[124] The lawsuit pretrial hearings were not deemed important enough for the *Monitor* to assign a reporter to cover and were not placed on the front page as the Senate probe stories often were.

By the end of November and into December, it looked as though the Hennings subcommittee had all but abandoned the McCarthy investigation. The *Monitor* wrote that the investigation was handled "spasmodically for a year" and with resignations by Senators Gillette and Smith, and with Senator Monroney in Europe, the subcommittee was left with just two members; the prospects of a report being filed in the remaining few weeks seemed unlikely. The two senators left believed that continuation under the circumstances was "pointless," according to the *Monitor*, so it looked like "curtains" on action related to Benton's charges against McCarthy.[125] But, just before the new Congress took over in January 1953, the Hennings subcommittee released the report on its 18-month investigation of charges originally levied by Senator William Benton against McCarthy. McCarthy biographer Reeves, in retrospect, saw the report as vindictive:

This hurried and unfair report should have been quickly dismissed by the nation's liberal and intellectual community, for it contained features often associated with extremist literature and McCarthyism. But the hostility toward McCarthy and the bitterness over the recent election defeats were such that many otherwise reasonable people welcomed the Hennings' report with fanfare and applause.[126]

The *Monitor*'s Neal Stanford was largely unimpressed with the overall content of the 400-page report—stating it had "relevant information and scores of questions—but no answers." Stanford contended that the most important part of the report accused McCarthy of refusing no fewer than six times to appear before the subcommittee to answer questions about business deals and other matters. The report flatly charged that McCarthy intentionally tried to "thwart" the investigation. The subcommittee report also touched on McCarthy's shady financial dealings.[127] The *New York Times* claimed the subcommittee "declined to offer either conclusions or recommendations as to his fitness to hold office," and the *Chicago Tribune* noted that the subcommittee's report "was admittedly disappointing to enemies of the Wisconsin Senator."[128] The new Congress and a Republican in the White House, coupled with no clear recommendation by the subcommittee, doomed the report to oblivion.

LETTERS TO THE *MONITOR*

The year 1952 was the first year that any significant number of letters about McCarthy and McCarthyism appeared in the *Monitor*. The choosing of a President was the subject of many letters. Benjamin Jacobs of North Carolina denounced a *Monitor* editorial implying that Democrat Presidential candidate Adlai Stevenson was "captive" of city bosses and Truman by pointing out that General Eisenhower (the Republican candidate) was hardly an "independent" thinker in succumbing to the "old GOP guard" by supporting Senator McCarthy.[129] However, a subsequent letter from C. W. Esmond of Ohio contended that "Ike" was not the captive of anyone because Senators McCarthy and Jenner (among others) "need Ike more than he needs them. He is not their captive. They are his captives."[130] Still another letter about the Presidential election from a self-proclaimed Republican, Fred LaBastille of Missouri, admonished the *Monitor* for providing thorough coverage of the strengths and weaknesses of Stevenson, but failing to expose to the public that "the good supporters of Eisenhower have disappeared and a thoroughly repulsive group has replaced them" (referring to Nixon, Jenner, and McCarthy). LaBastille concluded that the *Monitor* supported the Republicans who campaigned by "tearing down the opposing team" and he expressed anxiety that what was said did not bother him as much as what was left unsaid.[131] He clearly implied that the *Monitor* should find out what was "unsaid" and disclose it.

Another letter on a different topic, from Mildred D. Gutterson of Lisbon Falls, Maine, praised the independence of Senator Margaret Chase Smith. Gutterson declared that "all women voters in both parties should be proud" of Ms. Smith because she "stood four-square for fundamental civil liberties in a period of global cold war and of much domestic confusion."[132]

Willim Evjue, Editor and Publisher of the *Capital Times* of Madison, Wisconsin, took the *Monitor* to task for not crediting his newspaper for being the first to challenge McCarthy. Citing a March 20 Strout "Intimate Message from Washington" titled "Let's Look at the Evidence," Evjue stated he was "surprised and dismayed" that Strout failed to identify the *Capital Times* as exposing McCarthy as early as 1946, and continuing to publish the "truth" about McCarthy, whether it was the Senator's battle with the Wisconsin State Supreme Court or controversy over granting "quickie" divorces when McCarthy was a judge. This caused McCarthy to begin his "Communist smear campaign" against the *Capital Times* some three months prior to his Lincoln Day speech in Wheeling.[133] Evjue's letter clearly intended to set the record straight and give his newspaper's campaign against McCarthy the credit he felt it was due. In fact, Evjue and McCarthy's animosity toward one another had been documented nationally in November 1949, when the feud received coverage in *Time*.[134]

The *Monitor* published a long and detailed letter from W. B. Coates, Jr. of New Hampshire, chronicling McCarthy's "contributions" (or lack thereof) to fighting Communism in the United States. Coates first explained that McCarthy did not cause the "wave of anti-communism"; he was merely "smart enough to sense that he could use the furore to his own advantage."

Coates noted that anticommunist measures had been taken long before McCarthy's Wheeling speech, and in looking at the Senator's record since he made the issue his own, there had been no instances of a "conviction for Communist or subversive activity in government that could be remotely ascribed to evidence uncovered by Mr. McCarthy." Coates expressed concern that under the continued atmosphere of McCarthyism, liberties would be lost that "can never be recovered."[135] Perhaps spurred by the political atmosphere of a Presidential election year, published letters in the *Monitor* about McCarthy reached an all-time high with few displaying any support for the methods of the well-known Communist fighter.

MCCARTHY'S 1953 STRATEGY

As 1952 came to a close, McCarthy indicated that with a Republican administration taking over and therefore less suspicion of protecting subversives in the State Department and other government agencies, perhaps the Federal Communications Commission and colleges and universities would be the targets of his Communist hunting probes.[136] However, Neal Stanford of the *Monitor* theorized that the FCC and the nation's colleges and universities would merely be added to McCarthy's list of probes, a list that still included government agencies: "There is growing evidence that in the coming months the United States is in for a full-scale investigation of activities of subversives, communists and communist sympathizers in government, the nation's schools and the United Nations."[137]

Specifically, Stanford listed investigations that would begin in the new year, including a probe of the FCC, two separate committees looking at the nation's schools, one possibly investigating the labor movement, and an investigation into charges that congressmen helped four or five subversives get jobs at the United Nations.[138] McCarthyism was going strong.

MEDIA SELF-CRITIQUE

The debate in the press about the press remained constant throughout 1952. In January, *Monitor* editor Erwin D. Canham addressed the New Hampshire Weekly Publishers Association about the dangers of losing press freedom. Canham told the group that freedom was being threatened for three basic reasons: There had been a failure to inform the people of the importance of that freedom; power-hungry men were attempting to destroy the freedom; and newspapers needed to "more effectively and responsibly" do their jobs.[139] There were some hopeful signs related to press freedom, though. The Committee on Information of the American Society of News Editors (ASNE) reported that a survey indicated that for the first time since World War II there were gains for the press in access to records, from local school boards to the federal government. The Chair of the committee, James S. Pope of the *Louisville Courier-Journal*, concluded that there had been gains in press access to the military and public education, and several newspapers across the country had won fights against suppression.[140] The *Monitor*'s Washington Bureau Chief, Roscoe Drummond, was named head of a Senate advisory committee (of newspaper and radio correspondents) charged with assembling data about the status of access to government records in Washington, D.C. ABC's Elmer Davis and the *New York Times*' James Reston also served on the committee.

Most of the debate in the press involved specific people, companies, and events. *Editor and Publisher* condemned the practice of using economics to squelch a free press. The magazine referred to an October 1951 story in *Time* titled "Demagogue McCarthy," which the Senator responded to by contacting advertisers asking them to boycott the magazine. *E&P* noted that it was the second time McCarthy had tried such a tactic, the first being the intimidation of the Adam Hat Company, sponsor of the Drew Pearson radio show. McCarthy urged the company to drop Pearson because of the broadcaster's criticism of the Senator. Adam Hat dropped Pearson, but denied it was because of pressure from McCarthy. *E&P* wrote that the whole thing "reeks of totalitarianism."[141] A follow-up article in *E&P* two weeks later contended that the *Time* episode was actually the fifth instance McCarthy's wrath had been felt by organizations challenging him. Besides *Time* and Pearson, the *Milwaukee Journal* and the *Capital Times* on three other occasions had been singled out by McCarthy for criticism because they opposed him, though no boycotts were urged then.[142] Biographer Fred J. Cook contended that McCarthy ignored the many hundreds of newspapers and radio stations that supported him and focused on those dissenting, charging them with being pro-Communist because they were critical of him. Cook wrote that Strout and ABC Radio's Elmer Davis were among "the ablest journalists" in the country who, because they criticized McCarthy, had their character assassinated by him.[143]

The press continually debated the problem of providing publicity for McCarthy's charges when the reporter and newspaper knew they were not true; this practice made newspapers, in effect, co-conspirators with McCarthy. A Boston University professor wrote that the press "in its attempt to report 'objectively' Senator McCarthy or any other public figure who makes 'news' becomes an unwitting or unwilling accomplice in the cult of incredibility."[144] Alan Barth, a member of the editorial staff at the *Washington Post*, leveled harsh criticism against the newspaper industry charging that the "dirty work" for McCarthy was being done by the press. Barth contended that when headlines were written about wild charges against individuals, many of which were later learned to be false, "we [newspapers] inflict on his victim an irreparable injury." He called the press a "partner in a corruption of the democratic process" in adhering to the "detached and objective reporting" techniques largely used by newspapers. He stated the *Post* compensated for the inadequacies of the system in editorials.[145] An *E&P* editorial the following week defended the system of objective reporting, despite its shortcomings. Reacting to Barth's assessments, the editorial declared, "Newsmen cannot establish themselves as infallible judges of whether a member of Congress is telling the truth or not." It urged the industry to keep the current practices because "we know in spite of the faults and the potential abuses the good far outweighs the bad."[146]

In August 1952, ABC broadcaster Elmer Davis eloquently articulated the problem facing the press in the troubled and fearful times of the Cold War:

A good newspaper, the good broadcaster, must walk a tightrope between two gulfs—on the one side objectivity that takes everything at face value and lets the public be imposed on by the charlatan with the brazen front; on the other, the "interpretive" reporting which fails to draw the line between objective and subjective, between a reasonably well established fact and what the reporter or editor wishes were fact.[147]

Davis talked specifically about reporting about Congressional hearings. Providing "adequate coverage" of those stories, according to Davis, "entails reporting not only what a man says now, but the very different thing he may have said last year—or last week."[148]

At one point, the Associated Press Managing Editors (APME) attempted to take formal action about objective versus subjective reporting. Warden Woolard of the *Los Angeles Examiner* proposed a resolution calling for "safeguards" against "so-called interpretive writing" and urged that any complaints be forwarded to APME.[149] The resolution was tabled after Norman E. Isaacs of the *Louisville Times* argued that the idea of policing the AP had been rejected at a meeting in Atlanta, and the prospect of looking over the shoulder of every AP man would not make for good working conditions.[150] Alan Gould, an executive editor with the Associated Press, noted a policy statement from the *1948 APME Red Book* that "explanatory writing" should be permitted "assuming that certain safeguards are established to preserve the fundamental objectivity of the A.P. news report."[151]

While the press continued to wrestle with the advantages and disadvantages of objective versus interpretive reporting, two of the nation's most respected newspapers gained high marks for integrity. Business owners in the San Francisco area were polled about what they thought about the press. One respondent echoed many when he or she wrote that "the *New York Times,* and for the most part, the *Christian Science Monitor* and *Boston*

Transcript" had "complete editorial integrity, uninfluenced by owners, advertisers, etc."[152]

An end-of-the-year poll of United Press editors showed that the Republican nomination of General Eisenhower for President and his subsequent election was the top story for 1952. (The first test of the H-bomb by the United States ranked second and the third year of the Korean War was the third most important story, according to the editors.) The year had included events such as McCarthy's continuous harassment of Dr. Owen Lattimore; Senator William Benton's continued push for formal Senate action against the junior senator; McCarthy's brutal attacks on Adlai Stevenson; and McCarthy receiving credit from many for election victories of GOP candidates. Many believed Eisenhower's presence in the White House (after a resounding victory at the polls) would result in McCarthy toning down his attacks on the State Department and other government agencies, but as 1953 began, McCarthy took on the press, and became entangled in several controversies about foreign policy.

NOTES

1. Those interested in the details surrounding Lattimore are referred to: Newman, Robert P., *Owen Lattimore and the "Loss" of China* (Berkeley: University of California Press, 1992).

2. Quoted in Richard L. Strout, "Survey Repudiates McCarthy's Charges," *Christian Science Monitor*, 29 January 1952, 10.

3. Strout, "Survey Repudiates," 10.

4. Quoted in Neal Stanford, "Loyalty Board Chief Blasts McCarthy 'smear' Tactics," *Christian Science Monitor*, 12 February 1952, 13.

5. Quoted in "Assails McCarthy," *Chicago Tribune*, 12 February 1952, 18.

6. Richard L. Strout, "Lattimore Loyalty Case Gets New Senate Review," *Christian Science Monitor*, 26 February 1952, 3.

7. Roland Sawyer, "Lattimore Stays Unruffled under Fire of Committee," *Christian Science Monitor*, 29 February 1952, 3.

8. Editorial, "Clearing the Air," *Christian Science Monitor*, 29 February 1952, 18.

9. Editorial, "Politics, Not Persons," *Christian Science Monitor*, 7 March 1952, 20.

10. Roland Sawyer, "Reporting a Hearing: An Intimate Message from Washington," *Christian Science Monitor*, 12 March 1952, 22.

11. Williams S. White, "Senators Accuse Lattimore of Untruths in Testimony," *New York Times*, 22 March 1952, 1. "McCarran Rips Lattimore for Untruths," *Chicago Tribune*, 22 March 1952, 1, 4.

12. Editorial, "Free to Be 'Expert,' " *Christian Science Monitor*, 5 April 1952, 24.

13. "State Department Forbids Customs Exit to Lattimore," *Christian Science Monitor*, 21 June 1952, 3.

14. Neal Stanford, "Motive Still Veiled in Lattimore Case," *Christian Science Monitor*, 26 June 1952, 6.

15. "Washington Letter," *Christian Science Monitor*, 28 June 1952, 9.
16. Neal Stanford, "State Dept. Apologizes to Lattimore over False Tip," *Christian Science Monitor*, 30 June 1952, 13.
17. "Lattimore and Davies Charged with Perjury by Senate Group," *Christian Science Monitor*, 2 July 1952, 11.
18. C. P. Trussell, "Senate Unit Calls Lattimore Agent of Red Conspiracy," *New York Times*, 3 July 1952, 1.
19. Willard Edwards, "Report Calls for Perjury Indictments," *Chicago Tribune*, 3 July 1952, 1. Editorial, "Judgment on Lattimore," *Chicago Tribune*, 5 July 1952, 6.
20. Roscoe Drummond, "State of the Nation: Reassuring Facts in Lattimore Case," *Christian Science Monitor*, 18 December 1952, 1.
21. Joseph C. Harsch, "The Affairs of Nations: What's Wrong with the State Department—Part I," *Christian Science Monitor*, 19 December 1952.
22. Editorial, "Lattimore Indicted," *Chicago Tribune*, 18 December 1952, 12.
23. Editorial, "Good!," *San Francisco Examiner*, 18 December 1952, 34.
24. Earl Latham, *The Communist Controversy in Washington: From the New Deal to McCarthy* (Cambridge, Mass.: Harvard University Press, 1966), 305.
25. Joseph R. McCarthy, *McCarthyism: The Fight for America* (New York: National Weekly, Inc., 1952), 5–7.
26. Ibid.
27. Ibid.
28. Fred J. Cook, *The Nightmare Decade: The Life and Times of Senator Joe McCarthy* (New York: Random House, 1971), 183–184.
29. Richard L. Strout, "Opposite Views of McCarthy Published," *Christian Science Monitor*, 16 July 1952, 7.
30. Ibid.
31. Erwin D. Canham, "From the Bookself—McCarthyism: A Question of Fact, Review of *McCarthyism: The Fight for America*, by Joseph R. McCarthy, *Christian Science Monitor*, 3 September 1952, 9.
32. Ibid. Strout, "Opposite Views," 7.
33. Canham, book review of *McCarthyism*, 9.
34. Years later *Monitor* editors and Strout could not recall details of the suspension, but documentation in Strout's papers provides some answers.
35. Richard L. Strout, "Bridges Elected GOP Leader as Congress Opens," *Christian Science Monitor*, 8 January 1952, 1.
36. Quoted in Max K. Gilstrap, "Taft Praises McCarthy Stand in Opening Wisconsin Campaign," *Christian Science Monitor*, 22 January 1952, 3.
37. Max K. Gilstrap, "Wisconsin Democrat Offers Campaign Challenge to McCarthy," *Christian Science Monitor*, 23 January 1952, 7.
38. Richard L. Strout, " 'Liberal' Block Snubbed: Full Control," *Christian Science Monitor*, 2 July 1952, 1.
39. Editorial, "The 'Captives,' " *Christian Science Monitor*, 16 August 1952, 18.
40. Editorial, "The Problem of 'Bedfellows,' " *Milwaukee Journal*, 10 August 1952, 2V.
41. Editorial, " 'Burying' the 'Hatchet Men,' " *Christian Science Monitor*, 20 August 1952, 16.

42. Max K. Gilstrap, "McCarthy Primary Test Is Keyed by Talkathon," *Christian Science Monitor*, 29 August 1952, 1.

43. Editorial, "How Wisconsin Republicans Can Help Gen. Eisenhower," *Milwaukee Journal*, 31 August 1952, 2.

44. "Press Polled 75% for Eisenhower," *Christian Science Monitor*, 5 September 1952, 1.

45. Max K. Gilstrap, "McCarthy: Patriot or Smear?—Public Deeply Divided," *Christian Science Monitor*, 8 September 1952, 3.

46. Max K. Gilstrap, "Schmitt Given Slim Hope to Beat McCarthy at Polls," *Christian Science Monitor*, 9 September 1952, 15.

47. Everett Melvin, "Wisconsin Voters Go to the Polls Today . . . Smear of McCarthy Boomerangs," *Chicago Tribune*, 9 September 1952, 1.

48. George Rothwell Brown, "Political Parade: Attack on McCarthy," *San Francisco Examiner*, 9 September 1952, 20.

49. "McCarthy Wins Smashing Victory," *Christian Science Monitor*, 10 September 1952, 1.

50. Quoted in Max K. Gilstrap, "McCarthy Victor in Wisconsin—Texas Democrats Freed to Vote for 'Ike': Schmitt Declares Senator Has Perpetrated Fraudulent Hoax on People of the State," *Christian Science Monitor*, 10 September 1952, 4.

51. Editorial, "The Man They Nominated," *Milwaukee Journal*, 10 September 1952, 24.

52. Richard J. H. Johnston, "M'Carthy Asserts Wisconsin Spoke," *New York Times*, 11 September 1952, 23.

53. Editorial, "McCarthy Victory," *New York Times*, 11 September 1952, 30.

54. Editorial, "McCarthy's Triumph," *Chicago Tribune*, 11 September 1952, 18.

55. Max K. Gilstrap, "McCarthy Victory Shadows 'Ike' Campaign—Strategists: Why Did Wisconsin Senator Win?" *Christian Science Monitor*, 11 September 1952, 9.

56. Richard L. Strout, "Democrats Set Tactics," *Christian Science Monitor*, 11 September 1952, 1.

57. Editorial, "Two Jobs to Be Done," *Christian Science Monitor*, 13 September 1952, 18.

58. C. P. Trussell, "M'Carthy Victory Tops 8 Primaries," *New York Times*, 11 September 1952, 1.

59. David M. Oshinsky, *A Conspiracy So Immense: The World of Joe McCarthy* (New York: The Free Press, 1983), 242.

60. Richard L. Strout, "McCarthy Set to Fire," *Christian Science Monitor*, 25 October 1952, 1.

61. "The Stevenson Story," *Newsweek*, 3 November 1952, 30.

62. Quoted in "IKE Disclaims McCarthy Line," *Christian Science Monitor*, 27 October 1952, 1.

63. Quoted in "Stevenson Set Backfire against McCarthy Blaze," *Christian Science Monitor*, 27 October 1952, 2.

64. "Stevenson Set Backfire," 2.

1952: McCarthy in the National Spotlight 83

65. Richard L. Strout, "Korea Trip by 'Ike' and McCarthy Speech Held Key Issues," *Christian Science Monitor*, 27 October 1952, 3.

66. Clifton Brock, *Americans for Democratic Action: Its Role in National Politics* (Westport, Conn.: Greenwood Press, 1985), 141.

67. Quoted in "McCarthy Charges Set Off Tense Debate across the U.S.: Aid to Reds Alleged," *Christian Science Monitor*, 28 October 1952, 1.

68. Richard L. Strout, "Stevenson Derides McCarthy Attack," *Christian Science Monitor*, 28 October 1952, 1.

69. Quoted in Editorial, " 'In the American Way,' " *Christian Science Monitor*, 29 October 1952, 18.

70. Editorial, " 'In the American Way,' " 18.

71. Editorial, "The McCarthy Speech," *New York Times*, 28 October 1952, 30.

72. Editorial, "Now Marshall, Eisenhower and Stevenson Have Been Smeared," *Milwaukee Journal*, 28 October 1952, 20.

73. George Tagge, "Senator Hit Governor for 'Aid to Red Cause': Calls Nominee Part of Hiss, Lattimore, Acheson 'Group,' " *Chicago Tribune*, 28 October 1952, 1. "Fits Together 'Jigsaw Puzzle' of Candidate," *Chicago Tribune*, 28 October 1952, 1.

74. Editorial, "McCarthy," *Chicago Tribune*, 29 October 1952, 18.

75. John Casserly, "McCarthy Flays Stevenson Record; Cites Past Activities and Advisers," *San Francisco Examiner*, 28 October 1952, 2.

76. Editorial, "Soft!," *San Francisco Examiner*, 30 October 1952, 32.

77. Richard M. Fried, *Men against McCarthy* (New York: Columbia University Press, 1976), 234.

78. Richard L. Strout personal message to Saville [Davis], 16 September 1952, Richard L. Strout Papers, Weston, Mass.

79. Saville [Davis] personal message to RLS [Richard L. Strout], 16 September 1952, Richard L. Strout Papers, Weston, Mass.

80. Mr. Canham to the Board of Directors, 6 August 1952, 1–3. Church History Department, The First Church of Christ, Scientist, Boston, Mass.

81. R. [Richard L. Strout] to Dearest Family, 29 September 1952, Richard L. Strout Papers, Weston, Mass.

82. Ibid. A memo to Roscoe [Drummond] from Spike, 3 November 1952, Richard L. Strout Papers, Weston, Mass., indicated that Drummond and Strout had provided superb election coverage "despite the obvious difficulties." Spike wrote that he had not remembered a more intense violent reaction to each of the candidates, but readers found "relatively little" to complain about related to Drummond and Strout's copy covering the election.

83. Richard L. Strout, "Ike Endorses Wisconsin GOP," *Christian Science Monitor*, 3 October 1952, 1.

84. Robert Griffith, *The Politics of Fear: Joseph R. McCarthy and the Senate* (Amherst, Mass. UMass Press, 1987), 193–194.

85. Richard L. Strout, "Ike Nails Issue of Communism into Campaign," *Christian Science Monitor*, 4 October 1952, 1.

86. Editorial, "The *Monitor* and the Campaign," *Christian Science Monitor*, 9 October 1952, 22.

87. Richard L. Strout, "Editorial Pages Favor Eisenhower but Reporters Like . . . Stevenson," *Christian Science Monitor*, 17 October 1952, 6.

88. "Survey Shows Papers 4 to 1 for Ike," *Christian Science Monitor*, 30 October 1952, 10.

89. Strout, "Editorial Pages," 6.

90. Editorial, "Reasons for Our Confidence," *Christian Science Monitor*, 25 October 1952, 18.

91. Oshinsky, *A Conspiracy So Immense*, 232.

92. Edwin R. Bayley, *Joe McCarthy and the Press* (Madison, Wisc.: University of Wisconsin Press, 1981), 105.

93. Editorial, "Nature of the Election," *Christian Science Monitor*, 7 November 1952, 20.

94. Editorial, "Toward Better Debate," *Christian Science Monitor*, 17 November 1952, 18.

95. Richard J. H. Johnston, "M'Carthy Is Winner, but Is Last on Ticket," *New York Times*, 5 November 1952, 1, 22.

96. Richard J. H. Johnston, "Wisconsin Slashes M'Carthy Margin," *New York Times*, 6 November 1952, 30.

97. Editorial, "The Victors and Their Victory," *Chicago Tribune*, 5 November 1952, 16.

98. Editorial, "The Dems," *San Francisco Examiner*, 7 November 1952, 30.

99. Fulton Lewis, Jr., "The Passing of Truman," *San Francisco Examiner*, 5 November 1952, 23.

100. Quoted in Richard L. Strout, "Ike Faces Congress Difficulties," *Christian Science Monitor*, 5 November 1952, 1.

101. John P. Rossi, "The British Reaction to McCarthyism, 1950–54," *Mid-America: An Historical Review*, 70/1 January 1988, 5.

102. "Press Fraternity to Sift Reporting of Campaign," *Christian Science Monitor*, 24 November 1952, 4.

103. Editorial, "One Party Press?," *Christian Science Monitor*, 8 December 1952, 20. Additionally, *Washington Post* editorial writer Robert H. Estabrook defended his newspaper in a piece called "Press Performance in the Campaign," *Nieman Reports*, 7/1 January 1953, 12. He claimed the *Post* "went to special pains, because of its support of Eisenhower, to provide fair treatment." However, Estabrook realized the "real dangers" in a press so committed to Eisenhower that it may apologize for him "instead of giving him the independent, constructive criticism that any administrator needs."

104. James Aronson, *The Press and the Cold War* (Indianapolis and New York: Bobbs-Merrill Company, 1970), 81.

105. Nathan B. Blumberg, *One Party Press? Coverage of the 1952 Presidential Campaign in 35 Daily Newspapers* (Lincoln, Nebr.: University of Nebraska Press, 1954), 44.

106. Neal Stanford, "McCarthy Transactions Questioned by Senate Group; Non Cooperation Hit." *Christian Science Monitor*, 3 January 1953, 3.

107. Quoted in "McCarthy Again," *Newsweek*, 7 January 1952, 16.

108. Quoted in "Vote on McCarthy," *Newsweek*, 17 March 1952, 26.

1952: McCarthy in the National Spotlight

109. Quoted in Richard L. Strout, "Let's Look at the Evidence," *Christian Science Monitor*, 20 March 1952, 26.

110. Thomas C. Reeves, *The Life and Times of Joe McCarthy: A Biography* (New York: Stein & Day, 1982), 398.

111. More on this will be discussed later in the chapter.

112. Strout, "Let's Look at the Evidence," 26.

113. "McCarthy Files Slander Suit against Benton for $2 Million," *Christian Science Monitor*, 26 March 1952, 17.

114. Quoted in "Benton Dares McCarthy to Push Suit Before Fall," *Christian Science Monitor*, 27 March 1952, 3.

115. Editorial, "A Chance for the Facts," *Christian Science Monitor*, 28 March 1952, 22.

116. RLS [Richard L. Strout] to Dear Family, 11 April 1952, Richard L. Strout Papers, Weston, Mass.

117. Richard L. Strout, "McCarthy Storms—But Maine Senator Wins Joust," *Christian Science Monitor*, 11 April 1952, 3.

118. C. P. Trussell, "M'Carthy Inquiry Gets Senate Push," *New York Times*, 11 April 1952, 9.

119. Editorial, "60 to 0—Investigate McCarthy," *Milwaukee Journal*, 11 April 1952, 16.

120. Richard L. Strout, "Probers Eye $10,000 Fee to McCarthy," *Christian Science Monitor*, 12 May 1952, 1.

121. Richard L. Strout, "McCarthy Finances Eyed in Senate Fitness Probe," *Christian Science Monitor*, 13 May 1952, 5.

122. Reeves, *The Life and Times*, 153.

123. "Pre-Trial Benton Hearings Terminated by McCarthy," *Christian Science Monitor*, 6 June 1952, 3.

124. Quoted in "McCarthy Says Benton Worth Millions," *Christian Science Monitor*, 29 October 1952, 4.

125. "The Washington Letter," *Christian Science Monitor*, 22 November 1952, 9.

126. Reeves, *The Life and Times*, 413.

127. Stanford, "McCarthy Transactions Questioned," 3. More details about Stanford's story and the *Monitor's* coverage of the subcommittee report will be discussed in Chapter 6.

128. "Senate Unit Shies at M'Carthy Issue," *New York Times*, 3 January 1953, 5. Willard Edwards, "Probers' Report; No Conclusions," *Chicago Tribune*, 3 January 1953, 4.

129. Benjamin Jacobs, to editor, "Captives?," *Christian Science Monitor*, 29 September 1952, 14.

130. C. W. Esmond, to editor, "Best Insurance," *Christian Science Monitor*, 18 October 1952, 18.

131. Fred LaBastille, to editor, "Not Enough," *Christian Science Monitor*, 30 October 1952, 20.

132. Mildred D. Gutterson, to editor, "Margaret Chase Smith," *Christian Science Monitor*, 18 April 1952, 24.

133. William T. Evjue, to editor, "The Capital Times' Exposé," *Christian Science Monitor*, 14 April 1952, 16.

134. Reeves, *The Life and Times*, 192.

135. W. B. Coates, Jr., to editor, "Opinion on McCarthy," *Christian Science Monitor*, 20 October 1952, 16.

136. "McCarthy Hints Probe of FCC by Senate Unit," *Christian Science Monitor*, 29 November 1952, 20. "McCarthy Says He Plans to Investigate Colleges," *Christian Science Monitor*, 29 December 1952, 5.

137. Neal Stanford, "Full-Scale Probe Looms of Subversives in the U.S.," *Christian Science Monitor*, 30 December 1952, 1.

138. Ibid.

139. Quoted in "Editor Urges Newspapers to Maintain Objectivity," *Christian Science Monitor*, 18 January 1952, 4.

140. "Editors Report Gains in Fight on News Curbs," *Christian Science Monitor*, 19 April 1952, 14.

141. Editorial, "Intimidation," *Editor and Publisher*, 2 February 1952, 28.

142. Robert U. Brown, "Shop Talk at Thirty," *Editor and Publisher*, 16 February 1952, 72.

143. Cook, *The Nightmare Decade*, 183–184.

144. David Manning White, "The Cult of Incredibility," *Nieman Reports*, 6/2 April 1952: 10.

145. "Barth Asserts Press Is Used for 'Dirty Work,' " *Editor and Publisher*, 10 May 1952, 20.

146. Editorial, "Dirty Work," *Editor and Publisher*, 17 May 1952, 38.

147. Elmer Davis, "News and the Whole Truth," *Atlantic Monthly*, August 1952, 32–38.

148. Ibid.

149. Quoted in "The Woolard Resolution," *The AMPE Redbook 1952*, v. 5, 12–15 November 1952, 227.

150. Quoted in "The Woodland Resolution," 227.

151. Quoted in "The Woodland Resolution," 170–171.

152. F. Bourn Hayne, "What Do Readers Think of the Press?" *Nieman Reports*, 6/4 October 1952, 20.

4

1953: McCarthy versus the Press and the Eisenhower Administration

THE *MONITOR* PRESSURES STROUT

Strout and Ike's Cabinet

Richard L. Strout, in a January 1953 front-page interpretive piece about Eisenhower cabinet appointees, speculated about the strengths and weaknesses of bringing many business leaders into government. Strout reported that Washington correspondents "cannot help but be struck by their superbly dynamic quality, self-confidence, ease of manner, and powerful personalities." The bulk of the article centered on the nominee for Secretary of Defense, Charles E. Wilson—head of General Motors. Wilson stated he planned to retain millions of dollars in GM stock. With GM one of the largest defense contractors, Strout suggested possible problems with Wilson's confirmation because of a conflict of interest.[1] However, it was a general characterization Strout made about businessmen that irked Directors of the Mother Church: "These men [business men entering government jobs] are not used to bowing to Congress or anybody. They are not used to politics, they are not, indeed, used to being crossed."[2]

Monitor Editor Erwin D. Canham issued a memo to American News Editor Saville R. Davis about the statement. Canham wrote that the Directors, many of them successful businessmen, had "long admired and spoken most warmly of Mr. Strout's high journalistic contribution to our paper." However, since Eisenhower's election, the Directors felt that Strout was "no doubt unconsciously, 'needling,' the new Administration." Canham explained that he did not want the paper to turn to "slavish adulation" for Eisenhower, as it did for Hoover in the late 1920s and early 1930s, but a simple change in the "manner in which" things were written was needed.[3]

After this "problem" was brought to the attention of Strout, he wrote to the new Secretary of the Treasury (and a former steel maker), George M. Humphrey, and asked him to review the article. Strout asked Humphrey, "Have I been unfair?"[4] Strout included a copy of Humphrey's return letter (which indicated Strout had been fair) in his official response to Roscoe Drummond about complaints from the Directors (passed to Strout through Saville R. Davis and Washington Bureau Chief Roscoe Drummond). Strout defended his reporting, stating that Humphrey did not see the article as "anti-business."[5] The discussion about the "anti-business" tone of Strout's cabinet appointees' story served only as a prelude to larger disputes between Strout and the Mother Church's Directors. (There were no further memos about the matter.) A controversy about Strout's "dual-life" that had began more than a year earlier reached a climax.

Strout's Ban

In a confidential memo from American News Editor Saville R. Davis to Roscoe Drummond, Davis expressed concern that the TRB columnist in the *New Republic* might be Strout, and that if it were, "fairly sharp cracks at the Eisenhower group" may have gone beyond the *Monitor*'s policy to "injure no man." Davis noted that *Monitor* reporters, according to the standard employee contracts, "are expected not to write and interpret in one vein for us, and in quite another vein for another periodical." Davis concluded that if Strout was not writing the TRB column, then the issue was dead, but if he was, the "delicacy" of the problem must be conveyed so that Strout can "find ways to say what he wants to within the broad limits of *Monitor* style and policy."[6] Strout had compared McCarthy repeatedly to Hitler and other reviled foreign leaders in his TRB column, certainly violating the *Monitor*'s distaste for name-calling and a canon "to injure no man, but to bless all mankind." David M. Oshinsky, in his biography of McCarthy, found the name-calling by the anti-McCarthyites (such as TRB and others) as repulsive as McCarthy's tactics: "the righteous people who condemned his [McCarthy] name calling were the same people who called him a Nazi, a jackal, and a thug; that the people who yelled loudest at his dirty tactics were the same people who spread rumors of his alleged homosexuality and hired spies to infiltrate his office and dredge up material about the personal habits of his aides."[7]

In a second confidential memo from Davis to Drummond, which Davis asked Drummond not to share with anyone, Davis admitted he knew Strout was TRB. Further, he echoed concerns by Erwin D. Canham, editor, that if everyone became cognizant that Strout was TRB, "or if someone out to get us should come in with an attack from the outside... we would be in a very awkward position." Davis gave Drummond the option of "informally" talking to Strout about the concerns of the Directors, though he did not ask Drummond to request that Strout desist from writing his TRB column. Finally, Davis stated that "I would be happier if he [Strout] knew that we were living on a small volcano and trying to ignore it" because of great respect for Strout's work, and because Davis and Drummond considered Strout a "right good friend."[8] A final confidential memo from Drummond to Davis confirmed that Drummond had discussed that matter with Strout.[9]

The issue seemed to end, but nearly one year later it surfaced again in a memo from Strout to William H. Stringer (he replaced Drummond as Washington Bureau Chief in September 1953) and Saville R. Davis. Strout acknowledged that the Directors, sometime after the McCarthy book was published in September 1952, asked him not to write about McCarthy because anything written by him was being viewed by some readers as "vindictive." He complained that on January 9, 1953, "prayerfully and with all the care at my command," he wrote an "Intimate Message" about the Hennings subcommittee findings related to McCarthy's finances.[10] The piece never made it into the *Monitor*. The Directors rejected it despite approval from Don Richardson (editorial page editor) and editor Erwin D. Canham. Strout saw the rejection of his "Intimate Message" by the Directors as a "vote of no confidence" and expressed a desire to thrash out "a chasm between the men getting out the paper and people directing the paper."[11]

Davis responded to Strout's concerns in a confidential memo to Stringer. Davis recalled that there was not "anything formal" removing Strout from covering McCarthy or in rejecting his pieces. He admitted a period of sensitivity had existed, but wrote that "That period has long since passed." Davis concluded that he was "delighted" to have Strout cover McCarthy, and reminded Stringer that the only complaints about Strout's work came related to "Intimate Messages," not about his news copy.[12]

Meanwhile, on April 27, 1954, Davis sent Strout a five-page letter chronicling the events surrounding the concern that Strout was the TRB columnist. Davis noted that many people noticed "certain similarities of writing and style" between Strout and TRB, asking the question "When does the anonymity stop?" Davis described TRB's writing as contrary to what the *Monitor* espouses in that it included "personal attack, the shrewd and often brilliant sword thrust that wounds the other fellow." He was most concerned about the personal attacks on McCarthy, keeping in mind Mrs. Eddy's original mandate and the paper's policy to steer away from personalities and stick to issues. Davis reiterated management's respect for his work, and said the only problem was with "special crusading articles directed at McCarthy."[13]

Strout, apparently depressed at being directed not to write about McCarthy and the rejection of his "Intimate Message" 16 months earlier, wrote a letter to Davis where he openly contemplated resigning from the *Monitor*, saying he would be "sorry to leave."[14] Strout never sent the letter. However, in a May 10, 1954 letter to Davis, he challenged the meaning placed upon Mrs. Eddy's charge "to injure no man, but to bless all mankind." He wrote that she did not mean it "literally" and that "people like McCarthy, Hitler and the like must be attacked." He complained about the limited coverage the *Monitor* gave to the Hennings report on January 3, 1953.

Actually, what the *Monitor* carried about the Hennings report was a lengthy story by Neal Stanford. Stanford wrote that the report "detailed a maze of financial transactions, market speculations, income tax returns, campaign expenditure reports and other activities" and raised questions about possible "devious financial" dealings by McCarthy, labeling the $10,000 fee received from Lustron Corporation as "highly improper, to say the least." Stanford also highlighted the Hennings report section documenting the six times McCarthy was requested, but refused, to appear before the subcommittee. No editorial or "Intimate Message" from Strout appeared, but certainly Stanford's detailed story hit the major points of the 400-page report.[15] Meanwhile, the *Washington Post* seemed to agree with Strout, suggesting the Hennings report had been "suppressed" and should be examined by the Mundt committee.[16]

When did Strout's ban on writing about McCarthy begin and end? Was the ban strictly adhered to? The researcher was only able to uncover evidence suggesting possible answers.[17] It is clear, despite Strout's repeated complaints to *Monitor* editors from January through May 1954, the ban on Strout's writing about McCarthy was "officially" lifted on February 24, 1954.[18] However, a review of all stories about McCarthy revealed that Strout did not cover the Senator regularly until he became one of the primary reporters for the Army-McCarthy hearings, April 23, 1954. From that point on in the hearings, Strout received most of the page 1 stories; various other Washington bureau reporters wrote sidebars, and other supplemental stories appeared inside the newspaper. So, the ban was lifted on February 24, but Strout did not consistently cover McCarthy until April 23.

When the ban started and how strictly it was enforced are more difficult questions. A Stringer memo to Davis explained that nothing "formal" had been written about Strout's not being allowed to cover McCarthy, which would explain the lack of documentary evidence about the ban. Months after McCarthy's book was published, the *Monitor* had no problem with Strout's commenting about McCarthy. In a November 5, 1952 news story,

Strout surmised that the elections had "to some degree" showed McCarthy's strength on a national basis, and Strout quoted from a British publication about the damage being done to America's standing in the world due to McCarthyism.[19] Strout, in early 1953, was the primary *Monitor* reporter for the Bohlen confirmation fight (discussed in detail later in this chapter). McCarthy was among the major opponents to the confirmation, and Strout's stories during March and April chronicled the controversy, with no hesitation about mentioning McCarthy. However, after the Bohlen confirmation, and a few stories about McCarthy's clashes with Mutual Security Administrator Harold Stassen and Secretary of State John Foster Dulles, Strout wrote virtually nothing about McCarthy from April 24, 1953 until December 1, 1953.[20] On December 1, 1953, Strout wrote about the battle between Dulles and McCarthy regarding the fitness for service of John Paton Davies, and how the actual issue was McCarthy against Eisenhower.[21] This story, along with subsequent stories and "Intimate Messages" on December 2, 3, and 5, suggest that while no "formal" lifting of the ban against writing about McCarthy occurred, clearly the *Monitor* was no longer uncomfortable with Strout's mentioning him. Except for this series of stories and commentaries about McCarthy, which appeared after about seven months of the Washington correspondent writing virtually nothing about the Senator, Strout did not return to covering McCarthy consistently until April 23, 1954.

Early in 1954, William H. Stringer, Washington Bureau Chief, and other bureau reporters, such as Mary Handy, Neal Stanford, Mary Hornaday, Godfrey Sperling, Jr., and Roland Sawyer, covered the initial rumblings of problems between McCarthy and the Army and reaction to Edward R. Murrow's famous *See It Now* television program devoted to profiling McCarthy. Strout was conspicuous by his absence.[22] So, a thorough review of all the articles written about McCarthy appearing in the *Monitor* from July 16, 1952 (the day after Strout wrote about McCarthy's book, *McCarthyism: The Fight for America*) until Strout resumed full-time coverage of McCarthy during the Army-McCarthy hearings (April 23, 1954) suggested the "informal ban" on Strout's writing about McCarthy started on or about April 24, 1953 and lasted until nearly one year later, April 23, 1954. On the other hand, documentation from the *Monitor* clearly showed that editors had no problem with Strout's writing about McCarthy after February 24, 1954. In fact, Strout mentioned McCarthy as early as December 1953. So, depending on how you may view the ban, it appears to have lasted about 8 to 12 months.

Saville R. Davis, in an informal letter to Strout in July 1958, revealed that he was trying to identify how long the ban occurred. He "couldn't believe it lasted more than temporarily." He also expressed the desire to go back some day and review the coverage to "see how we made out in retrospect."[23] The period of 8 to 12 months certainly does not seem temporary; but the ban would hardly have been noticeable to the reader. During most of the 8 to 12 months, Strout covered the President, which would in no way be considered a demotion!

THE *MONITOR*, MCCARTHY'S NAME, AND THE TERM "MCCARTHYISM"

Some evidence indicates that late 1952 through early 1953 and leading into Strout's ban in April 1953 was an "appeasement" period for the *Monitor*.[24] By the middle of 1953, the newspaper was weary of problems that might be created by overpublicizing McCarthy's actions, and by its reporters labeling certain actions "McCarthyism." As far back as April 22, 1953, the Board of Trustees of the Christian Science Publishing Society had written to the Board of Directors stating that the term "McCarthyism" should not be used because it would not have met with approval from the Church's founder, Mrs. Eddy.[25] The Board of Directors assured the Trustees, in a communication on June 5, that the Directors would discuss the matter with Erwin D. Canham, along with other matters about covering McCarthy.[26] The result was a June 12, 1953 memo from Canham to Don Richardson and Saville R. Davis stating that the Directors were concerned that "frequent use of Senator McCarthy's name in the public press serves his chief purpose for publicity for public office." The memo also urged omitting McCarthy's name from the headlines. Further, Canham declared that the *Monitor* should avoid using the word "McCarthyism," wherever possible, "not originating [it] ourselves, and printing it only when it enters inescapably in the news." Finally, Canham warned against "excessive promotion—either positive or negative—for the junior Senator from Wisconsin."[27]

Davis relayed and clarified Canham's directive in a June 15, 1953 memo to Washington Bureau Chief Roscoe Drummond. Davis conceded that "McCarthyism" was a "dubious" term that should be used "without hesitation in quotes" but not originated by *Monitor* reporters. However, he suggested McCarthy's name in the headlines should be determined on a story-by-story basis. Additionally, McCarthy stories that were not worthy of front-page treatment could be placed inside.[28] The *Monitor* became cautious, though it continued to criticize McCarthy's methods, while McCarthy attempted to intimidate the *New York Post*, and send a message to the dissident press.

WECHSLER CASE

The *New York Post* constantly criticized McCarthy and his tactics. In September 1951, the *Post* published a 17-part series about the junior senator that was not flattering.²⁹ While James A. Wechsler, the editor, did not hide the fact that he had been a member of the Young Communist League from 1934 through 1937 (at age 22), he claimed he had been a devoted anticommunist since then. Wechsler "suggested that McCarthy possessed neither the wisdom nor the background to serve as an expert on communism and that 'McCarthyism' could in fact be defined as a kind of 'Political Murder, Inc.'"³⁰

In April 1953, under the guise of questioning Wechsler about books he had written that were available in U.S. libraries overseas, the *Post*'s editor was summoned before McCarthy's Permanent Subcommittee on Investigations of the Government Operations Committee. The questioning, however, involved the *Post* and its editorial policies, along with Wechsler's political beliefs. Wechsler, noting the nature of the questions and the direction the inquiry had taken, claimed that McCarthy sought reprisals because the *Post* editorially opposed him. The editor requested that the American Society of Newspaper Editors (ASNE) appoint a committee to investigate the Senator's practices. This request came after Wechsler, at McCarthy's request, provided McCarthy the names of 60 people who were members of the Young Communist League while Wechsler was a member.³¹ In essence, Wechsler damned McCarthy and his methods, yet fully cooperated. Despite the editor's cooperation, the *Monitor* described the testimony of Wechsler as a "five hour bitter exchange." The *Monitor* also gave its readers excerpts from the testimony and a promise to print "significant portions of the text" of Wechsler's testimony when it became available (the questioning of Wechsler was not open to the public or the press).³²

Editor and Publisher spelled out Wechsler's specific complaints against McCarthy. The editor wanted ASNE to investigate four areas: why he was never notified what book carried in foreign libraries the subcommittee was concerned about; why he was questioned about the *Post* when the hearing was supposed to be about State Department Information Centers; why McCarthy linked the editorial policy of the *Post* to the *Daily Worker*, yet the *Daily Worker* had attacked the *Post* for its anticommunist position; and, why McCarthy did not read the *Post* (yet criticized it), and showed no interest in reading copies of editorials provided by Wechsler.³³

The extensive excerpts of Wechsler's testimony promised by the *Monitor* were published on May 11, 1953. A separate *Monitor* article stated that "the independent, objective and critical attitude of James A. Wechsler toward communism is illustrated in his book, *Labor Baron—A Portrait of John L. Lewis.*"³⁴ Roscoe Drummond analyzed the Wechsler case. He conceded up front the right of Congress to investigate and stated, "Neither the press nor Mr. Wechsler is claiming any immunity from investigation of newspapermen."³⁵ (As a reader later pointed out, Congress has the right to investigate *only* "with intent to legislate," yet Drummond considered investigations of a general nature to be proper.)[36] Drummond raised the question of whether McCarthy "used his right of investigation as a cover to attempt to harass and intimidate Mr. Wechsler." Drummond described Wechsler as "a total, undeviating, dedicated, loyal, and particularly effective anti-Communist writer and worker." Drummond reported that out of the five hours Wechsler appeared before McCarthy's subcommittee, only about five minutes were devoted to books Wechsler had written—two while he was a Communist and two after. Further, Drummond reported that neither McCarthy nor his counsel knew which of Wechsler's books were involved in the inquiry. Drummond concluded that there was "extensive documentation" corroborating Wechsler's claim that McCarthy had reprisal in mind, not books Wechsler had written. Drummond wrote that McCarthy's actions may serve to alert the press "to a grave danger" and to expose a fatal mistake by McCarthy "disclosing some of the things he is up to which are different from his stated objectives."[37]

The day after Drummond's analysis, a *Monitor* editorial stated that the Wechsler incident alone "might not constitute attempted intimidation of the Press," but when added to previous actions by McCarthy, such as proposing a boycott of *Time* and urging Adam Hat Company to drop sponsorship of Drew Pearson's radio show, it became clear a pattern existed. The *Monitor* contended that McCarthy's questioning of Wechsler was "more like an indictment by denunciation and innuendo than a search for facts."[38] The editorial concluded by asking, "Are publications and their editors who thoroughly oppose communism but who happen to see dangers in the methods by which Senator McCarthy attacks it thus to be 'punished' and equated with 'the *Daily Worker* and every other Communist-line paper.' "[39]

The *Milwaukee Journal* described the questioning of Wechsler in the same manner as the *Monitor*. The *Journal* contended that the *Post* was "militantly anti-Communist, even as it has been anti-fascist and anti-McCarthy." The McCarthy subcommittee's proceedings, according to the *Journal*, again defined "McCarthyism," "the cynical, flagrant abuse of power in the effort to bulldoze any and all opposition into silence by means fair or foul."[40]

Editor and Publisher, meanwhile, stated bluntly that McCarthy's questioning of Wechsler was an attempt to intimidate a newspaperman who opposed the Senator. *E&P* called it an "abuse of his position and a dangerous precedent," and endorsed an investigation by an ASNE committee.[41] An 11-member ASNE committee was appointed to look at the Wechsler versus McCarthy case. On August 12, 1953, the committee's report was issued; it indicated that the members failed to come to a consensus. Seven of the members wrote that if McCarthy's questioning of Wechsler was an infringement on freedom of the press, it was a bad thing. But, they could not decide if freedom had been infringed upon and left it up to individual editors to decide the case on its own merits. Radio commentator Elmer Davis failed to see the logic in the majority opinion: "a number of highly respectable journalists argued that since McCarthy's attack had in fact failed to intimidate Wechsler, it was no attack on freedom of the press at all. This amounts to saying that attempted rape is no crime if the girl is lucky enough to fight off her assailant."[42]

Four dissenting members, Herbert Brucker, editor of the *Hartford Courant*, J. R. Wiggins, managing editor of the *Washington Post*, William Tugman, editor of the *Eugene Register Guard*, and Eugene Pulliam, Jr., managing editor of the *Indianapolis News*, wrote additional comments about the case, stating that McCarthy had infringed on freedom of the press.[43] The *Monitor* provided extensive details about the ASNE report and subsequent analysis. An August 13, 1953 issue published nearly the entire text of the ASNE report and the bulk of the "additional comments" were carried verbatim.[44] Roscoe Drummond's "State of the Nation" column also analyzed the ASNE report. Drummond wrote that the Congress had no right to summon into questioning a newspaper editor to answer for his editorial policies or political beliefs. He referred to the First Amendment to the Constitution, writing that if Congress was banned from "abridging the freedom of speech and of the press" then certainly a Congressional committee was bound by the same rules.[45] A *Monitor* editorial the next day revealed an understanding of the seven ASNE members' desire to avoid partisanship by restraining from any strong statement, but said "the forthright four have performed the greater service." The *Monitor* opposed not only intimidation of the press, but the mere attempt, much in line with Elmer Davis's opinion.[46] The *Milwaukee Journal* expressed disappointment that the entire ASNE committee could not come to a consensus. The newspaper wrote that perhaps the seven who found no infringement of freedom of speech in the Wechsler case showed a "disinclination to face up to an issue because of crossing Senator McCarthy's path or of becoming involved in a distasteful controversy."[47] The *New York Times* declared that the split decision was "entirely inadequate" in a clear case of McCarthy's violating "the spirit of the Constitution by using his governmental authority to pillory an editor."[48]

Reaction from the junior senator came within days. McCarthy called for an ASNE investigation of one of the committee members, J. R. Wiggins of the *Post*, whose newspaper McCarthy claimed was "endangering a free press by the manner of its criticism of the McCarthy approach."[49] The committeemen reacted immediately, each indicating no chance of investigating Wiggins.[50] But, McCarthy did not stop there. A month later he requested that ASNE strike from the report a statement indicating the Senator had questioned Wechsler about editorial policies at the *Post* under the guise of probing books available in overseas libraries. ASNE did not honor McCarthy's request.[51]

While the *Monitor* and many other McCarthy critics backed Wechsler in the name of freedom of the press, some historians have not been as kind. Victor S. Navasky noted that in essence, McCarthy failed to win a public-relations victory over Wechsler, while he won a more substantive issue. That is, Wechsler editorially opposed McCarthy's methods of naming names of people without allowing refutation, yet Wechsler named names and "thereby reinforced the very system his editorials had opposed."[52]

FOREIGN AFFAIRS

VOA/USIS

In the first half of 1953, McCarthy challenged two other sources for dissemination of information to the rest of the world, but this time they were government sources. He started with the Voice of America (VOA), and when that investigation went nowhere, he sent two "investigators" to Europe to research the books and materials provided by the United States Information Service (USIS) in overseas libraries. The VOA and USIS probes became high-profile news stories and the *Monitor* covered and commented about them frequently.

McCarthy's subcommittee started hearings on the VOA on February 16, 1953. Two topics were addressed: the proposed locations of two new transmitters, one in North Carolina and the other in Washington State, and possible Communist infiltration in the VOA.[53]

President Dwight D. Eisenhower's first news conference as President came the day after McCarthy's hearings began. At his second news conference (February 25), the President offered no comment about McCarthy's probe of the VOA.[54] Reporters waiting for Eisenhower to stand up to McCarthy were disappointed. Meanwhile, early in the investigation, the State Department ordered the "Voice" not to air any material provided by "controversial" authors, Communists, or fellow travelers.[55] The *Monitor*, during the initial days of the hearings, relied almost exclusively on dispatches from the Associated Press and the United Press, but as the probe became more controversial many articles provided by a *Monitor* "staff correspondent" were written, and columns and editorials were frequent.[56] During the questioning by McCarthy and others about the content of the "Voice," the *Monitor* received a strong compliment. Senator Edwin C. Johnson, a Democrat from Colorado, informed his colleagues that a constituent of his suggested that the *Monitor* provide the material for the radio broadcasts of the VOA. Johnson conceded that he was not sure that the "greatest of all American newspapers" could undertake such a "gigantic" task, but he characterized the publication as providing "objective reporting" and complimented the "clean, wholesome, courageous, patriotic and spiritual tone of the policies and editorials of the *Christian Science Monitor*."[57] The matter was never pursued, however.

The Eisenhower administration named the President of Temple University, Robert L. Johnson, to head the VOA (as chief of the International Information Administration). Secretary of State John Foster Dulles handled the early criticism of the "Voice" by stating that McCarthy's investigation was about policies and positions of administrators appointed by Democrats—administrators who were being methodically removed by the new Eisenhower administration. The *Monitor* contended that Washington, D.C. was fascinated by the prospect of Eisenhower being forced "to draw a fine line between Democratic policies and Republican policies within the Voice of America" and wondered what the President would do if McCarthy attacked Republican policies.[58]

The *Monitor* also was apparently eager to show America the good work being done by the VOA. The service could not be heard in the United States, so the newspaper announced that it would periodically print "significant excerpts" from broadcasts. This practice started March 7, 1953, and before the end of the year no fewer than 17 issues of the *Monitor* carried extensive excerpts with a final script published in the December 12 issue.[59] And, less than a month after the McCarthy hearings about the "Voice" started, an editorial stated the real dangers of injuring an "activity of incalculable importance to the United States and the World." The McCarthy inquiry, according to the *Monitor*, had brought "more confusion than light to the subject" and the paper felt that the new President and Secretary of State would improve the "Voice" "without the prodding and jabbing" of a Congressional subcommittee.[60] The *Milwaukee Journal* described the VOA as "the country's major weapon in the struggle to win men's minds." After describing in detail the operation of the "Voice," the *Journal* revealed that while it had weaknesses, a "panel from the radio industry and the United States advisory commission on information have found *no serious faults* with the Voice."[61] The *San Francisco Examiner* saw the situation quite differently. Citing testimony by one VOA official, the *Examiner* surmised that the Communists were laughing at the current investigation. The newspaper wrote that it was no laughing matter. It described the VOA as fitting "so well into Communist purposes in the past," and suggested correcting the problems so the VOA could become the "true voice of America in the future."[62]

VOA radio engineer Raymond Kaplan's suicide was one of the tragic results of the McCarthy probe. McCarthy's "sources" indicated that the two locations for new transmitters (North Carolina and Washington State) were totally inadequate and deliberately chosen as part of the Communists' efforts to silence the "Voice." Kaplan was involved in the site selection, and became so distraught at the accusations that he hurled himself under a truck. In a final letter to his wife, Kaplan stated that if the locations were wrong it was not deliberately done. He lamented that when "the dogs are set upon you" your entire life becomes "suspect."[63] The *Monitor* called Kaplan's death an "example of what officially developed terror can do to the innocent." The *Monitor* conceded that the government had made mistakes with the VOA but if a "treasonous atmosphere" was used to review each decision, then "the process of government becomes too hazardous and distasteful for men of competence and integrity."[64] Besides the death of Kaplan, there were other "casualties" in the probe of the "Voice" though none as severe. Reed Harris, a deputy administrator of the International Information Administration, resigned declaring that McCarthy had damaged America's Cold War efforts. The VOA dismissed official Theodore Kaghan for Communist activities while in college;[65] Kaghan's dismissal caused a chain reaction: Raymond Swing, who had delivered 383 commentaries on the VOA, resigned to protest Kaghan's firing. *Monitor* columnist Joseph C. Harsch wrote that "unless the purge is halted" other important "independent" voices would be silenced. Harsch explained the uniqueness of Swing's contribution: "He presented America to our allies in terms and tones which they could understand and accept, whereas too often now it is presented in terms and tones which alienate."[66]

The McCarthy probe into the transmitter locations caused a halt to the work and ultimately the cancellation of the construction by new VOA Director Robert L. Johnson.[67] But at nearly the same time (March 19, 1953), Secretary of State Dulles lifted the ban on quoting Communists on the VOA (which had been in place since February 19, 1953). Dulles's statement indicated that Communists could be quoted if their words "help to show up Communist lies or propaganda."[68] A *Monitor* editorial hailed the lifting of the ban as the "Voice of Common Sense." The VOA would again be able to "point to Soviet inconsistencies of a far more serious sort than even the worst inconsistencies of this odd episode."[69]

A "book-burning" controversy began when the State Department sent letters to American book publishers asking that they certify that books submitted for export were not written by Communists, fellow travelers, or "persons who might be considered controversial." The goal was to eliminate "subversive books" from the United States Information Service libraries around the world.[70] The *Monitor* labeled the strategy weak and asked if readers were likely to be impressed with "safe" books, "Or are they likely to be more impressed by the splendid vitality and variety, the stimulus and challenge, of books that mirror wide-ranging views and the fruitful clash of ideas, to be found only in a free society?"[71]

McCarthy subcommittee counsel Roy Cohn and an assistant, David G. Schine, traveled through Europe in April 1953, visiting U.S.-sponsored libraries searching for subversive materials. The antics of the two cast the United States into an awkward light on the world stage, and the trip became infamous over time.[72] A *Monitor* foreign correspondent, Edmund Stevens, wrote that moves by Cohn and Schine aided the Italian Communists. He contended that "bundles of books still smelling of the printer's ink" were put in storage, with many of them containing some of the "most effective anti-Communist propaganda ever to appear in Italy."[73]

As the State Department and USIS buckled under the pressure put on by McCarthy, books were pulled from the overseas libraries' shelves and some were burned. This prompted President Eisenhower to address the subject of book burning during a speech at Dartmouth College in Hanover, New Hampshire. He told the gathering, ". . . don't join the book burners," but he failed to mention McCarthy or anyone else's name associated with the purge of library materials overseas. *Monitor* New England correspondent Edgar M. Mills wrote that the book-burning mention "was immediately interpreted as being a criticism of Senator Joseph R. McCarthy."[74] A *Monitor* editorial called Eisenhower's words "crucially needed" because Europe was beginning to see the United States increasingly as a "police state" reminiscent of Nazi Germany.[75] Eisenhower, just one day later, clarified his Dartmouth speech, still declining to mention McCarthy's name, but spelling out specifically what he expected of the U.S. overseas libraries. Eisenhower wanted a variety of ideas represented, did not want to stifle controversy or exchanges of ideas, and conceded that there were times when people could learn more about Communism (and its dangers) from the mouths of Communists themselves.[76] The *Monitor* viewed Eisenhower's "clarification" as an "amplification" of ideas expressed in his Dartmouth College speech. The newspaper agreed with the President's opposition to the suppression of ideas and maintained that the "great tenet of free discussion requires not only noble words but courageous action."[77] About one week after the initial book-burning statements by Eisenhower, the *Monitor*'s Josephine Ripley expressed her dismay with the whole affair. She called the entire episode "reminiscent of the famous Nazi bonfires of 1933," and said the purge "was carried to such an extreme in some cases that books by authors active in the fight against communism were yanked from the shelves." She ended by explaining that the question "Burned any good books lately?" was being used frequently in Washington, D.C. to ridicule government and its handling of the entire issue.[78] The *Milwaukee Journal* declared that the President made a fine statement, but "*he* is the man—perhaps the one man—who can stop the dangers he warns about."[79] The *New York Times* stated that the President was "appealing for a vigorous and positive sort of citizenship" to "fight existing evils in their own country." The *Times* ended, "The book-burners, the exalters of ignorance, the censors and bullies, are, after all, an un-American faith."[80] After 'Ike' clarified his position on the stocking of books in the overseas libraries, the *San Francisco Examiner* applauded the President for assuring the public that he was not "attempting to propagate Communist beliefs by using Government money to buy Red-written books."[81] Meanwhile, Louis Lyons, at the 20th Annual Convention of the American Newspaper Guild in Boston, told editors that book burning infringed on a basic right of freedom of the mind, and that "no one who speaks has a right to be neutral" on the topic.[82] Certainly the *Monitor* was not one of the newspapers in the country to remain neutral.

Early in July, the State Department ordered reinstatement of many books that had been banned from overseas libraries. In fact, what had been a purge of some 300 titles now was reduced to a "black-list" of 25 books.[83] The *Monitor*'s Roland Sawyer wrote a lengthy article about the lifting of restrictions on overseas books, applauding the reinstatement of "controversial books" and explaining that "conspiratorial books ... which propose the destruction of the United States Constitutional government" would still be banned. He expressed relief that this embarrassing censorship episode was now behind the United States: "Once more men and women the world over will be able to visit American libraries and see for themselves that the United States is a land where [there is] freedom to read, to think, and to speak inviolably, though it has been challenged by the near hysteria that has grown out of Senator McCarthy's investigations."[84]

A final editorial about book burning in the *Monitor* (July 1953) explained that the new rules placed a "distinction between controversy and conspiracy, and would have the suitability of any book judged primarily by its content, not its author." It agreed with the government that books by Earl Browder and Ilya Ehrenburg, both espousing the value of Communism, should be among the 25 titles still banned. But the editorial stated that what was needed from the start was "common sense," and it appeared to the *Monitor* that the new directive showed that "common sense" had returned to the State Department.[85] The *New York Times* wrote that it was "too bad" the latest action reinstating most of the banned books was not "made several weeks or even months ago." The *Times* emphasized that the "very fact that they are free libraries is the best possible propaganda for America in a Communist-infested world."[86] Eight months later, two books written by McCarthy, *McCarthyism: The Fight for America* and *America's Retreat from Victory*, were rejected for distribution to the overseas libraries. A *Monitor* editorial supported the action reluctantly. The newspaper reasoned that since the overseas libraries, despite having the ban on "controversial" books lifted, were still "cautious" and contained nothing critical of McCarthy, then "what is sauce for the leftist goose is sauce for the rightist gander." However, the *Monitor* contended that it would rather allow McCarthy's books in the overseas libraries along with "counter-balancing books" by Jack Anderson and Ronald May, and Dr. Owen Lattimore. This, according to the newspaper, would "allow Europeans and Asians to examine all sides of this burning issue and judge for themselves in the democratic American way."[87]

Greek Ships

During the same time McCarthy took on the VOA/USIS, his Government Operations Committee announced a "negotiated" agreement with 242 merchant ships to stop trade with Korea, Communist China, and Russia's far eastern ports. The following day, March 28, 1953, the State Department announced that the Greek government had agreed to forbid Greek ships from carrying cargo to Communists. On March 30, 1953, the Director of the Mutual Security Agency, Harold E. Stassen, claimed McCarthy had "undermined" the nation's foreign policy by his improper negotiations with ship owners.[88] Strout reported that a "breach between the senator from Wisconsin and the Eisenhower administration was widening."[89] Strout's assessment proved wrong. Two days later, after Secretary of State John Foster Dulles had met with McCarthy, President Eisenhower softened Stassen's words, claiming the administrator probably meant "infringed" on the nation's foreign policy, not "undermined," forcing a humiliated Stassen to back down from his original comments.[90]

The *Monitor* surmised that Eisenhower was more "pacific" than many Americans had expected, especially in his treatment of "the sovereign state of McCarthy."[91] It applauded Eisenhower for handling a delicate situation without admonishing either side. The editorial said the President "neatly" lifted McCarthy off the hook for "negotiating" with Greek shipowners, because under the Constitution a senator has no authority to negotiate for the country. Eisenhower stated that "undermined" was too strong a word to describe McCarthy's actions, but did not state directly that he was "unhappy over the Stassen stand."[92] The *Monitor* saw the President as having a "talent for teamwork" and supported his belief that to govern best, one must govern "by coalitions of diverse interests" and maintain "a strategy of peace."[93] Oddly enough, the McCarthy subcommittee interim report about Western trade with Red China avoided any theories of Communist conspiracies and was "well researched" and "judicious" in tone, winning the praises of many people from both parties.[94]

Dulles

As he had previously with Secretary of State Dean Acheson, Joseph R. McCarthy complicated John Foster Dulles's job. It mattered not that Dulles was an Eisenhower appointee. Strout wrote that even with the new Eisenhower administration, an "uneasy relationship" between the Senate and the State Department "may have a substantial effect on American Foreign Policy." Strout surmised that "alarm" was too strong a word and "anxious" not strong enough to describe the relationship.[95] The statements made by Strout came in mid-April. Tension and disagreement between McCarthy and Dulles existed throughout the year, but a major controversy did not come until December.

Senator McCarthy contended throughout 1953 that Communism would be an issue in the 1954 elections. President Eisenhower stated that the government was handling the problem and that it should not be an issue. Then, in a speech (November 24), McCarthy denounced the Eisenhower administration (Dulles, specifically) for failing to dismiss John P. Davies, U.S. counselor of the embassy in Lima, Peru for Davies' alleged "Communist" connections. McCarthy also continually encouraged the United States to withhold giving any aid to countries trading with Communist China.[96] Joseph C. Harsch of the *Monitor* wrote that these issues and others had increased the "breach" between McCarthy and Eisenhower, but that "Neither side has passed the point of no return." However, Harsch admitted that the break "has long been regarded as probably unavoidable" and that left unanswered the question of whether the White House would decide that now was the time to accept the "ultimate total breach."[97] Harsch criticized the Republican Party for not coming to the aid of Eisenhower and Dulles; rather, fellow Republicans "moved to neutral corners." And, Harsch concluded, the action by Dulles "was political war" not the "appeasement" of McCarthy that many reporters had expected from Dulles.[98]

Dulles went public with his support for Davies. And while he did not name McCarthy, he denounced any attack on the diplomat's integrity and character, causing some reporters to speculate that a "break" between Eisenhower and McCarthy *must* occur, or Davies would have to be dismissed from government service. However, Neal Stanford of the *Monitor* wrote that "a majority opinion was inclined to believe that such action would so defeat the purpose and intention of this public reply to the senator as tantamount to capitulation by the administration to the senator."[99]

Strout reported that Eisenhower firmly supported Dulles, and he felt that the "rift" was the beginning of "a struggle for party leadership which many observers believe inevitable." Strout agreed with Harsch and Stanford that most believed the "breach" had widened between Eisenhower and McCarthy, though many politicians had "soft-pedaled their feeling" to avoid charges of partisanship.[100]

McCarthy, undaunted by the alliance between Eisenhower and Dulles, made a public appeal for people to flood the White House with letters requesting that U.S. aid to nations trading with China be cut off. The *Monitor* ran a front-page story on the announcement, and inside the paper ran the entire text of the McCarthy statement, along with reaction from the White House.[101] While *Monitor* reporters and columnists (Strout, Stanford, and Harsch) continually mentioned an ever-increasing breach between Eisenhower and McCarthy, *Monitor* editorials seemed to be championing the cause of keeping the Republican Party united. The *Monitor* contended that the "rift" about foreign policy and trade with China "does not necessarily herald a split in the Republican ranks." The *Monitor* believed that when Dulles stated that "demagogic baiting of allies" was contrary to U.S. foreign policy, he was not criticizing McCarthy in general, but intended to clarify Dulles's position. Finally, the newspaper saw the actions of Eisenhower and Dulles defending U.S. foreign policy as "an act of leadership" and an effort to develop "teamwork to grapple with ... great national problems," not a repudiation of the junior senator from Wisconsin.[102]

When the dust had settled from the immediate controversy between McCarthy and Dulles, with Dulles being backed by the administration, the *Monitor* concluded that McCarthy did not want to "capture leadership in the Republican Party," though he was not halting his criticism of Dulles's foreign policy with respect to countries trading with China. The newspaper explained that McCarthy's contention that if England stopped trade with China, it would kill China's "warmaking power" was not true because China got most of its war materials from Russia; the paper went on to point out that many Americans believed it caused "bitterness" among Americans toward our allies. This, according to the *Monitor*, caused "more harm than good." The newspaper contended that disagreements between McCarthy and the administration had been "papered over," but if both parties continued to travel in their respective directions, "a divergence in basic purposes" would develop.[103]

The *Monitor*'s Washington Bureau, in a "Washington Letter" insiders' piece, described McCarthy as a "sideline" critic of the President "on an increasing number of events." It conceded that the "break" that all of the *Monitor*'s reporters in Washington (along with journalists at other newspapers) had predicted had not occurred.[104] Finally, in a column several days later, Joseph C. Harsch described a "quiet revolution" occurring in Washington. Harsch claimed that Dulles's standing up to McCarthy publicly caused a feeling among government employees that contesting charges of Communist affiliation was no longer hopeless, and resigning no longer the only option: "There has been an invisible flow of power from the hands of those men constitutionally entrusted with government toward the hands of Senator McCarthy, whose mandate comes only from the people of Wisconsin, not from the people of the whole country. Mr. Dulles' action has checked that flow. Where he can challenge, perhaps others can, too."[105]

Repeatedly throughout 1953, reporters (particularly in the *Monitor* Washington Bureau) anticipated that certain actions (whether about Dulles and McCarthy or others) would finally result in an obvious break between Eisenhower and McCarthy—all suggesting that "Ike" would prevail. The previous comment by Harsch, where he clearly interpreted the action of one man (Dulles) as changing the attitude of Washingtonians about taking on McCarthy, illustrated more about the reporters' hope than about a genuine sense of change. The big "break" all had anticipated did not come in 1953.

Bohlen Nomination

Still another foreign affairs–related issue occurred early in 1953, during the VOA/USIS and Dulles controversies. Secretary of State John Foster Dulles nominated Charles "Chip" Bohlen to be the American ambassador to the Soviet Union. Bohlen's nomination was questioned by some senators, not because of his character or competence, but because of past affiliations with the Truman administration, and specifically former Secretary of State Dean Acheson.[106] Dulles testified before the Senate Foreign Relations Committee that the FBI summary statement about Bohlen showed no derogatory material about the nominee.[107] The *Monitor*, from the very beginning of the confirmation fight, portrayed the case as a test of Eisenhower's strength against the conservative right wing of the party. The *Monitor* stated that "either Eisenhower must assert considerable pressure or the Bohlen appointment" would fail.[108] The possibility of Bohlen ultimately being confirmed by the Senate was seen as "highly encouraging" by the *Monitor*. The *Monitor* also saw the possibility of confirmation as a victory for Eisenhower, calling it a "turning point" in restoring the "efficiency and morale of the foreign service."[109]

The Senate Foreign Relations Committee eventually voted 15 to 0 in favor of the nomination, but senators such as Joseph R. McCarthy continued to link Bohlen with the FDR and Truman administrations.[110] The *Monitor*'s Neal Stanford saw the vote as spotlighting the "cleavage developing" between McCarthy and the right wing of the Republican party and "the Eisenhower-Dulles policies controlling the State Department."[111] Richard L. Strout reported that nearly everyone agreed that the nomination would be approved by the full Senate, but that did not stop a "clash between certain extreme Congressional elements" causing deep tension in the nation's Capitol.[112] Strout pitted McCarthy directly against Eisenhower in the nomination fight, contending that McCarthy could not be "reduced in importance in his party" without the administration's launching a "direct frontal assault" led by one man—Dwight D. Eisenhower.[113] The *Milwaukee Journal*

1953: McCarthy versus the Press

viewed the unanimous approval by the committee as a rebuke of McCarthy and others who were "still trying to destroy confidence in a man we are about to send on one of our most important diplomatic missions." The *Journal* also failed to see the logic of many senators who would like the new Republican administration to oust any foreign service official who had worked for the Democrats over the last 20 years. The *Journal* stated, "They don't seem to want our foreign affairs directed by men trained for the job."[114] The *New York Times* was equally pleased with the appointment of Bohlen. The newspaper claimed there was no better candidate for the post than Bohlen because he not only could read and speak Russian fluently, he "probably knows more about Russia than most Russians outside the relatively small ruling class."[115]

Just days before the confirmation vote, the *Monitor* ran editorials on two consecutive days applauding those Republicans who had decided to endorse the nomination. The *Monitor* argued that had McCarthy been successful, it would have allowed him veto power "on almost any appointment, and additional power to terrorize individual citizens." Bohlen's inevitable approval, according to the newspaper, had shown "responsible" Republican leaders that government cannot be run by "rumor and suspicion."[116] Further, the *Monitor* criticized McCarthy for making much of his case against Bohlen from derogatory material in the nominee's FBI file that turned out to be "gossip, rumor and anonymous letters." The *Monitor* concluded that when Eisenhower was voted into office, the people wanted "change" but that did not include the administration losing the "freedom and responsibility to carry out its foreign affairs program."[117]

The 74-to-13 vote in favor of confirmation was no surprise—it came after McCarthy conceded the day before that he had no chance of blocking approval.[118] After the vote, Strout wrote that the confirmation showed Congressmen's "faith" in "Ike."[119] Roscoe Drummond saw the confirmation as a defeat for the "McCarthy-led opposition," which proved that the junior senator could be defeated on the Senate floor.[120] Still, he down-played any major victory by Eisenhower, stating that "some say the administration has won the battle, but hardly a war. At this stage it may well be nearer the truth to say that the administration has won a skirmish, but hardly a battle."[121]

Oddly enough, the pro-McCarthy *San Francisco Examiner* ran an Associated Press dispatch about the 74-to-13 vote in favor of confirmation. The AP story described the overwhelming approval as a "smashing vote of confidence in President Eisenhower."[122]

At least one McCarthy biographer, David M. Oshinsky, contended that the news media played up the importance of the Bohlen confirmation as a victory for Eisenhower, yet the President only narrowly backed the ambassador nominee, and did not support other members of the foreign service who became victims of McCarthy and other red-baiters.[123] Excepting the column by Roscoe Drummond after the confirmation, the *Monitor* certainly falls into the category of those characterizing the confirmation battle as one of Eisenhower (with Taft's support) versus McCarthy. In the editorials, and articles and columns by Strout, they were more about what the newspaper and writer hoped would be proved, not the reality of the situation. And, at least in the case of Strout, he wanted "Ike" to stand up to the demagogue McCarthy, so perhaps Strout saw what he wanted to see in the Bohlen nomination struggle.[124]

THE ROSENBERGS' EXECUTION

The *Monitor* clearly stated in 1951 that it believed that Julius and Ethel Rosenberg, convicted of conspiracy to commit espionage, received a fair trial. When the carrying out of the death sentence appeared imminent, the *Monitor* did not directly support the penalty, but showed very little compassion for the couple's plight.

In January, an editorial declared that the two received "a full, fair and reliable hearing" in their appeal, and criticized the couple for displaying a "defiant" attitude.[125] Columnist Joseph C. Harsch, more than one month later, described the trial as "due process" but was troubled by the possible consequences of either carrying out the death penalty or setting the couple free. Harsch proposed trading the Rosenbergs to the Russians in exchange for the release of all political prisoners in the Soviet Union. Harsch claimed that if the Rosenbergs were executed, the Russians would get themselves "off the hook of their anti-Semitism."[126]

John F. Neville's book about the Rosenbergs and the media stated that the *National Guardian* was the only publication that printed an article explaining that a table containing compartments for spy activities and reportedly given to the Rosenbergs actually was bought by the couple at Macy's and had not disappeared—it was at a relative's house. Neville identified the *Monitor* among nine mainstream newspapers that ignored the story about the desk—a key piece of evidence. And Neville was accurate—the *Monitor* never investigated or reported the story about the table. In addition, Neville identified the *New York Times* as the only mainstream newspaper to admit that the Rosenbergs did not receive a fair trial.[127]

In the days leading up the execution of the Rosenbergs, the *Monitor*, using a combination of Associated Press– and United Press–generated stories and staff dispatches, covered the rejection of the final appeal, including a description of a thousand people marching outside the White House asking for the President to intervene.[128] One article also identified the outrage displayed by the French who likened the execution to Nazi tactics in World War II.[129]

Julius and Ethel Rosenberg were executed June 19, 1953, just 11 minutes apart.[130] The *Monitor* reported that the Rosenbergs' request for a reduction in their sentences had been rejected "by the highest appellate tribunal of a patient nation." And the editorial did not stop there: "All this has taken place in no atmosphere of hysteria or ferocity; it has been a cold judicial search for the right course." The *Monitor* contended that Moscow really did not want the Rosenbergs freed—it preferred their being martyrs. Further, the newspaper believed that had Eisenhower commuted the sentences, it would have sent a message that "pressure tactics" could win over "the processes of law."[131] The *Chicago Tribune* called the Rosenbergs "wretched spies" and labeled the interminable appeals and delays in carrying out the execution "cruel" because it prolonged "the mental suffering of the defendants." However, the *Tribune* explained its main opposition to the delays was because it undermined "respect for law and the courts and invites propagandists here and abroad to defame American law as cruel and American courts as engines of justice."[132]

JOSEPH C. HARSCH VS. THE ROMAN CATHOLIC CHURCH

Columnist Joseph C. Harsch, who served as a radio and television commentator for three decades, and worked for the *Monitor* 60 years,[133] wrote perhaps his most controversial piece late in 1953. The front page "State of the Nations" column centered on the growing concerns of many "Protestants" fearful that McCarthy teamed with the Roman Catholic Church to persecute Protestants. This was not the first time in 1953 that religion entered the story surrounding McCarthy. McCarthy had come under fire in early July, when it became known that J. B. Matthews, a staff assistant hired to help in the Senator's subcommittee work, had charged that the Protestant clergy was the largest group in America supporting the Communist effort.[134] And late in July, Dr. G. Bromley Oxnam, Bishop of the Methodist Church in the Washington area, testified before a Senate committee and was forced to discredit people he knew because of their affiliations (guilt by association). The Bishop was considered a humanitarian with libertarian ideas, and overall he was applauded for his own self-defense while testifying.[135] Regarding McCarthy and the Catholic Church, McCarthy biographer Thomas C. Reeves felt the evidence gathered in retrospect was such that he could conclude, "Conservative newspapers in cities and towns across the country but especially Wisconsin, had refused to publish stories critical of the Senator. The Catholic press was predominately pro-McCarthy."[136]

Harsch's column in November 1953, "Religious Controversy," written in a Christian Science–sponsored newspaper, seemed to serve as a catalyst for increased suspicion between Protestants and Catholics. He prefaced his opinion by stating that "the facts are not available in full" and proceeded to make some startling comments and reveal some startling statistics. Harsch wrote that McCarthy's actions "have had the incidental effect ... of increasing the proportion of Roman Catholics to Protestants employed in public service." He contended that to be immune from attack, government agencies "have increasingly resorted to the practice of employing Roman Catholics as security and personnel officers.... The sequel is that the proportion of Roman Catholics included in dismissals is low and the proportion of Protestants high." Harsch further contended that in the Foreign Operations Administration, 80 percent of the people fired had been Protestants and that not one Roman Catholic had been dismissed from the State Department.[137]

While the letters poured into the *Monitor* offices 10 to 1 praising Harsch,[138] church publications and some popular press columnists either applauded or damned Harsch's position. For the most part, and not surprisingly, Protestants and Protestant publications voiced support for Harsch, while Catholics and Catholic publications sought to discredit his information.

The Christian Century wrote that "one of the most conservative and respected newspapers in the country set off a bomb which could start a chain reaction more explosive than the one touched off by Elizabeth Bentley and Whittaker Chambers."[139] The publication stated that Harsch accurately described "concerns" of Protestants with "facts to support the reasonableness of that concern."[140] *Church and State*, published by Protestants and Other Americans United for Separation of Church and State (POAU), supported Harsch's concern, claiming "it is being widely whispered around Washington that if the notation, 'attends mass regularly,' appears in the security data on a government employee, a further check of his loyalty is considered unnecessary."[141] The *Michigan Christian Advocate* declared that Harsch's column was "one of the most disturbing articles we have read in a long time or will be disturbing to every Protestant who knows its contents."[142] The editorial charged that "it is no secret that Catholicism, having lost ground in Europe, is concentrating on the United States to help recoup some of those losses."[143] Among the many readers who sent letters of support was Bishop G. Bromley Oxnam. Dr. Oxnam wrote to Harsch expressing gratitude, "not only for this fine piece of work but for the superb reporting and interpretation you always have in your column."[144]

Critics of Harsch's column were many. *The Tablet*, a publication of the Roman Catholic Diocese of Brooklyn, New York, declared that a "movement appears to be gaining headway ... to create cleavages by reviving antipathies against American Catholics." The editorial stated that Harsch failed to point out that two of the most prominent Communist hunters (associated with McCarthyism), Senator William Jenner and Representative Harold Velde, were Protestants. *The Tablet* contended that Harsch's argument was false and that "any intelligent person, Catholic and non-Catholic" should realize this.[145] J. J. Gilbert wrote in *The Pilot*, a publication of the Roman Catholic Archdiocese of Boston, that it was "almost impossible to determine the 'religious preference' of government employees" because none are asked on a standard employment form for religious preference.[146] Hearst columnist George E. Sokolsky, a staunch McCarthy supporter, stated that Harsch's conclusions were based on "his private estimate" not on any available statistics. Sokolsky wrote that Secretary of State John Foster Dulles was a Protestant, so why would he be part of a Roman Catholic movement to dismiss Protestants from the State Department? Sokolsky concluded, "We have troubles enough in our country without anybody permitting private bigotry to disturb the national unity of our people."[147]

Evidence suggests that Harsch answered every letter written to him, whether pro or con, and expressed gratitude to people who sent clippings from publications that reacted to his column. Harsch, in a memo to Saville R. Davis, American News Editor, and Editor Erwin D. Canham, proposed sending a letter of response to Sokolsky. However, evidence suggests that Harsch never sent the letter, and Harsch never wrote a column in the *Monitor* answering Sokolsky.[148]

Crosby's book, *God, Church, and Flag: Senator Joseph R. McCarthy and the Catholic Church, 1950–1957*, ignored the controversy stirred by the column, despite Harsch's high profile at the time as an NBC radio commentator. Harsch remembered that the head of the Washington bureau of NBC, Bill McAndrew (a "good Catholic"), read the column and expressed concern. Of course, Harsch, a "good" Christian Scientist, received no negative comments from The First Church of Christ, Scientist, Board of Directors.[149]

MEDIA SELF-CRITIQUE

As McCarthyism flourished in its fourth year, the press discussed what the most effective ways were to report the Senator's actions without being used by McCarthy and unnecessarily alarming citizens. Richard Fried wrote, in *Nightmare in Red: The McCarthy Era in Perspective*, that the "press was obsessed" with McCarthy from 1953, through his censure. Fried contended that the press was "in love with their enemy"—that is, suffering from what he called "phobofilia."[150] And while many in the press, and also in the Republican Party, hoped that the victory by Eisenhower would conclude McCarthy's crusade, "the often intoxicated marauder simply turned his sights on the Eisenhower team."[151]

In a book review about *McCarthy: The Man, the Senator, the "ISM"* appearing in *Nieman Reports*, Melvin Mencher laid out four suggestions for dealing with McCarthy. He urged that when McCarthy singled out an individual for attack, the individual be given equal space in the lead of the story. Mencher told reporters to demand texts of McCarthy's speeches four hours before released, so charges could be confirmed or denied, and included in the story. Further, when McCarthy referred to documents, reporters should demand to see them, or leave them out of the story. And finally, Mencher suggested that McCarthy, or any other speaker attacking individuals, be available for questions about additions or omissions from the prepared text of speeches normally provided.[152]

Meanwhile, Gordon A. Sabine, Dean of the University of Oregon School of Journalism, proposed a five-point "admonition" to the press about dealing with McCarthy. Sabine warned that the press has the "power to make monsters as well as move mountains." Among his suggestions were that reporters become knowledgeable in history to place character assassinations in the past in perspective with McCarthyism; avoid panicking the public because it could "produce a sickbed from which America might not be able to rise"; never let your guard down to people such as McCarthy; and work as hard as you can to "increase the respect by the public of the press."[153]

While Mencher and Sabine suggested methods for newspapers to use to more fairly cover McCarthy, the editor and publisher of the *Denver Post* made public an internal memorandum demanding "fair play" in his newspaper's coverage. Palmer Hoyt stated that his newspaper was "alert to the problem of McCarthyism and we are anxious to take every possible step to protect the innocent." Hoyt asked his staff to, among other things, "always evaluate the source of the charge"; decide what you might do if "official immunity were lacking"; hold the story till "proper proof can be obtained" if possible; apply reasonable doubt to the treatment of the story; and decide whether the words are used for shock treatment or to truly summarize the story.[154] The memo gained widespread acclaim during 1953. The *Monitor* ran a lengthy article outlining the specifics of the Hoyt memo and then published verbatim a Hoyt speech at Harvard University in Boston.[155] Wherever Hoyt spoke, he was widely covered by the press. *Time* quoted Hoyt as declaring that newspapers should try to be as objective as possible, but "should have no taboos against 'interpretation' when necessary to an understanding of a happening."[156]

Mary McCarthy, in the *Nieman Reports*, lamented the liberal voice being lost in the reactionary times of Joseph R. McCarthy. Ms. McCarthy documented her claim that "no respectable magazine" supported Joseph R. McCarthy: "He has been criticized by *Time*, the *New Yorker*, by the liberal fortnightly the *Reporter*, by the liberal weeklies, the *Nation* and the *New Republic*, by the Jesuit weekly *America*, by the lay Catholic weekly *Commonweal*, by the *Christian Science Monitor*."[157]

The *Nieman Reports, Editor and Publisher*, and events and publications sponsored by the American Society of Newspaper Editors (ASNE) and the Associated Press Managing Editors (APME) all carried the ongoing debate about McCarthy and the press. While Richard F. Rourade of the *San Diego Union* contended the Washington correspondents were printing denials to McCarthy's charges more prominently than the charges, most, like Tom Reynolds of the *Chicago Sun-Times*, saw McCarthy as the "master of the press" and urged that some copy coming from McCarthy be withheld until charges were "checked, refuted or answered."[158] J. R. Wiggins of the *Washington Post* spoke about the long-term effects of serious charges (that are never proved true): "I say to you solemnly that if we circulate or permit others to circulate day after day, week after week, month after month, the infamous allegation that there's treason in the White House, in the Chief of Staff, in the Secretary of State, and in all of the departments of government, we need not be surprised if an hour comes when American people have confidence in no one."[159]

William H. Heath, editor of the *Haverhill Gazette*, wrote that after McCarthy spoke at an ASNE-sponsored event, he was perceived by his enemies as transformed from "buffoon to menace" and the coverage given to his activities had aided that transformation.[160] Editor of the *Cedar Rapids Gazette* E. C. Hoyt used a sports metaphor in describing what the press needed to do: "Let's learn to keep our eye on the ball—meaning accuracy and honesty—rather than swing wildly for homeruns—meaning sensationalism."[161] An editorial writer for the *New York Times*, John B. Oakes, writing in the *Nieman Reports*, feared for the survival of this country. Oakes worried that "when a democracy no longer wishes to be informed because it is so emotionally wrought up that it cannot tell truth from falsehood, then it has already lost its freedom."[162]

All during the debate about covering McCarthy, the *Monitor* and its reporters were quoted often, showing the respect for the newspaper among the highest ranks in journalism. For instance, to illustrate the diversity of opinions about the coverage of the 1952 elections, Oakes quoted both Roscoe Drummond and William H. Stringer of the *Monitor*. Drummond claimed the Democrat nominee for President received a "less than even break" in news columns while Stringer thought "on balance" the press "did a fairly credible job" in reporting the campaign, with obvious exceptions noted. Ralph McGill, editor of the *Atlanta Constitution*, speaking at Southern Methodist University, quoted Drummond as "highly critical" of the one-sided coverage the press gave the 1952 campaign.[163] And at an editorial writers' meeting discussing ethics, the *Monitor*'s Richard L. Strout was cited as a reporter "whose integrity as a Washington correspondent stands in the front rank."[164]

Editor and Publisher polled its ranks to determine the top ten 1953 newspaper *industry* stories, and found the number one story to be the strikes of several newspapers in major cities (notably New York and Seattle). The relaxation of press relations by the White House, allowing more freedom of quotation and tape recording for broadcast, ranked as the second most important newspaper-related story. *New York Post* Editor James A. Wechsler's celebrated battle with McCarthy ranked as the seventh most important story. As for the top-ranked stories overall, International News Service (INS) editors reported that Stalin's death and other events in the Soviet Union ranked first, while the Rosenbergs' execution ranked fourth. United Press (UP) editors agreed with INS that Stalin's death (and the Soviet Union) was the most important story and ranked the Rosenbergs' execution fifth.[165] But, as 1954 began, McCarthy became embroiled in a dispute with the Army that earned him more prominence in the news and ultimately led to his demise.

NOTES

1. Richard L. Strout, "Senate Eyes GM Holdings," *Christian Science Monitor*, 19 January 1953, 1.
2. Ibid.
3. Mr. Canham to Mr. Davis, 27 January 1953, Richard L. Strout Papers, Weston, Mass.
4. Richard L. Strout to The Hon. George M. Humphrey, 3 February 1953, Richard L. Strout Papers, Weston, Mass.
5. Richard L. Strout to Mr. Drummond, 6 February 1953, Richard L. Strout Papers, Weston, Mass. Strout, in a handwritten message (dated March 13, 1976) at the bottom of a carbon copy of this memo, wrote that the Humphrey letter was never returned to him.
6. Saville [R. Davis] to Roscoe [Drummond], 28 January 1953, Richard L. Strout Papers, Weston, Mass.
7. David M. Oshinsky, *A Conspiracy So Immense: The World of Joe McCarthy* (New York: Free Press, 1983), 309.
8. Saville [Davis] to Roscoe [Drummond], undated, Richard L. Strout Papers, Weston, Mass.
9. Roscoe Drummond to Saville [Davis], 12 February 1953, Richard L. Strout Papers, Weston, Mass.
10. Dick [Richard L. Strout] to Bill [Stringer] and Saville [Davis], (on or about) 24 February 1954, Richard L. Strout Papers, Weston, Mass.
11. Ibid.
12. Saville [Davis] to Bill [William H. Stringer], 24 February 1954, Richard L. Strout Papers, Weston, Mass.
13. Saville [Davis] to Dick [Richard L. Strout], 27 April 1954, Richard L. Strout Papers, Weston, Mass.

14. Dick [Richard L. Strout](unsent) to Saville [Davis], 30 April 1954, Richard L. Strout Papers, Weston, Mass.

15. Neal Stanford, "McCarthy Transactions Questioned by Senate Group; Non-Cooperation Hit," *Christian Science Monitor*, 3 January 1953, 3.

16. Dick [Richard L. Strout] to Saville [Davis], 10 May 1954, Richard L. Strout Papers, Weston, Mass.

17. From the original mention of McCarthy's book in the *Monitor*, July 16, 1952, until Strout resumed covering McCarthy on a regular basis, April 23, 1954, every story Strout wrote was identified by the primary subject matter and logged. Additionally, all stories generated by the *Monitor* staff primarily about McCarthy were logged by subject matter and who wrote them. This information was used to determine when the ban occurred and how strictly it was adhered to.

18. Saville [Davis] to Bill [Stringer], 24 February 1954, Richard L. Strout Papers, Weston, Mass.

19. Richard L. Strout, "IKE Faces Congress Difficulties," *Christian Science Monitor*, 5 November 1952, 1.

20. There were two minor exceptions. Richard L. Strout, "Eisenhower Takes Leadership Role," *Christian Science Monitor*, 26 May 1953, 5. (This mentioned that if Eisenhower was not interested in running for reelection, McCarthy might seek the GOP nomination in 1956.) Richard L. Strout, "Three Victories Chalked Up by the President," *Christian Science Monitor*, 18 July 1953, 10. (This mentioned one of Eisenhower's victories over a McCarthy attack on the administration.)

21. Richard L. Strout, "Davies Case Hints Big Test between Dulles, McCarthy," *Christian Science Monitor*, 1 December 1953, 13.

22. This information was lifted from the logs mentioned in note 17.

23. Savills [sic] [Davis] to Dick [Richard L. Strout], 31 July 1958, Richard L. Strout Papers, Weston, Mass.

24. Dick [Richard L. Strout] personal note to Bert [Person Unknown], 5 August 1953, Richard L. Strout Papers, Weston, Mass.

25. Board of Trustees to the Board of Directors, 22 April 1953, Church History Department, The First Church of Christ, Scientist, Boston, Mass.

26. Board of Directors to the Board of Trustees, 5 June 1953, Church History Department, The First Church of Christ, Scientist, Boston, Mass.

27. Erwin D. Canham to Mr. Davis and Mr. Richardson, 12 June 1953, Richard L. Strout Papers, Weston, Mass.

28. Saville R. Davis to American News Department and Roscoe Drummond, 15 June 1953, Richard L. Strout Papers, Weston, Mass.

29. James A. Wechsler, *The Age of Suspicion* (New York: Random House, 1953), 5.

30. Ibid, 246.

31. "McCarthy in Clash with *New York Post* Editor," *Christian Science Monitor*, 6 May 1953, 4. "McCarthy versus Wechsler: New York Editor Charges Reprisal against the Press," *Christian Science Monitor*, 8 May 1953, 5.

32. Oshinsky, *A Conspiracy So Immense*, 282.

33. "Wechsler Implores ASNE to Speak Out Eloquently," *Editor and Publisher*, 9 May 1953, 7–8.

34. "Wechsler Wrote: Book Links Lewis to Left-Wing Block," *Christian Science Monitor*, 11 May 1953, 13.

35. Roscoe Drummond, "State of the Nation: The Case of McCarthy vs. Wechsler," *Christian Science Monitor*, 11 May 1953, 1.

36. Mildred Morrison, to editor, *Christian Science Monitor*, 5 June 1953, 24.

37. Drummond, "State of the Nation: The Case of McCarthy vs. Wechsler," 1.

38. Editorial, "Attempted Intimidation," *Christian Science Monitor*, 12 May 1953, 20.

39. Ibid.

40. Editorial, "You Gotta Be for Me, or Else—," *Milwaukee Journal*, 11 May 1953, 22.

41. Editorial, "Wechsler vs. McCarthy," *Editor and Publisher*, 16 May 1953, 38.

42. Elmer Davis, *But We Were Born Free* (New York: The Bobbs-Merrill Company, 1954), 34.

43. James Aronson, *Press and the Cold War* (New York: The Bobbs-Merrill Company, 1970), 91–93.

44. "Editors Appraise Free-Press Issue in Probe of Wechsler by McCarthy," *Christian Science Monitor*, 13 August 1953, 7. " 'Additional Comment on Case,' " *Christian Science Monitor*, 13 August 1953, 5.

45. Roscoe Drummond, "State of the Nation: Press Freedom and the Wechsler Case," *Christian Science Monitor*, 13 August 1953, 1.

46. Editorial, "Defend the Frontiers!," *Christian Science Monitor*, 14 August 1953, 18.

47. Editorial, "McCarthy and the Editors," *Milwaukee Journal*, 23 August 1953, 2.

48. Editorial, "Wechsler vs. McCarthy," *New York Times*, 13 August 1953, 24.

49. "ASNE Expected to Snub Senator's Call for Probe of Critical Editor," *Christian Science Monitor*, 17 August 1953, 7.

50. "Reaction from Committeemen," *Christian Science Monitor*, 17 August 1953, 7.

51. "Senator Asks Editors to Revise Statement," *Christian Science Monitor*, 14 September 1953, 4.

52. Victor S. Navasky, *Naming Names* (New York: Viking Press, 1980), 68.

53. Oshinsky, *A Conspiracy So Immense*, 269.

54. Richard L. Strout, log of Presidential Press Conference, 25 February 1953, Richard L. Strout Papers, Weston, Mass.

55. " 'Voice' Ban Set on Communists," *Christian Science Monitor*, 19 February 1953, 6.

56. The possibility exists that Strout covered some of the hearings, but he received no bylines.

57. "*Monitor* Material Proposed for Radio Casts by 'Voice,' " *Christian Science Monitor*, 27 February 1953, 3.

58. "No Administration Brakes Yet Applied to McCarthy's Loyalty Probing," *Christian Science Monitor*, 5 March 1953, 6.

59. "Excerpts from Voice of America Broadcasts Show How Soviet Life Is Refuted," *Christian Science Monitor*, 7 March 1953, 6. The researcher, in reviewing

every page of every issue of the *Monitor* in 1953, logged the number of excerpts from the VOA printed.

60. Editorial, "To Lift Up the Voice," *Christian Science Monitor*, 9 March 1953, 17.

61. Editorial, "Who's Running the Voice?," *Milwaukee Journal*, 11 March 1953, 24.

62. Editorial, "We're Not Laughing," *San Francisco Examiner*, 11 March 1953, 24.

63. "Letter to Wife Disclosed from 'Voice' Aide Suicide," *Christian Science Monitor*, 7 March 1953, 3.

64. "Pressure Probe Tactics Studied in Kaplan Case," *Christian Science Monitor*, 14 March 1953, 7.

65. "Harris Resigns from 'Voice' in McCarthy Clash," *Christian Science Monitor*, 15 April 1953, 8. Alan Barth, *Government by Investigation* (New York: Viking Press, 1955), 52.

66. Joseph C. Harsch, "The Affairs of Nations: Independents in America's 'Voice,'" *Christian Science Monitor*, 28 March 1953, 9.

67. " 'Voice' Station Contracts Canceled," *Christian Science Monitor*, 21 March 1953, 3.

68. "'Voice' Can Quote Communists," *Christian Science Monitor*, 19 March 1953, 5.

69. Editorial, "Voice of Common Sense," *Christian Science Monitor*, 21 March 1953, 22.

70. Editorial, "Controversial?," *Christian Science Monitor*, 11 March 1953, 24.

71. Ibid.

72. Richard H. Rovere, *Senator Joe McCarthy* (New York: Harper & Row, 1959), 199.

73. Edmund Stevens, "M'Carthy Committee Move Aids Italian Communists," *Christian Science Monitor*, 23 May 1953, 8.

74. Edgar M. Mills, "'Ike' to Conciliate Congress, Hits Anti-Red 'Book Burners': McCarthy Not Named," *Christian Science Monitor*, 15 June 1953, 1.

75. Editorial, "Don't Join the Book Burners," *Christian Science Monitor*, 16 June 1953, 16.

76. Quoted in Josephine Ripley, " 'Ike' Clarifies 'Book-Burning,' " *Christian Science Monitor*, 17 June 1953, 3.

77. Editorial, "Burning and Banning," *Christian Science Monitor*, 19 June 1953, 20.

78. Josephine Ripley, "Smoke from the 'Book Burnings': An Intimate Message from Washington," *Christian Science Monitor*, 26 June 1953, 19.

79. Editorial, "'Don't Join the Book Burners,' " *Milwaukee Journal*, 18 June, 1953, 24.

80. Editorial, "Mr. Eisenhower at Dartmouth," *New York Times*, 15 June 1953, 28.

81. Editorial, "Bravo, Ike!," *San Francisco Examiner*, 19 June 1953, 26.

82. Quoted in "Proceedings: 20th Annual Convention of the American Newspaper Guild," 29 June–3 July 1953, 73.

83. "State Department Orders Books Reinstated," *Christian Science Monitor*, 7 July 1953, 3. "U.S. Announces Names of 25 Black-List Books," *Christian Science Monitor*, 8 July 1953, 11.

84. Roland Sawyer, "America Drops Restrictions on Library Books," *Christian Science Monitor*, 9 July 1953, 1.

85. Editorial, "Smoke, Fire, and Daylight," *Christian Science Monitor*, 11 July 1953, 20.

86. Editorial, "Books Not for Banning—II," *New York Times*, 10 July 1953, 18.

87. Editorial, "Book Ban in Reverse," *Christian Science Monitor*, 22 March 1954, 16.

88. Barth, *Government by Investigation*, 40–41.

89. Richard L. Strout, "Stassen Hits McCarthy Deal," *Christian Science Monitor*, 30 March 1953, 1.

90. Oshinsky, *A Conspiracy So Immense*, 295.

91. Editorial, "The Quiet Crusade," *Christian Science Monitor*, 6 April 1953, 15.

92. Quoted in "The Quiet Crusade," 15.

93. Editorial, "The Quiet Crusade," 15.

94. Oshinsky, *A Conspiracy So Immense*, 298.

95. Richard L. Strout, "GOP Senators Put Squeeze on Dulles," *Christian Science Monitor*, 16 April 1953, 1.

96. Quoted in Joseph C. Harsch,"State of the Nations: Eisenhower-McCarthy Rift," *Christian Science Monitor*, 27 November 1953, 1.

97. Joseph C. Harsch, "State of the Nations: Eisenhower-McCarthy Rift," *Christian Science Monitor*, 27 November 1953, 1.

98. Joseph C. Harsch, "State of Nations: Dulles Accepts McCarthy Challenge," *Christian Science Monitor*, 2 December 1953, 1.

99. Neal Stanford, "Dulles Defends U.S. Policy; Split with McCarthy Looms," *Christian Science Monitor*, 1 December 1953, 1.

100. Richard L. Strout, "Communists in Government: GOP Seeks to Heal Spy Rift," *Christian Science Monitor*, 2 December 1953, 7.

101. Neal Stanford, "McCarthy Voices Appeal to People," *Christian Science Monitor*, 3 December 1953, 1. Text of McCarthy statement and GOP response, 23.

102. Editorial, "Taking Command," *Christian Science Monitor*, 3 December 1953, 30.

103. Editorial, "Papering Over a Crack," *Christian Science Monitor*, 4 December 1953, 24.

104. "Washington Letter," *Christian Science Monitor*, 5 December 1953, 17.

105. Joseph C. Harsch, "State of the Nations: Quiet Revolution in Washington," *Christian Science Monitor*, 8 December 1953, 1.

106. Barth, *Government by Investigation*, 33.

107. Oshinsky, *A Conspiracy So Immense*, 289.

108. "Senate Balks at Bohlen in Moscow Post," *Christian Science Monitor*, 13 March 1953, 1.

109. Editorial, "A Turning Point," *Christian Science Monitor*, 18 March 1953, 22.

110. Richard L. Strout, "Senate Unit Approves Bohlen," *Christian Science Monitor*, 18 March 1953, 1.

111. Neal Stanford, "Senate Unit's Vote for Bohlen Gives Eisenhower Major Victory," *Christian Science Monitor*, 19 March 1953, 9.

112. Richard L. Strout, "Split on Bohlen Symbol of Deep Capital Tension," *Christian Science Monitor*, 25 March 1953, 1.

113. Richard L. Strout, "Bohlen Fight to Hurt U.S. In Moscow?," *Christian Science Monitor*, 26 March 1953, 8.

114. Editorial, "The Attack on Bohlen," *Milwaukee Journal*, 19 March 1953, 24.

115. Editorial, "Mr. Bohlen Wins Out," *New York Times*, 20 March 1953, 22.

116. Editorial, "Republicans Stand to Be Counted,"*Christian Science Monitor*, 25 March 1953, 22.

117. Editorial, "Some Changes Not Ordered," *Christian Science Monitor*, 26 March 1953, 24.

118. "Dozen Votes Seen against Bohlen in 'Confidence Test,' " *Christian Science Monitor*, 27 March 1953, 1.

119. Richard L. Strout, "Faith in 'Ike' Seen in Vote for Bohlen," *Christian Science Monitor*, 28 March 1953, 1.

120. Roscoe Drummond, "State of the Nation: Significance of the Bohlen Test," *Christian Science Monitor*, 30 March 1953, 1.

121. Ibid.

122. "Senate Approves Bohlen, 74–13; Big Victory for Ike," *San Francisco Examiner*, 28 March 1953, 1.

123. Oshinsky, *A Conspiracy So Immense*, 292.

124. Various letters from Strout to family members, in the researcher's possession, indicated his desire for Eisenhower to wield the power of the Presidency against McCarthy.

125. Editorial, "The Rosenberg Appeal," *Christian Science Monitor*, 8 January 1953, 18.

126. Joseph C. Harsch, "The Affairs of Nations: The Rosenbergs and Psychological Strategy," *Christian Science Monitor*, 27 February 1953, 9.

127. John F. Neville, *The Press, the Rosenbergs, and the Cold War* (Westport, Conn.: Praeger, 1995), 114, 125.

128. Arthur Everett, "Thousand March Past White House in Plea to Save Rosenbergs: Background of the Case," *Christian Science Monitor*, 15 June 1953, 5.

129. Volney D. Hurd, "Virtually All of France Pleads for Rosenbergs," *Christian Science Monitor*, 18 June 1953, 11.

130. Neville, *The Press, The Rosenbergs*, 132.

131. Editorial, "Justice and the Rosenbergs," *Christian Science Monitor*, 20 June 1953, 18.

132. Editorial, "The Rosenberg Appeal," *Chicago Tribune*, 20 June 1953, 10.

133. Joseph C. Harsch, telephone conversation with author, 20 August 1996.

134. Thomas C. Reeves, *The Life and Times of Joe McCarthy: A Biography* (New York: Stein & Day, 1982), 499.

135. Barth, *Government by Investigation*, 155, 161–162. Of course, McCarthy's relationship with the Roman Catholic Church was such a complex one that Donald F. Crosby, S.J. wrote the book (mentioned in the literature review) *God, Church, and*

Flag: Senator Joseph R. McCarthy and the Catholic Church, 1950–1957, published by the University of North Carolina Press in 1978.

136. Reeves, *The Life and Times*, 326.

137. Joseph C. Harsch, "State of the Nations: Religious Controversy," *Christian Science Monitor*, 10 November 1953, 1.

138. A document dated 26 January 1954, found among papers provided by the Church History Department, The First Church of Christ, Scientist, Boston, Massachusetts, stated the count of 107 readers liked Harsch's column and approximately 10 did not.

139. Editorial, "The *Monitor* Bomb," *The Christian Century*, 25 November 1953, 1350.

140. Ibid, 1351.

141. "Agency Heads Accused of Favoring Catholics," *Church and State: A Monthly Review*, 6/11, December 1953, 2.

142. John E. Marvin, "Expressed Editorially: Not Conclusive but Cause for Concern," *Michigan Christian Advocate*, 10 December 1953, 4.

143. Ibid., 5.

144. G. Bromley Oxnam to Mr. Joseph C. Harsch, 22 March 1954, Church History Department, The First Church of Christ, Scientist, Boston, Mass.

145. Editorial, "Revival of Bigotry," *The Tablet*, 5 December 1953, editorial page.

146. J. J. Gilbert, "*Christian Science Monitor* Charges Exploded by Investigation of Facts," *The Pilot*, 9 January 1954, 1.

147. George E. Sokolsky, "These Days: Bigotry Can Only Help Kremlin," *New York Journal-American*, 6 January 1954.

148. JCH [Joseph C. Harsch] to Davis [Saville R.], 7 January 1954, Church History Department, The First Church of Christ, Scientist, Boston, Mass.

149. Harsch, telephone interview.

150. Richard M. Fried, *Nightmare in Red: The McCarthy Era in Perspective* (New York: Oxford University Press, 1990), 132.

151. Christopher Matthews, *The Rivalry that Shaped Postwar America: Kennedy and Nixon* (New York: Simon & Schuster, 1996), 96.

152. Melvin Mencher, Review of *McCarthy: The Man, the Senator, the "ISM"*, by Jack Anderson and Ronald W. May, *Nieman Reports* 7/1 January 1953, 47.

153. Gordon A. Sabine, "McCarthy Abuse Is Text for Dean's Advice," *Editor and Publisher*, 6 June 1953, 59.

154. "Hoyt Insists on 'Fair Play' in Staff Memo," *Editor and Publisher*, 28 February 1953, 12.

155. "Denver Editor Cautions on How to Cover Probes," *Christian Science Monitor*, 20 March 1953, 14. Palmer Hoyt, "Educator's Duty," reprinted in *Christian Science Monitor*, 10 August 1953, 16.

156. "The Fetish of Objectively," *Time*, 4 May 1953, 49.

157. Mary McCarthy, "The Menace to Free Journalism in America," *Nieman Reports* 7/4 October 1953, 46.

158. Quoted in "McCarthy," *APME Red Book 1953*, 50–51.

159. Ibid, 57.

160. William H. Heath, "Unfair Headline and Story Emphasis," ASNE *The Bulletin*, 1 September 1953, 3.

161. E. C. Hoyt, "Unfair Headline and Story Emphasis," ASNE *The Bulletin*, 1 September 1953, 2.

162. John B. Oakes, "The Dangerous Obligations of a Newspaperman," *Nieman Reports*, 7/4 October 1953, 6.

163. "New Responsibilities of U.S. Journalists Debate," *Christian Science Monitor*, 4 May 1953, 3.

164. "Study of Newspaper Ethics Asked by Editorial Writers," *Christian Science Monitor*, 17 April 1953, 2.

165. "Our Own 10 Biggest Stories," *Editor and Publisher*, 26 December 1953, 13.

5
1954: MCCARTHY'S DEMISE

PRELUDE TO ARMY-MCCARTHY

Peress Case

The beginning of the end of the junior senator's battles with the military involved the case of an Army dentist named Dr. Irving Peress. In October 1952, Peress was commissioned as a dentist, and in November 1953, he was promoted to major under the Doctor Draft law, despite the objections of Brigadier General Ralph W. Zwicker. In mid-January 1954, the Army ordered Peress discharged, and the dentist chose March 31 for termination.[1] However, on February 2, 1954, Peress—one day after McCarthy had requested that he be court-martialed—was granted an honorable discharge.[2] McCarthy questioned the loyalty of Peress after the dentist had refused to answer questions about his political beliefs once commissioned in the Army; McCarthy was enraged when he heard about Peress's discharge.[3]

McCarthy's subcommittee summoned General Zwicker to answer questions, but Zwicker would not identify who was involved in the Peress case. McCarthy became exceedingly abusive, calling Zwicker "not fit to wear the uniform" and a "disgrace to the army."[4] Secretary of the Army Robert T. Stevens, upset about the abuse endured by Zwicker, called McCarthy and indicated he would not allow any more officers to testify before the committee if they were treated badly. The pronouncement by Stevens led to what became a famous "chicken dinner"—actually a lunch on February 24 to work things out, involving Stevens, McCarthy, and Republican leaders.

Stevens agreed to cooperate with McCarthy's investigations while McCarthy seemingly agreed to nothing. It appeared that the Army had backed down from a McCarthy challenge.[5] Realizing how weak the Army appeared, Stevens later read a statement to the press attempting to redeem himself. Stevens stated that Zwicker had been severely mistreated, had been denied counsel that he was entitled to, and that McCarthy—at the luncheon—had agreed to treat Army representatives better when they appeared before his committee.[6] The President also took time at a news conference to address the Peress case. Eisenhower conceded the case had been handled badly, but praised General Zwicker's courage. He informed Congress that cooperation was a two-way street, stressing the need for courtesy between the two branches of government. And, the President placed the burden of making sure witnesses were treated fairly squarely on the shoulders of Republicans in Congress.[7]

The *Monitor* denounced McCarthy's abuse of General Zwicker, as it had McCarthy's treatment of others in previous hearings. It noted that several members of McCarthy's subcommittee had withdrawn from participation in investigations because of the Senator's actions, and suggested that it would be "even more important that the whole Senate should object to tyrannical and abusive handling of citizens appearing as witnesses."[8] In a second editorial, after Stevens' "retreat" and subsequent effort to redeem himself with a clarifying news conference, the *Monitor* again expressed its desire for fair treatment of witnesses appearing before Senate committees. While stating that "We doubt very much whether the nation's security was endangered by the dentist major's Army career," the newspaper conceded bumbling by the Army in rectifying the situation. The *Monitor* wrote that the "Army has taken steps to prevent any recurrence of the Peress case" and the newspaper urged the Senate to "take steps to prevent any recurrence of the Zwicker case."[9]

Though defeated in his 1952 bid for the Presidency, Adlai Stevenson remained the spokesperson for the Democratic Party. On national television, Stevenson attacked President Eisenhower for his failure to criticize McCarthy and his tactics. Instead of allowing McCarthy to respond directly to Stevenson's attack, Eisenhower named Vice President Richard M. Nixon to answer the charge. This meant McCarthy would be forced into the background. And, because of Nixon's anticommunist history, the President would be safe from any charge that he was soft on Communism in answering Stevenson.[10]

The *Monitor*'s Richard L. Strout interpreted Nixon's selection as intending to sidetrack McCarthy, and anticipated that Nixon would focus on Eisenhower's 196-item legislative program.[11] A *Monitor* editorial viewed Nixon's speech, which "avoided naming Senator McCarthy, but had plenty to say against his investigating methods," as a "step toward cutting away the public support for the senator [McCarthy] which has based much of his power—and abuse of power." On a positive note, the *Monitor* declared that Nixon believed that "to be fair is both right and more effective." Finally, the *Monitor* called some of Nixon's "partisan remarks on foreign policy ... divisive and confusing" but contended "his handling of McCarthyism should tend to unite Americans behind better methods of Red hunting."[12] The *Milwaukee Journal* began to report hopeful signs. An editorial lauded the President's choice of Nixon over McCarthy to answer Stevenson's allegations, because "it was the party's business not McCarthy's." Added to Eisenhower's action was that of Senator Ralph E. Flanders of Vermont who declared on the Senate floor that McCarthy was causing a split in the Republican Party.[13]

Before the McCarthy-Zwicker-Stevens incidents, a Gallup poll showed 50 percent of the public approved of McCarthy and his methods. That dropped to 46 percent immediately following the Peress controversy. More important, 29 percent had an unfavorable opinion of McCarthy before the controversy, and that leapt to 36 percent immediately following. However, perhaps most important, 82 percent of those surveyed had some opinion about McCarthy, "a standing seldom attained by any politician."[14] With McCarthy one of the best-known politicians in the country, and after many newspapers had questioned the junior senator's tactics for almost five years, the new medium of television finally joined in the battle against McCarthy.

Murrow vs. McCarthy

Edward R. Murrow, CBS news legend, and Robert E. Kintner, then ABC President, have been credited by some as the most important television people involved in McCarthy's downfall:[15] Murrow for his *See It Now* program devoted to exposing McCarthy for the demagogue he was, and Kintner for authorizing the live television broadcast of the Army-McCarthy hearings, which also exposed McCarthy and his methods.

A March 9, 1954 Murrow broadcast about McCarthy (while the Peress controversy was still raging) was actually one of several programs denouncing the practice of guilt by association and other McCarthy tactics.[16] Murrow had "come to believe about McCarthy, as he had about Hitler, that when a journalist was confronted with an unmitigated evil, there was no 'other side' to present."[17] Murrow, through film clips collected of McCarthy in action over the previous two years, simply let the junior senator's actions speak for themselves. He ended the broadcast with an eloquently written summation quoting Shakespeare and placing the blame for McCarthy's success at the feet of the American people who allowed McCarthyism to flourish. Murrow became an instant hero to McCarthy critics, while conservative Hearst newspaper columnist Fulton Lewis, Jr. spoke for many McCarthyites when he declared that "Mr. Egghead R. Murrow leans to the left."[18]

The *Monitor* ran both a front-page United Press story and page 14 story by *Monitor* reporter Mary Hornaday about Murrow's broadcast and the public's response. CBS received 1,000 congratulatory telegrams and only 14 protesting Murrow's program. More than 2,300 phone callers expressed their approval while only about 150 disapproved of Murrow's handling of the subject.[19] McCarthy took it on the chin from two fronts that day. Vermont Senator Ralph E. Flanders, who was becoming increasingly irritated with the junior senator, issued a statement ridiculing the success of McCarthy's red hunt in the government, specifically citing the Peress case: "He dons his war paint. He goes into his war dance. He emits war whoops. He goes forth to battle and proudly returns with the scalp of a pink dentist."[20]

About one week after Murrow's McCarthy broadcast, the *Monitor*'s William H. Stringer attempted to size up the arguments made by Murrow and McCarthy's response. Stringer concluded that "Mr. Murrow seems to have had the better of the argument."[21] It was also not long after Murrow's broadcast that McCarthy made it clear he was about to carry out a "personal project" in exposing Communists in the press. *New York Times* editor John B. Oakes viewed the investigation as "an obvious attempt at political intimidation," but he welcomed the probe because the newspaper industry had nothing to hide.[22] Robert U. Brown of *Editor and Publisher* spoke for many in the industry when he wrote, "Let him personally investigate the press to his heart's content. The press operates in a goldfish bowl. It has nothing to hide. Any person so inclined can investigate it."[23]

On April 6, 1954, McCarthy provided a rebuttal to Murrow's *See It Now* broadcast. The *Monitor* included McCarthy's remarks as part of an Associated Press story on page 9, but did not editorialize about them. Meanwhile, the always critical *Milwaukee Journal* called McCarthy's comments about Murrow "the latest in a long series of vindictive attacks" clearly illustrating "oppose McCarthy and you are smeared as a Communist."[24] Banner headlines announced McCarthy's response to Murrow in the *Chicago Tribune*. But the *Tribune*, unlike during the early years of McCarthyism, published a companion article to McCarthy's rebuttal with reaction from Murrow. The *Tribune* focused largely on McCarthy's contention that America deliberately delayed research on the hydrogen bomb for 18 months, a comment that came within the text of McCarthy's rebuttal to Murrow. Regarding Murrow, McCarthy took exception to the newscaster's contention that the junior senator had given "considerable comfort to the enemy," asking viewers to answer the question "What do the Communists think of me and what do the Communists think of Mr. Murrow?"[25]

Murrow's *See It Now* broadcast, perhaps more than precipitating the downfall of McCarthy, reflected the country's growing uneasiness with the Senator's tactics and set the stage for the live television broadcast of the Army-McCarthy hearings—which ultimately showed the American people McCarthy in action. On the heels of the Murrow broadcast came a 13–part series by the Associated Press (carried in many daily newspapers) called "The McCarthy Story." It was researched and written by five reporters from the AP, two of whom had won Pulitzer prizes. The stories were fed to newspapers and run in mid-April.[26] By the end of April though, McCarthy took on the Army, and live national television exposure played a vital role in his ultimate undoing.

ARMY-MCCARTHY HEARINGS

The hearings that preceded the censure drive against McCarthy involved charges by the Army that McCarthy and his chief counsel Roy Cohn had sought preferential treatment for Private G. David Schine. Schine had worked for McCarthy as an "investigative" assistant to Cohn. McCarthy countered that the Army blackmailed and bribed him by holding Schine "hostage" for the express purpose of thwarting any future investigations of the Army.[27]

Going into the hearings, the *Monitor* suggested that the GOP faced a McCarthy-related dilemma. In the "Washington Letter" column, the Washington bureau reporters stated that if McCarthy were "deflated" by the Army-McCarthy dispute, then he would not be a "vote-winning speaker for the autumn campaign." On the other hand, if he "emerges triumphant, he will be more difficult than ever to deal with."[28]

William H. Stringer, Roland Sawyer, and Richard L. Strout were the principal *Monitor* reporters covering the Army-McCarthy hearings. On the first day of the hearings, Stringer described the scene and put the Congressional inquiry into historical perspective: "Correspondents could remember no Washington hearing other than the Pearl Harbor investigation and the great probe of General Douglas MacArthur's dismissal which anywhere equaled this inquiry opening April 22 before a nationwide television audience and an unprecedented 120 reporters in the spacious—but jam-packed—Senate Caucus room, marble pillared and crystal-chandeliered."[29]

A *Monitor* editorial simply stated that "neither the Army nor the administration is likely to emerge wholly unscarred." And the newspaper saw at stake in the hearings, "control of the Republican Party, the preservation of the Chief Executive's power, and the American people's confidence in their government and each other."[30] *Monitor* Columnist Joseph C. Harsch claimed the hearings were not about the Senate choosing between McCarthy's story and the Army's; they were about "whether the American people in their own good time will accept or reject the essential claim of the Senator from Wisconsin to be the indispensable man in American public life." Harsch later clarified his belief that McCarthy was on trial, stating that actually the Senator was "on exhibition" with the American people getting a chance to see him in action as McCarthy's Senate colleagues had witnessed for more than four years.[31]

As the hearings opened, Richard L. Strout (in essentially his first news story about McCarthy since his "suspension") identified the Army as having transcripts of telephone conversations between Army officials and McCarthy's office where McCarthy's staff sought preferential treatment for Schine. Strout declared that the Army had "a mine of documentary material with which to support its case."[32] A "Washington Letter" column cautioned against expecting a "vigorous report condemning either Senator McCarthy or the Army."[33] In the early days of the hearings, a *Monitor* editorial identified the "most heartening feature of the hearings" as being "the evidence that the spell of terror once wielded by the junior senator from Wisconsin has been broken" with the committee and others standing up to McCarthy.[34]

While Strout described the Army-McCarthy hearings accurately and fairly in the *Monitor*, privately he blamed Eisenhower for McCarthy's prominence, and articulated emotions close to hatred for the junior senator. Strout wrote that the President was the American "spiritual leader" and had Eisenhower attacked McCarthy earlier many newspapers would have followed his lead. He concluded that he hated to say that the President showed "signs of moral weakness."[35] But, Strout's feelings for McCarthy ran much deeper. He wrote in a letter that he felt as if he were in a "pigstye" covering the Army-McCarthy hearings: "I loathe him and yet am fascinated by him. It seems unbelievable to me that he has fooled a portion of the American people. On the other hand I feel that the USA has again shown it is unequaled: certainly he is better raw material for a fuhrer than Hitler or Mussolini. Anything any other country can do we can do better."[36]

On April 27, Joseph N. Welch, the special counsel representing the Army, called into question a photograph submitted in McCarthy's (and Cohn's) defense. Welch had determined that a photo seemingly depicting Army Secretary Robert T. Stevens smiling at Private David G. Schine at Fort Dix had actually been cropped from a larger photo including several other men.[37] Strout reported the allegation that McCarthy's people deliberately misled the committee by implying Stevens was obviously smiling and enjoying Schine's company and not upset at being persuaded to provide special treatment. Describing the atmosphere of the hearings as that of a "circus," Strout reported that the cropped photo incident to "objective observers" was not thought to be of "great relevancy... to either side."[38] This statement came after a member of McCarthy's staff (James Juliana) explained a "misunderstanding" in the presentation of the photo. A *Monitor* editorial contended the photo's major significance may have been that it "typified an unscrupulous kind of attack anyone risks who dares to question McCarthy method" and stirred up the recollection of the doctored photo of Senator Millard Tydings shaking the hand of former Communist Party leader Earl Browder.[39] Senator Charles Potter (writing years later) identified the cropped photo incident as much more serious. Potter claimed he told President Eisenhower (at the time) that "McCarthy is finished" because of the faked photograph.[40]

In the early days of the hearings, *Monitor* columns lamented the excessive coverage about McCarthy at the expense of other important news from around the world. Joseph C. Harsch wrote that "in general the headlines and the mass type of dealing with the hearings have exceeded substantially the headlines and the mass of type devoted to the 'crisis' " [in Indochina].[41] A "Washington Letter" piece reported that a "score of big Eisenhower measures" in Congress were at a "crucial stage," but were largely being ignored. It went on sarcastically that "Many broadcast, television and newspaper outlets don't bother covering these 'minor matters'—like taxes, tariffs, farm prices, housing, Taft-Hartley Law, and similar items—because teams of reporters are busy with the McCarthy show."[42]

From nearly the start, the *Monitor* also analyzed the battle between McCarthy and his own party—namely President Eisenhower. Harsch contended that the "news will come into balance" when McCarthy is answered by someone as powerful as himself, and "The only such name in Washington is that of Dwight David Eisenhower."[43] Similarly, Strout wrote that the "mist of the McCarthy hearings" had obscured Eisenhower's legislative program, and that the President was the only person who could "dissipate the mist" as Secretary Stevens "battles alone" against McCarthy.[44]

Just 12 days into 36 days of hearings, Strout wrote about McCarthy's declining popularity even within his own party. Strout reported that the Republican National Committee had decided not to use McCarthy for any speeches during the fall election campaign. He observed that the relationship between McCarthy and Eisenhower was "close now to open war."[45] Realizing that the hearings were adversely affecting the Republican Party and the country, Republican Senator Everett M. Dirksen of Illinois proposed conducting the proceedings in private once Senator McCarthy's testimony concluded. Additionally, Dirksen proposed that McCarthy be allowed to resume hearings by his own committee.[46] Secretary Stevens opposed the proposal and eventually the Senate committee voted it down.[47] A *Monitor* editorial supported Stevens' insistence that open hearings be continued. The newspaper agreed with those who believed that efficiency was needed in carrying out the hearings, but stated that "secrecy could obtain that only in limited degree." It further contended that the Army felt an advantage in having the hearings open, to let the "public have a full view of their experience with McCarthy operations."[48] Clearly, one of McCarthy's staunchest opponents—the *Milwaukee Journal*—believed the public hearings were "worth the disgrace." A *Journal* editorial stated that "in the national spotlight" the people of the country were finally "being exposed to the real essence, the basic phoniness, the dangers of McCarthyism that have long been evident to those willing to take the trouble to look carefully."[49]

As the hearings reached the halfway point, McCarthy continued to defy President Eisenhower with respect to requests of federal employees. McCarthy asked that federal employees report to Congress any corruption, Communism, or wrongdoing in the agencies in which they worked. This directly contradicted the Espionage Act, Section 793, and the President's orders.[50] A *Monitor* editorial described McCarthy's actions as an effort to "set up a personal spy system of his own, with a promise of protection to those who disclose classified material to him." The newspaper conceded that corruption, Communism, and wrongdoing of any nature should be identified and dealt with, but through proper channels—with Congress being a last resort if they obtained no results. The *Monitor* stated that McCarthy "has encouraged the belief . . . that no one else wants to oust Reds or knows how." And, the Senator also assumes he "stands above—all three branches of government."[51] Accepting these provisos would be dangerous at best: "To accept his conscious or unconscious concept of his powers would lead first to anarchy—by the destruction of orderly, constitutional government—and then to dictatorship."[52]

Meanwhile, the *Monitor* made it clear that there should be cooperation between the legislative and executive branches of government in dealing with the problem of Communists in government. However, McCarthy's request that federal employees report Communists and other activities directly to him was not seen as "cooperation" by the *Monitor*. The newspaper suggested that neither Congress nor Senator McCarthy would be happy with staff members acting as "stool pigeons."[53]

Erwin D. Canham, editor of the *Monitor*, broadcast a regularly scheduled commentary on ABC radio that was reprinted in the newspaper. With the hearings over half completed, Canham identified six "fundamental points" that "should be crystallizing in the thinking of the American people." Among the six were that the government's security program should be carried out by the executive branch; that Congressional probes into ex-

1954: McCarthy's Demise

ecutive performance must be carried out with "decency and integrity"; and that generally speaking "the institutions of America are after all genuinely sound."[54] A *Monitor* editorial also summarized what had been learned during the hearings. The newspaper called McCarthy's methods confusing, contended they hampered the real search for Communists in government, and claimed the Senator was "unwilling or unable to work with other loyal Americans" in weeding out Communists. The *Monitor* declared that McCarthy was ready to destroy individuals and split the Republican Party, plus "upset the Constitutional division of powers among the three branches."[55]

Repeatedly over the five years of "McCarthyism" the press wrestled with the charge that it created and sustained the Senator's power. An *Editor and Publisher* editorial declared that "newspapers didn't 'make' Senator McCarthy." *E&P* argued that the newspapers "had a duty to report McCarthy's activities ... even though they knew that is what McCarthy wanted." It stated that if the press had not reported on McCarthy, and people had been exposed to his tactics for the first time in the Army-McCarthy hearings, they would have been astounded at what they saw. So, *E&P* concluded that newspapers were in the middle and could not win regardless of the kind of coverage given to McCarthy.[56] During the heart of the hearings, *E&P* wrote of the insidious effect McCarthyism had on the media. On the one hand, "reporters are sick and tired of it all," yet the media have been giving the spectacle "around the clock coverage." Further, *E&P* contended that the press was "irked at the sameness of what goes on day after day," yet when the hearings conclude they will miss them.[57] At the same time, the industry magazine urged newspapers to make sure they "make every effort to point up the truth in big bold type," and termed "disgraceful" Senator McCarthy's use of senatorial immunity to perpetuate libel.[58]

One of the most dramatic moments in the Army-McCarthy hearings occurred on June 9, 1954. While the Army's attorney Joseph N. Welch questioned Roy Cohn, McCarthy rose and contended that Frederick Fisher, a member of Welch's law firm (Hale and Dorr of Boston), had Communist ties, yet had been asked by the Army to help in its case. Welch calmly explained that Fisher was not part of the Army's team of lawyers, and besides he had no current ties to the Communist Party. McCarthy persisted, and Welch stormed back: "Let's not assassinate this lad further, Senator. You have done enough. Have you no sense of decency, sir, at long last? Have you no sense of decency?"[59]

Historians would point to the exchange between Welch and McCarthy as one of the defining moments in the Senator's ultimate demise, and at the time the *Monitor* clearly recognized the impact of the incident. Roland Sawyer wrote that the audience applauded Welch for his handling of McCarthy's smear against Fisher, and "many in the audience wept." Sawyer deduced that in "the hard, cynical, sensation-accustomed atmosphere of Washington, it is not often that men and women are reduced to genuine tears."[60] Similarly, the *New York Times* called the Welch-McCarthy exchange "bitter" and described how the "crowded hearing room burst into applause for Mr. Welch."[61] Even the staunchly pro-McCarthy *San Francisco Examiner* took time to note the applause afforded Welch and the tears in his eyes denoting the hurt inflicted by McCarthy's "recklessness."[62] The accounts by the *Monitor*, the *Times* and the *Examiner* slightly contrasted with a report in the *Chicago Tribune* that focused on McCarthy's testimony tracing the path of the Communist conspiracy nationwide—but it did mention the exchange between Welch and McCarthy.[63]

On June 17, the hearings were adjourned. They had covered 36 days, had 35 witnesses, 42 exhibits, and nearly 3,000 pages of testimony.[64] And, from an early January poll showing McCarthy with a 29 percent unfavorable rating, a June poll placed that figure at 45 percent.[65] Sawyer predicted no clear verdict, and concluded that McCarthy could not be "drawn for long into an orderly sequence of discussion and that the normal rules of personal conduct . . . cannot be relied upon in a situation where he is the protagonist."[66]

The *Monitor* editorialized about the proceedings and looked to the future. The newspaper believed the Army-McCarthy hearings displayed for the entire country the struggles between the legislative and executive authority—with "the sharpest picture of this conflict" being McCarthy's "repeated invitation to employees in executive departments to act as his spies within those areas." The *Monitor* conceded (as many had) that the hearings produced no absolute winner or loser, and hardly came close to settling the conflict between legislative and executive authority. It also conceded that the "hearings distracted American attention from a very great Communist danger in Indochina." Ultimately, the *Monitor* brought attention to the proper method for dealing with the internal threat from Communism. It stated that citizens must ask themselves if they are "being gulled into unthinking support of unfair, dishonest, and dictatorial means of fighting communism" by someone "chiefly interested in personal and political power."[67]

Monitor columnist Joseph C. Harsch interpreted the hearings as a blow to McCarthy, but not a deadly one. He declared that "no battles have been won or lost, but Senator McCarthy's strategic situation is different and less favorable to him than it was before the famous hearings opened."[68] Nonscientific polls contradicted one another about the results of the hearings. For instance, readers of the anti-McCarthy *Chicago Sun-Times* voted three to two that the Army held the edge, but readers of the pro-McCarthy *Chicago Tribune* voted nine to one in favor of the junior senator.[69]

1954: McCarthy's Demise

Following the hearings, Roy Cohn resigned from McCarthy's subcommittee staff—a resignation "in name only, for he faced certain dismissal as soon as they could take a formal vote registering the house-cleaning demand of Senator Potter and the three Democratic members." The *Monitor* labeled the forced change of McCarthy's hand-picked staff as censure of McCarthy's abuses. Additionally, the Senate's agreeing to set up a code of fair procedures, when added to the forced McCarthy staff dismissals, showed a "tacit admission that abuses" had occurred.[70]

With the Army-McCarthy hearings behind the country and censure hearings on the horizon, the *Monitor* put together a series of four "well-documented" articles about the Communist-hunting career of Senator McCarthy.[71] Reporter Robert M. Hallett received the byline for most of the stories, but the entire *Monitor* staff contributed to this "exhaustive survey" of McCarthy's activities.[72] Among the findings revealed in the series was that McCarthy had not uncovered a single Communist spy whose guilt was proved in court; no person charged with treason by McCarthy had been indicted; and no proven Communists worked for the Voice of America. However, in the Army-McCarthy controversy, four Army officers critical of McCarthy were reassigned and eventually Army Secretary Robert T. Stevens was pressured into ordering Army personnel to answer whether they were Communists or not.[73] Additionally, Hallett documented that 15 General Electric employees were dismissed for security reasons after a McCarthy probe into the defense contractor, but "not one . . . had been given government clearance or worked on a classified job."[74] This series of researched news articles clearly displayed for *Monitor* readers the overall ineffectiveness of McCarthy and his methods—methods that led to a censure motion by fellow Republican Senator Ralph E. Flanders of Vermont.

CENSURE

Over time, Senator Flanders had grown ever more uneasy with McCarthy. On March 9, 1954, he ridiculed McCarthy on the Senate floor for making such a big issue of the Dr. Irving Peress case.[75] On June 1, Flanders mentioned McCarthy in the same breath as Hitler and at the same time likened him to Dennis the Menace—setting party members against party members and neighbor against neighbor, thus doing more to help the Communist cause than thwart it.[76] On June 11, Flanders called for McCarthy's removal from his chairmanships on committees and subcommittees until the junior senator answered questions raised in the Hennings Report.[77] The *Monitor* quickly endorsed Flanders' request that McCarthy answer to the many allegations in the lengthy Hennings subcommittee report (among them, various campaign financing irregularities, including the $10,000 fee from Lustron Corporation received by McCarthy). The newspaper stated,

"We see no reason why the Senate should not before adjournment take a day or two and face this ultimately inescapable issue" declaring that the Senate had "too long dodged responsibility for the conduct of its committees and their chairman."[78]

By July 30, Senator Flanders had a much more extreme action he wanted taken against McCarthy. Flanders withdrew his original request that McCarthy be stripped of his chairmanships on committees and subcommittees and substituted Senate Resolution 301. The resolution called for Senator McCarthy to be "condemned" for conduct "unbecoming of the United States Senate" and for bringing the Senate "into disrepute."[79] On August 2, 1954, the Senate voted 75 to 12 for the creation of a select committee of three Republicans and three Democrats to look into Flanders' resolution. Vice President Richard M. Nixon named Utah Republican Arthur V. Watkins to head the committee and he was joined by fellow Republicans Frank Carlson of Kansas and Francis H. Case of South Dakota. Seventeen-year veteran of the Senate Edwin C. Johnson of Colorado, Mississippi's John C. Stennis, and North Carolina's Samuel J. Ervin, Jr. were the Democrats.[80] The *Monitor*'s William H. Stringer believed the naming of the select committee "this close to the November elections" showed "that he [McCarthy] is regarded as a waning political asset in at least some Republican quarters."[81] The *Monitor*'s Richard L. Strout noted that to this point most senators had been critical of McCarthy when speaking off the record, "but they have found it expedient to remain silent" while speaking on the record.[82] With a resolution to condemn, senators would be forced to end their silence. Strout's penchant for descriptive writing surfaced in setting the scene of Congress dealing with McCarthy. Strout saw Flanders as a person "quiet and relaxed" who remained "cool and calm," and not flustered "at immediate thrusts against him." Strout described McCarthy as "dark and somewhat Napoleonic," and "reading a newspaper" while Flanders spoke, yet "listening appreciatively" while friends defended him.[83]

Pro- and anti-McCarthy newspapers applauded the naming of the select committee. The *Times* expressed hope that the new panel would "rise above politics" while in the meantime the legislative branch of government could search for better ways to combat Communism than the present system of sensationalized committee hearings.[84] The *San Francisco Examiner* called Senator Flanders' attempt at censure a "farce" but applauded handing the investigation over to a "bi-partisan committee . . . to decide in the quiet of a closed meeting if there is any meat to the charges."[85]

Chairman Arthur V. Watkins was determined to control the proceedings and not thrust upon the American people the same spectacle that occurred during the Army-McCarthy hearings. Watkins closed the hearings to broadcasters (radio and television), causing *Editor and Publisher* to be among the media representatives upholding the right of radio and television to broadcast the sessions.[86] Nearly a month later (September 11), *E&P* called the hearings a "pretty dry affair" but reiterated its position that radio and television should have been able to broadcast them.[87]

The censure resolution contained five general categories of charges: showing contempt for senatorial committees, encouraging federal employees to break the law, receiving classified documents from executive files, abusing Senate colleagues, and the abuse of General Zwicker.[88] Once the hearings were well underway, Strout sensed an easiness in the way Washington was dealing with the crisis. In fact, Strout wrote that the atmosphere at the hearing was "matter-of-fact, business-like, prosaic" and that Watkins' control of the proceedings "has Senator McCarthy baffled."[89] Senator Flanders—on the final day of the hearings—charged that McCarthy had "persistently" tried to "intimidate" the press and radio. Flanders admitted that the intimidation attempt had not yielded very good results for McCarthy, but he declared that fact "in no way minimizes the gravity of the attempt."[90] The committee withdrew to write its final report on September 15, and emerged recommending two counts of censure. One was for the abuse of General Zwicker during the Peress investigation and the second was contempt for the Senate for McCarthy's lack of cooperation and harsh criticism of investigating committees.[91]

Nearly three months before the Senate was asked to vote on the condemnation of McCarthy, a "Washington Letter" column in the *Monitor* accurately predicted the result. The Washington bureau stated that "observers think there is a good chance that it [the Senate] will vote to censure Senator Joseph R. McCarthy," but it explained that "no one can foretell how strongly the report would be worded or whether a majority of the Senate would go along."[92]

In the end, the recommended censure resolution dropped the denunciation of McCarthy's treatment of General Zwicker. The resolution cited two counts against the junior senator—showing contempt toward the Gillette subcommittee by obstructing constitutional processes, and abusing colleagues. McCarthy described the process as a "lynching bee" and declared that the Watkins select committee was an "unwitting handmaiden" of the Communist Party."[93] A *Monitor* editorial saw absolutely no merit in the characterizations, and asked McCarthy to put a "curb on such reckless accusations, on sowing of suspicion, confusion and internal strife" and produce a much more effective anticommunist campaign.[94] Another editorial objected to an attempt to reach a "compromise" to avoid McCarthy's censure. As McCarthy characterized colleagues as "imbecilic" and "dishonest," the *Monitor* opposed any agreement. In fact the newspaper stated that, "In view of a four-year record of delays, evasions or appeasements it is difficult to see how the Senate could now dodge the censure recommendations of its own committee."[95] In fact, a nationwide review of newspaper "opinion" revealed "widespread satisfaction with the Watkins committee."[96] Of course the Hearst press and McCormick newspapers did not share the views of the majority. Largely, they (and others of the "Far Right") condemned the report "for bias, ignorance and un-American activity."[97]

The changing feeling in America about McCarthy may have been reflected in the turnout for a New York City rally in support of the Senator. "Ten Million Americans Mobilizing for Justice" gathered at Madison Square Garden on November 30, just days before the Senate censure vote. A disappointing 13,000 showed up to support McCarthy—with Flanders, former President Truman, and the *New York Times* serving as the chief targets of the organization.[98]

The vote on condemnation of McCarthy for contempt of the Gillette subcommittee and for abuse of its members was 67 to 22, splitting the Republican Party down the middle. Strout saw the vote having "profound consequences abroad," showing that American institutions were stronger than many foreign countries realized.[99] And privately, Strout was elated with the developments. He wrote his family that it had been a "good week" and that despite working extremely hard "writing a couple of pieces a day," McCarthy censured was something he had waited five years to see: "I could not leave it and lived with it as my baby."[100] McCarthy (in his book) had tried to discredit Strout and the *Monitor*, and now Strout's revenge had come as a Senate censure.

A *Monitor* editorial answered critics of the vote with rebuttals to specific points. The newspaper contended that the censure was not the result of Congress' becoming an "unwitting tool" of the Communist Party—witness the three-to-one margin in favor. Free speech would not be hampered because of the vote and that was proven by the "decidedly unrestrained exchanges" during the censure debate. And, the censure vote did not "undermine the powers of its [Senate] committees or halt effective investigations of communism," it merely stated that investigations would be carried out with certain standards of conduct. The censure vote was—according to the *Monitor*—"essentially a decision to uphold standards of honor, accuracy, impersonal justice, reasonableness and responsibility which are in the highest American tradition."[101]

Meanwhile, the *New York Times* stated that the Senate had "done much to redeem itself in the eyes of the American people" in voting overwhelmingly for censure. The *Times* contended that to preserve its own dignity, the Senate could not have issued anything "milder" than the censure.[102] A follow-up editorial stated that the lopsided vote was a "vivid demonstration of the essential political truth that this is not a country of extremes or extremists."[103] The *Milwaukee Journal* took it upon itself to identify those brave souls who "led the fight for decency" and listed among the heroes responsible for the censure Margaret Chase Smith of Maine, author of the famed Declaration of Conscience speech in 1950; former Senator William Benton for pressing charges against McCarthy that resulted in the Gillette investigation in 1952; and, of course, Senator Flanders, author of the censure motion.[104] In another editorial a couple of days later, the *Journal* meticulously reviewed the reasons for the censure vote, vividly describing (in most unflattering terms) "The Man They Censured."[105] The *Chicago Tribune* was chagrined at the censure vote, blaming the Democrats and the Eisenhower Republicans. The *Tribune* wrote that Eisenhower's support of the censure vote "clearly revealed" President Eisenhower's "ineptitude as a political leader." It stated that Eisenhower failed to "influence Mr. McCarthy for his own good and that of the country."[106] The *San Francisco Examiner* predicted that many senators who supported the censure would inevitably have second thoughts. It stated that the actions of the U.S. Senate had "whittled the prestige of the Senate to a modern day low." Further, it described the act of censure as "politically misguided" and called the senators' act of voting in favor a "spasm of cowardice."[107]

POSTCENSURE

The censure of Senator McCarthy effectively ended the junior senator's extensive coverage by the press. Historians and McCarthy biographers have no disagreement about that point. Robert Griffith, in *The Politics of Fear: Joseph R. McCarthy and the Senate*, wrote, "The press, long an unwilling instrument of McCarthy's campaigns, now entered a tacit compact to ignore him."[108] Richard Rovere, in *Senator Joe McCarthy*, observed that upon the announcement of a McCarthy speech, reporters would leave for lunch or gossip instead of listening. Rovere stated that "handouts from McCarthy's office would land in the wastebaskets, and the group that had called itself 'the goon squad' was disbanded."[109] David Oshinsky, in *A Conspiracy So Immense: The World of Joe McCarthy*, surmised that more "heartbreaking" for McCarthy than being censured was being ignored by the press. Oshinsky claimed that McCarthy would "rather be hated than ignored."[110] And, Oshinsky cited an episode where McCarthy delivered an "eloquent" speech about the GOP's campaign pledge to liberate "captive peoples." Despite assurances of full coverage from William S. White of the *New York Times*, the story ended up only a paragraph on page 40.[111]

Less than one week after the censure, the *Monitor* analyzed what the Senate's action meant for both the long and the short term. An editorial asked the Senate "amid a widespread rumble of satisfaction over the censure vote" to realize the "disapproval of one action." The *Monitor*, referring to the decision to drop the charge that McCarthy abused General Zwicker, expressed disappointment that the Senate denounced McCarthy's treatment of its own investigating subcommittees, but "seems to dodge completely the question of the Senate's obligation to maintain the rights of individuals." It admonished the senators for putting themselves in "the ugly position of defending themselves but leaving ordinary citizens undefended against their own agents' abuse."[112] An editorial three days later called the censure action against McCarthy "by no means a complete job." It called for "new approaches" by investigating committees, particularly in protecting individual rights. The *Monitor* wrote that Congressional inquiries into Communism should alert the public to the dangers but not try to duplicate the FBI's work. This "educational task," the *Monitor* continued, must be carried out "carefully, honestly, and effectively with genuine information rather than by flash-in-the-pan headlines designed chiefly to promote personal or partisan ends."[113]

Columnist Joseph C. Harsch explored (in a three-part series, "Mr. Eisenhower and His Party") what the McCarthy censure meant to the Eisenhower administration. Harsch stated "the great political question in Washington is whether President Eisenhower will now assume active leadership of his own political party and attempt to lead it vigorously and positively away from the opposition of his program inside the Republican Party."[114] Harsch answered his own question—at least in part. He concluded that the inside word from the White House was that the President "intends to seize the political as well as the foreign policy initiative: that he intends to go over from a passive to a positive political role." Harsch cited Eisenhower's congratulations to Senator Watkins for his handling of the censure hearings as "the first move" toward more active leadership.[115]

The declaration by Griffith, Rovere, Oshinsky, and other historians and McCarthy biographers that the press largely ignored the Senator after the censure certainly held true at the *Monitor*. McCarthy was mentioned in conjunction with speculation about Eisenhower's possible new "power," but other than that the newspaper had little to print about the discredited Senator from Wisconsin.

MCCARTHY'S DEATH

About three years after Joseph R. McCarthy lost his "power" in Washington, he was admitted to the Bethesda Naval Center Hospital in Maryland. He died May 2, 1957, largely from liver failure due to complications related to alcoholism.[116] The *Monitor*'s Washington News Bureau Chief, William H. Stringer, wrote that McCarthy's passing left "an important gap" in the far rightwing of the Republican Party, but Stringer admitted that the junior senator in recent years had "exerted little political power." Stringer

1954: McCarthy's Demise 137

recounted some events of McCarthy's notorious career, but concluded that "he never recovered politically from this censure by his peers."[117] Joseph C. Harsch attempted to put McCarthy's career in perspective with that of other similar men in United States' history. He called McCarthy's reign "not an isolated phenomenon" and listed Thaddeus Stevens (who tried to impeach President Johnson), Bishop James Cannon, Jr. (who engineered the campaign against Al Smith for President in 1928), and Huey P. Long (one of the "great rabble rousers of all time"), as sharing similarities to McCarthy. Harsch concluded that the only protection against McCarthy and the others was "the maturity and common sense of the citizenry."[118] However, other than these two brief mentions of McCarthy's passing (without any hint of banner headlines), the *Monitor* did not afford much coverage.

This was in stark contrast to the *New York Times*. On May 3, the *Times* ran a front page story about his death as well as other stories covering nearly all of pages 14 and 15. On May 4, the *Times* carried a story about the Senate's plan to honor McCarthy, along with a reprinting of comments from newspapers throughout the country about the Senator's death; this covered all of page 12. On May 5, McCarthy's death received mention in the "Week in Review" section, and in a column by Arthur Krock. Clearly, in devoting the space it did to McCarthy's death, the *Times* saw the Senator as a major figure in American history. Yet with all the space devoted to the Senator's passing, Arthur Krock could only conclude that "his death culminated a personal tragedy too near for present sound analysis."[119]

Many "rabid" McCarthy supporters sought to blame the Senator's opponents for his demise. The *Chicago Tribune* and others claimed that McCarthy had been "A Valiant Fighter" and that "The White House palace guard plotted his ruin." The *Tribune* argued that "No man in public life was ever persecuted and maligned because of his beliefs as was Sen. McCarthy."[120] The *San Francisco Examiner* labeled McCarthy a "Valiant Warrior" whose enemies "sought to pervert and disgrace his motives." The *Examiner* simply stated that "His country has lost a champion of liberty."[121] William Randolph Hearst, Jr., in an "Editor's Report," called charges of demagoguery "completely unfounded," and he suggested that the best replacement for the deceased Senator would be McCarthy's wife, Jean.[122]

A COMMUNIST AT THE *MONITOR*?

More than 40 years after the McCarthy era, startling new evidence surfaced about one of the *Monitor*'s most prized reporters, Edmund Stevens. Stevens won the newspaper's first Pulitzer Prize in 1950, and served as a foreign correspondent for decades with the *Monitor* (and other news organizations). Only once during the McCarthy era was any question raised publicly about Stevens' loyalty to the United States, and that was a case of mistaken identity.

It was reported in some newspapers that Stevens had strongly "assailed" President Harry S. Truman calling him a "warmonger."[123] Even though the Stevens so identified was "Frank," who was not one of the newspaper's correspondents, *Monitor* editor Erwin D. Canham decided to prevent any misunderstanding. Canham wrote that the public should not confuse the *Monitor*'s Pulitzer Prize–winning Edmund Stevens with Frank Stevens. Canham admitted that while Frank Stevens submitted pieces to the *Monitor* in the 1930s and some were published, Frank Stevens was never a member of the newspaper staff.[124] Canham wrote in his history of the *Monitor* that Frank Stevens again offered his services to the newspaper in 1950—claiming he had written for Reuters, the United Press, and others—but when the copy arrived it was procommunist and never printed.[125] Essentially, the controversy ended in 1950—until 1995.

With the Soviet Union's collapse and the opening of many archives that had been sealed for decades, historians expected to find a "treasure trove" of information about Russian purges; but they also found information about the American Communist Party (CPUSA). A book, published by Yale University and based on the newly released documents of the old Soviet Union, titled *The Secret World of American Communism*, confirmed what many conservatives had argued for years—namely that the American Communist Party was funded by the Soviets, that there were covert operations in the United States, and that "some prominent Americans and journalists aided the Communist espionage effort." Surprisingly, Edmund Stevens—one of the *Monitor*'s most distinguished correspondents—was identified as a Communist.[126]

The chronology (in a nutshell) from the 1995 book was as follows. Edmund Stevens traveled to the Soviet Union in 1934, and, one year after arriving, married a Soviet citizen. Stevens wrote for the American-Russian Chamber of Commerce and worked part-time for several British papers and magazines. The book claimed suspicions about Stevens' connections in the Kremlin surfaced at about this time because he purchased a "luxuriously equipped log cabin," which was an "unusual privilege granted to only a handful of foreigners." In 1939, Stevens returned to the United States with his wife, which the authors of the book claimed was another "unusual" event because Stalin "rarely" permitted Russians to leave the country. The *Christian Science Monitor* hired Stevens as a war correspondent in 1942, and for part of the year he served in a temporary position as an advisor to the United States on Soviet matters. After taking "lengthy tours" in Russia (1943–1944), he published *Russia Is No Riddle*, a book that was favorable toward Stalin and Russia and defended the Nazi-Soviet Pact of 1939. In

1946, he returned to Russia as the resident correspondent for the *Monitor* and in 1949, left Moscow and published a book, *This Is Russia Uncensored*, which won the Pulitzer Prize. It included a harsh critique of Stalin. After Stalin's death, Stevens returned to the Soviet Union and worked as a Moscow correspondent until his death in 1992 (though he resigned from the *Monitor* in 1955).[127] *The Secret World of American Communism* quoted fellow correspondent Whitman Bassow: "Stevens concealed his membership in the CPUSA throughout his journalistic career. Whether Stevens had an understanding with the Soviet government may never be known, but these documents [pages 81–82 in book] greatly strengthen the suspicion that he was not a neutral journalist."[128]

When the book was released, the *Monitor* reacted to the revelations with two news stories and one message from the editor. The *Monitor* explained that there was no evidence in the documents uncovered that Stevens ever did any espionage work for the Soviets, but documentation did confirm that Stevens joined the Young Communist League in 1931 and the American Communist Party in 1938. The newspaper reported that from time to time it tried to follow up on rumors and suspicions that Stevens was a Communist, but never found any evidence. Suspicions were raised, the *Monitor* article continued, when Stevens was allowed to "own a three-story mansion in the city [Moscow]."[129]

David T. Cook, editor of the *Monitor*, issued an official reaction from the newspaper. He stated that if the information about Stevens belonging to the Communist Party proved true "the fact should not have been hidden" from the *Monitor*. Cook explained how revered Stevens was in journalistic circles, pointing out that Stevens reported for *Look*, *Time*, *Newsday*, *The Saturday Evening Post*, NBC Radio, and *The Times* of London after leaving the *Monitor*. Cook wrote that Stevens' son and widow both contended that if he joined the Communist Party it was to obtain visas for his Russian-born wife and son to escape Stalin's purges. In 1963, Stevens and the *Monitor* talked about his rejoining the staff, and even with the rumors persisting through the years that he was a Communist, Cook claimed U.S. government officials reported that Stevens was not a Communist. Nevertheless, Cook issued an apology to the newspaper's readers: "The *Monitor* deeply regrets that, if the newly disclosed documents are correct, a valued colleague withheld information from his editors and readers."[130]

On April 28, 1995, the *Monitor* published a letter from Stevens' son defending his father and criticizing the newspaper's handling of the latest information. Edmund Stevens, Jr. stated that if his father had been accused of being a Communist while he was alive, he would have reacted with a "wry smile" because the very idea "would have seemed too outrageous to deserve a more elaborate answer." The younger Stevens claimed his father was "kicked out" of Russia in 1949, and his reporting about the Soviet Union "repeatedly got him into hot water with Soviet authorities." Stevens reasoned that his father may have claimed to be a Communist in an attempt to "extract my mother and me from Soviet clutches" in 1938, and, Stevens said, no one can think wrongly of him for doing so.[131]

A second letter, from a disgruntled reader, criticized the *Monitor* for apologizing for "whatever political affiliation a former or current employee had or has" calling the act "frightening." Steven S. Rothblatt of Los Angeles stated that everyone has political views, but "Either Mr. Stevens was an excellent journalist or he wasn't."[132]

The Edmund Stevens case provides an interesting epilogue to the McCarthy era at the *Monitor*. The *Monitor's* reaction to the revelations about Stevens revealed that the newspaper still preferred to err on the side of caution. And, even though consistently critical of McCarthy's methods from 1950 through 1954, and apparently less reactionary against its personnel during the era than other newspapers, the *Monitor* felt obligated to attempt to uphold the integrity and the fairness of its news coverage. But the *Monitor*, in apologizing for a Pulitzer Prize–winning writer's actions nearly 50 years ago, appeared timid and overly sensitive, as if the Cold War and the McCarthy era still existed in 1995.

NOTES

1. Thomas C. Reeves, *The Life and Times of Joe McCarthy: A Biography* (New York: Stein & Day Publishers, 1982), 538.
2. Robert Griffith, *The Politics of Fear: Joseph R. McCarthy and the Senate*, 2d ed. (Amherst, Mass.: UMass Press, 1987), 246–247.
3. Edwin R. Bayley, *Joe McCarthy and the Press* (Madison, Wisc.: University of Wisconsin Press, 1981), 187.
4. David M. Oshinsky, *A Conspiracy So Immense: The World of Joe McCarthy* (New York: The Free Press, 1983), 373.
5. Ibid, 385–386.
6. Ibid, 388.
7. Ibid, 391.
8. Editorial, "Zwicker Case: Two Issues," *Christian Science Monitor*, 24 February 1954, 18.
9. Editorial, "A Basic Struggle Continues," *Christian Science Monitor*, 27 February 1954, 18.
10. Oshinsky, *A Conspiracy So Immense*, 393.
11. Richard L. Strout, "Nixon to Air GOP Strategy," *Christian Science Monitor*, 9 March 1954, 1.
12. Editorial, "Answers Plus Action," *Christian Science Monitor*, 16 March 1954, 16.

13. Editorial, "Signs of Awakening at Last?," *Milwaukee Journal*, 11 March 1954, 24.

14. Quoted in "Rating McCarthy," *Newsweek*, 22 March 1954, 26.

15. Robert J. Donovan and Ray Scherer, *Unsilent Revolution: TV News and American Public Life, 1948–1991* (Cambridge, England: University of Cambridge Press, 1992), 23.

16. For other shows related, refer to a book by Thomas Rosteck titled, See It Now *Confronts McCarthyism: Television Documentary and the Politics of Representation* (Tuscaloosa and London: University of Alabama Press, 1994).

17. Stanley Cloud and Lynne Olson, *The Murrow Boys: Pioneers on the Front Line of Broadcast Journalism* (Boston and New York: Houghton Mifflin Company, 1996), 307.

18. Quoted in Oshinsky, *A Conspiracy So Immense*, 399.

19. "Murrow Attack Stirs Response," *Christian Science Monitor*, 10 March 1954, 1. Mary Hornaday, "Murrow Gets 20–1 Response over Senator," *Christian Science Monitor*, 10 March 1954, 14.

20. Quoted in Griffith, *The Politics of Fear*, 273.

21. William H. Stringer, "The Washington Scene: Turn of the Tide," *Christian Science Monitor*, 15 March 1954, 1.

22. "McCarthy Studies Press 'Infiltration,'" *Editor and Publisher*, 27 March 1954, 13.

23. Robert U. Brown, "Shop Talk at Thirty," *Editor and Publisher*, 3 April 1954, 64.

24. Editorial, "He Who Criticizes McCarthy Is Target for Violent Revenge," *Milwaukee Journal*, 7 April 1954, 26.

25. Quoted in "Hints Reds Delayed U.S. H-Bomb Work: Charges Murrow Aped Communists," *Chicago Tribune*, 7 April 1954, 1, 4.

26. "Five Men Do 13-Part Profile on McCarthy," *Editor and Publisher*, 3 April 1954, 8.

27. Oshinsky, *A Conspiracy So Immense*, 413.

28. "Washington Letter," *Christian Science Monitor*, 27 March 1954, 13.

29. William H. Stringer, "General Says McCarthy Aide Used Pressure Tactics on Him: Senate Probe Opens," *Christian Science Monitor*, 22 April 1954, 1.

30. Editorial, "As the Hearings Begin," *Christian Science Monitor*, 22 April 1954, 20.

31. Joseph C. Harsch, "State of the Nations: Senator McCarthy Stands Trial," *Christian Science Monitor*, 22 April 1954, 1.

32. Richard L. Strout, "Stevens Says Army Took Transcripts of Telephone Calls from McCarthy," *Christian Science Monitor*, 23 April 1954, 1.

33. "Washington Letter," *Christian Science Monitor*, 24 April 1954, 13.

34. Editorial, "A Good Start," *Christian Science Monitor*, 24 April 1954, 22.

35. Strout [Richard L. Strout] to Strout [Himself], 26 April 1954, Richard L. Strout Papers, Weston, Mass.

36. r [Richard L. Strout] to Family, 29 April 1954, Richard L. Strout Papers, Weston, Mass.

37. Oshinsky, *A Conspiracy So Immense*, 428.

38. Richard L. Strout, "Schine Picture Rocks Hearing," *Christian Science Monitor*, 27 April 1954, 1. Richard L. Strout, "Shrunk Photo Explained," *Christian Science Monitor*, 30 April 1954, 1.

39. Editorial, "Mr. Stevens' Handicaps," *Christian Science Monitor*, 29 April 1954, 20. The photo was used in Butler's successful campaign to unseat Tydings and has been referred to previously.

40. Charles E. Potter, *Days of Shame* (New York: Coward-McCann, 1965), 183.

41. Joseph C. Harsch, "State of the Nations: On Balancing the News," *Christian Science Monitor*, 30 April 1954, 1.

42. "Washington Letter," *Christian Science Monitor*, 1 May 1954, 19.

43. Harsch, "Balancing the News," 1.

44. Richard L. Strout, "The Price of Cooperation: An Intimate Message from Washington," *Christian Science Monitor*, 1 May 1954, 22.

45. Richard L. Strout, "Duel Effect: McCarthy Star Dims?," *Christian Science Monitor*, 7 May 1954, 1.

46. Richard L. Strout, "GOP Strives to Cut Quiz," *Christian Science Monitor*, 10 May 1954, 1.

47. Oshinsky, *A Conspiracy So Immense*, 436.

48. Editorial, "In the Open," *Christian Science Monitor*, 13 May 1954, 22.

49. Editorial, "Value of McCarthy-Army Hearings Worth the Disgrace," *Milwaukee Journal*, 9 May 1954, Sec. V, 2.

50. Roland Sawyer, "McCarthy Again Defies Authority of President," *Christian Science Monitor*, 27 May 1954, 1.

51. Editorial, "Challenge to the Constitution," *Christian Science Monitor*, 29 May 1954, 20.

52. Ibid.

53. Editorial, "Cooperation? Surely," *Christian Science Monitor*, 5 June 1954, 22.

54. Erwin D. Canham, "Beyond the Sound and Fury: Down the Middle of the Road," *Christian Science Monitor*, 9 June 1954, 18.

55. Editorial, "To Combat Confusion," *Christian Science Monitor*," 11 June 1954, 22.

56. Editorial, "In the Middle," *Editor and Publisher*, 8 May 1954, 42.

57. "McCarthy Tones Down Attack on *New York Post*," *Editor and Publisher*, 29 May 1954, 13.

58. Editorial, "Disgraceful," *Editor and Publisher*, 29 May 1954, 30.

59. Quoted in Oshinsky, *A Conspiracy So Immense*, 463.

60. Roland Sawyer, "McCarthy Contradicts Stevens," *Christian Science Monitor*, 10 June 1954, 1.

61. W. H. Lawrence, "Welch Assails M'Carthy's 'Cruelty' and 'Recklessness' in Attack on Aide; Senator, on Stand, Tells of Red Hunt: Exchange Bitter—Counsel Near Tears as Crowd Applauds him at Finish," *New York Times*, 10 June 1954, 1.

62. "McCarthy Takes Stand after Hot Row with Welch: Army Lawyer in Tears," *San Francisco Examiner*, 10 June 1954, 1.

63. Willard Edwards, "Traces Path of Conspiracy by Reds in U.S.: Tells of Peril to Whole World," *Chicago Tribune*, 10 June 1954, 1.

64. Oshinsky, *A Conspiracy So Immense*," 470. "Hearing Piles Up Mass of Figures," *Christian Science Monitor*, 18 June 1954, 1, displays different figures. It claims there were over 7,000 pages of testimony, but only 30 witnesses. And, out of the 36 days of testimony, Secretary of the Army Robert T. Stevens was on the stand for "all or part" of 15 days.

65. Oshinsky, *A Conspiracy So Immense*, 464.

66. Roland Sawyer, "Nation Watches Committee: Senators Seek Verdict," *Christian Science Monitor*, 18 June 1954, 1.

67. Editorial, "Review—Look Ahead," *Christian Science Monitor*, 19 July 1954, 18.

68. Joseph C. Harsch, "State of the Nations: Situation Report—McCarthy Front," *Christian Science Monitor*, 20 July 1954, 1.

69. "Army-McCarthy: Clouded Verdict," *Newsweek*, 28 June 1954, 20.

70. Editorial, "Censure by Committee," *Christian Science Monitor*, 22 July 1954, 18.

71. Reeves, *The Life and Times of Joe McCarthy*, 647.

72. Robert M. Hallett, "Results of McCarthy Investigations into Communist Activities Analyzed," *Christian Science Monitor*, 24 August 1954, 3.

73. Ibid. Robert M. Hallett, "McCarthy Try Fails to Prove 'Voice' Red," *Christian Science Monitor*, 25 August 1954, 14. Robert M. Hallett, "Army Probe Began with Little Fanfare," *Christian Science Monitor*, 26 August 1954, 3.

74. Robert M. Hallatt, "GE Hails Record in McCarthy Probe," *Christian Science Monitor*, 27 August 1954, 3.

75. Griffith, *The Politics of Fear*, 273.

76. Oshinsky, *A Conspiracy So Immense*, 451.

77. Griffith, *The Politics of Fear*, 271.

78. Editorial, "Contempt of the Senate," *Christian Science Monitor*, 17 June 1954, 18.

79. Quoted in Oshinsky, *A Conspiracy So Immense*, 474.

80. William H. Stringer, "Nixon Picks M'Carthy 'Jury,'" *Christian Science Monitor*, 5 August 1954, 1. Griffith, *The Politics of Fear*, 295.

81. William H. Stringer, "McCarthy 'Jury' Maps Action," *Christian Science Monitor*, 6 August 1954, 1.

82. Richard L. Strout, "Senate Begins Debate on M'Carthy Censure," *Christian Science Monitor*, 30 July 1954, 1.

83. Richard L. Strout, "Senate Tense in Move to Censure McCarthy," *Christian Science Monitor*, 31 July 1954, 1.

84. Editorial, "Investigating McCarthy," *New York Times*, 7 August 1954, 12c.

85. Editorial, "Farce Ended," *San Francisco Examiner*, 5 August 1954, 22.

86. "McCarthy and TV," *Editor and Publisher*, 14 August 1954, 38.

87. "TV, or Not," *Editor and Publisher*, 11 September 1954, 40.

88. Oshinsky, *A Conspiracy So Immense*, 477.

89. Richard L. Strout, "Decorum of McCarthy Hearing Startles Washington," *Christian Science Monitor*, 7 September 1954, 5.

90. Quoted in "McCarthy Charged with Abusing Press," *Editor and Publisher*, 18 September 1954, 8.

91. Oshinsky, *A Conspiracy So Immense*, 479.
92. "Washington Letter," *Christian Science Monitor*, 11 September 1954, 9.
93. Quoted in Oshinsky, *A Conspiracy So Immense*, 491.
94. Editorial, "That Lynching Bee," *Christian Science Monitor*, 12 November 1954, 22.
95. Editorial, "Compromise?," *Christian Science Monitor*, 16 November 1954, 22.
96. Reeves, *The Life and Times*, 652.
97. Quoted in Reeves, *The Life and Times*, 655.
98. Reeves, *The Life and Times*, 662.
99. Richard L. Strout, "Censure Vote Sets Precedent, Raises U.S. Prestige Abroad," *Christian Science Monitor*, 2 December 1954, 1.
100. r [Richard L. Strout] to Folks, 3 December 1954, Richard L. Strout Papers, Weston, Mass.
101. Editorial, "Standards Upheld," *Christian Science Monitor*, 3 December 1954, 24.
102. Editorial, "Censure," *New York Times*, 3 December 1954, 26.
103. Editorial, "After Censure," *New York Times*, 5 December 1954, 10E.
104. Editorial, "They Led the Fight for Decency," *Milwaukee Journal*, 3 December 1954, 26.
105. Editorial, "The Man They Censured," *Milwaukee Journal*, 5 December 1954, Sec. V, 2.
106. Editorial, "Vote of Censure, *Chicago Tribune*, 3 December 1954, 18H.
107. Editorial, "Joe's Censure," *San Francisco Examiner*, 3 December 1954, 34.
108. Griffith, *The Politics of Fear*, 318.
109. Richard H. Rovere, *Senator Joe McCarthy* (New York: Harcourt Brace Jovanovich, 1959), 239–240.
110. Oshinsky, *A Conspiracy So Immense*, 496.
111. Ibid., 499.
112. Editorial, "To Protect Citizens," *Christian Science Monitor*, 7 December 1954, 20.
113. Editorial, "More Effective Investigating," *Christian Science Monitor*, 10 December 1954, 16B.
114. Joseph C. Harsch, "State of the Nations: Mr. Eisenhower and His Party—Part I," *Christian Science Monitor*, 8 December 1954, 1.
115. Joseph C. Harsch, "State of the Nations: Mr. Eisenhower and His Party—Part III," *Christian Science Monitor*, 10 December 1954, 1.
116. Rovere, *Senator Joe McCarthy*, 246.
117. William H. Stringer," "McCarthy Stirred U.S. with Probes," *Christian Science Monitor*, 3 May 1957, 1.
118. Joseph C. Harsch, "The State of the Nations: The McCarthy Phenomenon," *Christian Science Monitor*, 8 May 1957, 1.
119. Arthur Krock, "M'Carthy's Influence an Uncertain Factor," *New York Times*, 5 May 1957, E3.
120. Editorial, "A Valiant Fighter," *Chicago Tribune*, 4 May 1957, 12H.
121. "Valiant Warrior," *San Francisco Examiner*, 3 May 1957, 2.
122. William Randolph Hearst, Jr., "Editor's Report: Nation to Miss Senator McCarthy," *San Francisco Examiner*, 5 May 1957, 1, 2.

1954: McCarthy's Demise

123. "U.S. Writer Assailing Truman Not Member of *Monitor* Staff," *Christian Science Monitor*, 16 July 1950, 3.

124. Erwin Canham, "Editor Replies," *Christian Science Monitor*, 16 July 1950, 3.

125. Erwin D. Canham, *Commitment to Freedom: The Story of the Christian Science Monitor* (Boston: Houghton Mifflin Co., 1958), 344.

126. Ron Scherer, "Soviet Archives Detail How U.S. Communists Aided USSR," *Christian Science Monitor*, 11 April 1995, 1.

127. Harvey Klehr, John Earl Haynes, and Frididrikh Igorevich Firsov, *The Secret World of American Communism* (New Haven and London: Yale University Press, 1995), 299.

128. Quoted in Klehr, Haynes, and Firsov, *The Secret World*, 300.

129. Ron Scherer, "Book Links Winner of 1950 Pulitzer Prize to Communist Party," *Christian Science Monitor*, 11 April 1995, 3.

130. David T. Cook, "From the Editor," *Christian Science Monitor*, 11 April 1995, 20.

131. Edmund Stevens, Jr., to editor, "In Defense of My Father's Political Ties," *Christian Science Monitor*, 28 April 1995, 19.

132. Steven S. Rothblatt, to editor, "No Political Affiliation Needed," *Christian Science Monitor*, 28 April 1995, 19.

6

The Legacy: The *Christian Science Monitor* and Joseph R. McCarthy

An extensive review of the *Monitor*'s editorials, columns, and news articles about McCarthy suggests that had all media outlets been as thorough and fair in reporting, and as outspoken yet responsible in criticism, perhaps the public would have been better informed about McCarthy, and therefore better able to judge McCarthy's actions earlier. The *Monitor* was not perfect in its handling of McCarthy, as reflected in some of its internal debates. But, judging from the other newspapers reviewed (*New York Times*, *Milwaukee Journal*, *Chicago Times*, and *San Francisco Examiner*) and secondary sources (such as Bayley, Aronson, and Tuck's books and Deaver's dissertation), the *Monitor* fares well. And in response to those who believe that the important voices of the press abdicated responsibility in cowering to McCarthy, the research on the *Monitor* suggests otherwise. Here was a conservative newspaper, a paper that repeatedly endorsed Republicans for President, yet it consistently over a five-year period attacked McCarthy's methods. True, the newspaper buckled under the pressure of McCarthyism from time to time—the suspension of Strout from covering the Senator and removing the term "McCarthyism" from use unless in direct quotations—but nearly all prestigious and popular press newspapers and other media also wavered at one time or another. And, many are still considered courageous for their actions. For example, the *New York Times* fired several employees with Communist ties, and Edward R. Murrow's CBS show *See It Now* came late in the McCarthy era, probably following the change in public opinion rather than leading it.

If Edwin R. Bayley is correct that those who criticized McCarthy when it counted were courageous (before the press's "wolf pack descent," which started sometime *after* the 1952 election and early 1953)[1] then the *Monitor* must be considered among that group. It was not until late 1952 and early 1953, that repercussions from McCarthy's book (released in mid-1952) caused caution at the *Monitor*, yet that caution did not stop the newspaper from criticizing McCarthy's methods. The newspaper already had spent nearly three years "when it mattered" criticizing McCarthy and his effects on the United States internally and abroad.[2] Bayley concluded that the "majority of American editors took no stand at all, expressed no opinion" for or against McCarthy, during a time in our history when "the editorial page was the principal source of guidance to the understanding of news."[3] Clearly the *Monitor* was not in Bayley's "majority."

The *Monitor* was an early and consistent critic of Joseph R. McCarthy and his methods, but never jumped on the bandwagon to keep up with the competition. Immediately following Senator Joseph R. McCarthy's Lincoln Day speech, the *Monitor*, by providing limited coverage, in a sense, dismissed the importance of his allegations against the State Department. A February 20, 1950 McCarthy speech which received widespread coverage in many prestigious and popular press newspapers and has been written about extensively in histories and McCarthy biographies, received no comment in *Monitor* editorials, and earned no greater than a short news story on page 17. However, when McCarthy's suspicions about Communist infiltration in the State Department received congressional attention, the *Monitor* quickly covered and commented about the situation.

Its first editorial about McCarthy, on March 11, 1950, set the tone for the next five years of editorials—it denounced the smearing of individuals in the name of cleansing the government of Communists, and argued that the junior senator's methods would destroy mutual trust, which was not the answer to rooting out Communists in government. The editorials strictly adhered to Mrs. Eddy's original vision for the newspaper—namely to "injure no man, but to bless all mankind." There were no personal attacks against McCarthy; the *Monitor* criticized the Senator's actions through carefully crafted logic.

By March 30, the *Monitor*, though always quick to insist that eliminating Communists from the government was important, launched a major effort to inform its readers about McCarthy. Two editorials, an editorial cartoon, and an "Intimate Message from Washington" all focused on the unfair methods McCarthy employed, irresponsibility by the press in providing sensationalized headlines and stories about McCarthy's reckless charges, and McCarthy's abuse of senatorial immunity. Those themes recurred throughout the nearly five years of editorials and columns about McCarthy. And emerging not long after these themes were developed was the idea that the junior senator was destroying the United States' standing in the world. Richard L. Strout, one of the resident "historians" at the *Monitor* (along with Joseph C. Harsch), wrote that something rare was occurring regarding foreign policy—the lack of a unified voice emanating from Washington.

The *Monitor*'s criticism of McCarthy did not waver in 1951. The newspaper called for an independent commission to handle the task of ridding the government of Communists. The *Monitor* objected to McCarthy's ruthless attack on General George Catlett Marshall's patriotism and approved of President Truman's decision to order General MacArthur home from the Far East because MacArthur's opinion about what should be done in China (bomb bases in Manchuria) was contrary to the President's. Meanwhile, McCarthy and many right-wing newspapers severely criticized Truman, and some even called for his impeachment.

By the 1952 Presidential election, editorials repeatedly expressed wariness with the reactionary and isolationist wing of the Republican Party, yet the *Monitor* endorsed Eisenhower, the Republican nominee. And after the General won easily, the *Monitor* cautioned against giving McCarthy credit for Republican wins (many pundits lauded McCarthy's display of power), suggesting that many candidates actually won on Eisenhower's coattails. With the endorsement of Eisenhower, the *Monitor* supported virtually every decision the new President made (related to controversies concerning McCarthy and the Cold War), and often credited him with holding the Republican Party together. When the Eisenhower administration seemingly backed down from initial criticism of McCarthy for "negotiating" with Greek ship owners about stopping trade with China in 1953, the *Monitor* viewed the General's actions in a positive light, citing "Ike's" talent for teamwork in stopping further disagreements between administration officials and McCarthy. Other newspapers viewed the President's action as appeasing McCarthy, showing weakness by the President, which may have been closer to the truth.

When McCarthy attacked the Voice of America (VOA) in February 1953, not only did the *Monitor* write about the vital service the Voice provided, but for the rest of the year, it published excerpts from VOA broadcasts to allow readers to decide its value for themselves. And by 1954, the *Monitor* and its columnists were relentless in their criticism. Whether it was patting Edward R. Murrow on the back for exposing McCarthy to a national television audience, commenting about how McCarthy hurt himself during the Army-McCarthy hearings, or noting the courageousness of the elderly statesmen from Vermont, Ralph Flanders, in standing up to McCarthy, the *Monitor* did not wane in its denunciation of McCarthy's methods.

From the *Monitor*'s original editorial in March 1950, until McCarthy's censure in December 1954, there was a steady, yet thoughtful, stream of criticism against McCarthy's methods, tempered with the proviso that the newspaper was empathically anticommunist. The chief concerns of the *Monitor* and its columnists were about the methods McCarthy employed to remove Communists-in-government, and about his damaging the United States at home and abroad.

What also emerged from the review of *Monitor* editorials and columns was a pattern where the newspaper's columnists took stronger stands—and used stronger language—in criticizing McCarthy than did the editorials. This may not seem remarkable on the surface, but it is worth noting. The Mother Church Board of Directors tightly controlled the *Monitor*, and was determined to present a unified voice throughout its editorials and columns. Yet, the Directors allowed stronger language to be used in columns and did not stop some columnists from criticizing McCarthy more frequently than in the editorials.

Monitor coverage of the Tydings subcommittee report was a prime example of the newspaper's columnists taking a stronger stand than the editorials. A *Monitor* editorial conceded that the Tydings report was born of partisanship. It also, in the first of what would be many pleas over nearly five years, called for a nonpartisan or independent commission to be named to carry out loyalty investigations. Meanwhile, columnists Strout and Harsch focused on the volatile language of the report. Strout labeled it a strong denunciation of McCarthy and his methods, while Harsch characterized the Senator's actions as "medievalism" in the 20th century.

Another illustration came in 1951, after the Gillette subcommittee issued its report about the 1950 Senate campaign of Republican John M. Butler of Maryland, who (with the assistance of McCarthy's staff) defeated Democrat Millard Tydings. Strout wrote that the report effectively censured the Butler campaign (and indirectly McCarthy), while an editorial lamented that people were not surprised with the unscrupulous tactics, believing all elections were corrupt.

News stories and columns by Richard L. Strout, Joseph C. Harsch, and Neal Stanford in December 1953 repeatedly reported a widening breach between Eisenhower and the right wing of the Republican Party—including specifically McCarthy. However, in another example of differences between *Monitor* columnists and editorials, an editorial conceded a division existed about foreign policy, but contended it would not necessarily lead to a split of Republicans. Still another example came in early 1954. President Eisenhower named Vice President Richard M. Nixon to respond to a speech by Democrat Adlai Stevenson. Stevenson criticized the Republican administration for, among other things, its tolerance of "McCarthyism." The

Monitor applauded the selection of Nixon for the rebuttal, which effectively prevented McCarthy from grabbing the spotlight on the issue. And after the Vice President's speech, a *Monitor* editorial stated that Nixon's criticism of McCarthy (without naming names) was appropriate, while the speech's larger theme of unity brought Americans together rather than divided them. Several days earlier, Harsch viewed Eisenhower's naming of Nixon as part of a bigger picture of events demonstrating that the President finally realized he was in a "struggle for the succession to political powers in the United States." Harsch characterized the "struggle" as "not unlike the struggle for succession which shook the Soviet realm after the passing of Stalin."[4] The *Monitor* and one of its highest profile columnists did not disagree, but clearly Harsch expressed a much stronger reaction to the President's actions.

Some interoffice memos reviewed for this study indicated grumbling and dissatisfaction by reporters and columnists about the Directors not allowing certain views to be expressed. For instance, some reporters complained that columns and news stories favorable toward 1952 Democrat Presidential candidate Adlai Stevenson were not printed (or were edited severely) because the newspaper endorsed Eisenhower, a Republican. But overall, during the McCarthy era, the *Monitor*'s columns and news stories did not seem muted. The *Monitor* consistently criticized McCarthy's methods while reiterating the newspaper's belief that the Communists-in-government issue was serious and needed to be dealt with in a fair manner.

The *Monitor*'s coverage and opinion about McCarthy showed courage yet restraint compared to other newspapers. The newspaper's news stories about McCarthy were characterized by the paper's dedication to presenting rebuttals to McCarthy just as prominently as his charges. The *Monitor* also made a great effort to put events and issues in proper perspective.

In many books written about that era, the overriding criticism was that too many newspapers took McCarthy's charges, created sensationalized headlines, and never gave those implicated equal treatment in rebuttal. The *Monitor* does not fit that description. For instance, during the Tydings investigation in 1950, State Department employees and others who were implicated as having Communist ties received rebuttals on the front page right next to the charges. Dorothy Kenyan was quoted by Strout characterizing McCarthy as a "liar," and the State Department issued a comment immediately about the integrity of Haldore Hanson. Both had been "smeared" by McCarthy. Another instance occurred during testimony before McCarthy's subcommittee in the investigation of Dr. Owen Lattimore in 1952. Strout painstakingly included responses to the Senator's accusations—not on the next day or buried on a page inside the newspaper—but in the front-page article directly after McCarthy's comments. The rebuttal was also reflected in the headlines. Further, detailed excerpts from Lattimore's statements and testimony were included on a jump page. Perhaps James Reston of the *New York Times*, writing in retrospect, hit on general criticism of newspapers that may apply directly to the *Monitor*. Reston wrote that "many newspapers condemned him on their editorial pages but gave him plenty of space on the front pages, which had more effect on public opinion."[5] McCarthy stories did not automatically appear on the front page of the *Monitor* (as they did in many newspapers), but they appeared prominently enough often enough to question the practice in retrospect.

The *Monitor* and its columnists also attempted periodically to calm the nerves of people who, because of all the publicity surrounding the "red scare," believed that the Communists were about to take over the country. Further, the newspaper reflected critically about the overall press coverage of McCarthy. For example, the newspaper ran a lengthy story in December 1950, revealing how the Communist Party actually had dwindled in numbers since World War II, and therefore was not as big a threat as it had been in the past. Of course, this did not stop the paper from repeatedly reminding its readers that the Communists-in-government issue was serious and needed to be dealt with fairly. Richard L. Strout's *Monitor Magazine* article "Ordeal by Publicity" has been widely quoted in history books and in McCarthy biographies as a thoughtful analysis of how the canon of "objectivity" did not serve the nation well regarding McCarthy. Whether or not "objectivity" is still largely blamed today for McCarthy's success is irrelevant. At least Strout and the *Monitor* were aware almost immediately (May 1950) that McCarthy created a dilemma for the press, and they were seeking to identify the reason with a mind toward a remedy.

There were times during the McCarthy era when the *Monitor* either did not cover with its own reporters or downplayed an event that history viewed as very significant or was played up as very significant in other newspapers at the time. The previously mentioned McCarthy speech on February 20, 1950, which outlined his allegations against the State Department, was one example of a very important story that ended up on page 17 in the *Monitor*. Another example was McCarthy's "most famous" speech, a 60,000-word statement in June 1951 about the alleged ineptness of General Marshall as Secretary of State. Although over half the speech was entered into the record without being read aloud, and virtually none of the oratory was written by McCarthy, a senator criticizing a national hero with such vigor probably warranted the banner headlines the story received in many newspapers. The *Monitor* did not carry details of the speech until two days later, and then the story was banished to page 3. Further, the pretrial histrionics in McCarthy's libel lawsuit against Senator Benton was covered ex-

The *Christian Science Monitor* and Joseph R. McCarthy

tensively by many newspapers, while the *Monitor* relied on Associated Press dispatches.

In 1952, Richard L. Strout (who at the time had covered McCarthy extensively) wrote the initial story about McCarthy's book, *McCarthyism: The Fight for America*. This may be viewed either as very bold and courageous of the *Monitor* or as a blatant breach of ethics. Strout's reputation in Washington, D.C. may have caused the *Monitor* to allow the correspondent to comment on the book, although Strout was mentioned in it. Under the premise of boldness, perhaps the *Monitor* tried to convey to McCarthy that it stood by its veteran reporter. On the other hand, having a reporter comment about a book in which he was mentioned in a negative light was ethically unwise under the journalistic canon of conflict of interest. The book, and other concerns about Strout at the *Monitor* (such as the possibility that Strout writing as the TRB columnist at the *New Republic* violated the "injure no man" policy of the *Monitor*), eventually led to Strout's removal from the McCarthy story for eight to 12 months.

Compared to the harshest critics and the staunchest supporters of McCarthy, clearly the *Monitor*'s opinion was the voice of reason. There were even instances that, when compared to the *New York Times*, at least in editorials, the *Monitor* was milder in language (though many of the same themes existed). But looking at many of the editorial comments made by the *Monitor* during the McCarthy era (with the benefit of the passage of time), there were specific instances when the *Monitor* handled a controversy with better logic and reason than did other newspapers, including the *Times*. After the midterm election in 1950, the *Times'* William S. White expressed the strong belief that nearly all of the McCarthy-backed candidates had won, implying that the junior senator wielded tremendous power. Other newspapers across the country expressed similar views. However, while a *Monitor* editorial conceded that John Butler's defeat of Millard Tydings of Maryland was a major upset, and could be attributed in part to the Tydings subcommittee report criticizing McCarthy, the newspaper mentioned other factors contributing to the defeat, and linked no other Republican victories to McCarthy. Meanwhile, Joseph C. Harsch (the other resident historian at the *Monitor*) labeled the Republican gains normal for a midterm election. The opposition party to the President, the Republican Party in this case, historically gained seats. Harsch's view of the election, very different from that of the *Times* and others, has passed the test of time.

There were several instances when the *Monitor*'s conservative leaning blinded it—with the case of Julius and Ethel Rosenberg a prime example. When the death sentences were handed down in 1951 (after their convictions for conspiracy to commit espionage), a *Monitor* editorial essentially supported the judge's sending a message to the world about threatening

United States' national security. And in 1953, when the Rosenbergs were put to death, the *Monitor* noted the professionalism and lack of "hysteria" and "ferocity" surrounding the event. To make that statement, the newspaper, which prided itself on its world perspective, ignored demonstrations in France and other parts of Europe that compared the U.S. to Nazi Germany and discounted the dissent and demonstrations in America.

Pro-McCarthyite William F. Buckley wrote as late as July 1994, "I swear, nothing McCarthy ever did—and he did many indefensible things—can ever compare with the lengths to which his enemies went and continue to go."[6] The *Monitor*, though always critical of the junior senator's actions, never stooped to name-calling, never intentionally distorted McCarthy's positions, and never sought to make "enemies" with McCarthy or anyone else.[7]

The pressures of McCarthyism affected the *Monitor* in its handling of personnel, yet editorially it remained consistent and largely unchanged during the McCarthy era. Specific individuals at the *Monitor* were affected and some new policies were created to deal with McCarthy and McCarthyism. Those aspects of the "effects" of McCarthyism on the *Monitor* are relatively easy to document. The "effect" of McCarthyism on editorials and the actual news coverage of the newspaper is much harder to document because it is much more subtle.

A Joseph C. Harsch column in 1953, about McCarthy and the Roman Catholic Church, drew raves from many and raised the ire of Catholics (since The First Church of Christ, Scientist, often has been accused of fearing Catholics). Harsch claimed the Roman Catholic Church aided McCarthy and therefore Catholics received preferential treatment concerning loyalty probes. Facts supporting his position were dubious at best. However, because he worked for Christian Scientists he was shielded from any negative effects that might have been felt had he worked for another newspaper. And, ultimately, it did not affect his broadcasting career, either.

Richard L. Strout felt the wrath of McCarthyism by being suspended from covering the Senator for eight to 12 months. But, this was hardly a major hardship because Strout was assigned to cover President Dwight David Eisenhower. Had the documentation of the suspension not been available (in Strout's papers, corroborated by reviewing the articles Strout wrote), the action might have never been detectable. After all, having the White House "beat" is preferred to covering a senator.

During the research for this book, evidence surfaced of an "appeasement" period at the *Monitor*, or perhaps better stated, a period of extreme caution. The fear expressed in memos and personal notes to and from Richard L. Strout, Saville R. Davis, and Roscoe Drummond about Strout's possibly being the TRB columnist at the *New Republic* illustrated that phase at the

Monitor, which extended from late 1952, months after McCarthy's book had been issued, to just after Strout stopped covering McCarthy in April 1953. But if "appeasement" is the proper term to use in describing the period, it was difficult to detect from a review of editorials, columns, and news stories. During the time, the *Monitor* and its columnists expressed support for Dr. Owen Lattimore (just before indictments against him); explored the disagreements between Eisenhower and right-wing Republicans in Congress; supported the "Voice of America" against McCarthy's criticism; criticized McCarthy for trying to suppress the press and intimidate *New York Post* editor James Wechsler; and fought against "book burning" proposed by McCarthy. It is fair to point out, however, that many of these news stories and columns were *not* placed on the front page; McCarthy was in effect relegated to the inside pages. But, was this due to "appeasement" or a move to undermine the publicity-hungry McCarthy? Perhaps it was simply a dispassionate decision regarding the newsworthiness of the stories? There was no way to answer the questions.

The fact that the *Monitor*, at one time, had a screening committee (confirmed by former Far East and London correspondent Henry Hayward and alluded to indirectly in Canham's book) to review stories and columns of reporters or "stringers" suspected of having Communist leanings or sympathies (such as Gunther Stein) showed the caution the newspaper used toward its editorial content and personnel during the McCarthy era. And while this seems paranoid behavior by 1990s standards, it was not unlike other newspapers' actions during the 1950s. The *New York Times* apparently dealt with employees suspected of being Communists in a much harsher fashion than did the *Monitor*. Turner Catledge wrote in his book, *My Life and The Times*, that in 1955, two former Communists who worked for the newspaper were fired and one resigned under pressure. Catledge claimed the three did not cooperate with the *Times* in its internal investigation and therefore the newspaper could not "retain" them.[8] Clearly this incident at the *Times*, just after McCarthy's censure, coupled with incidents at other newspapers show that many papers reacted much more radically toward employees under the threat of McCarthyism than did the *Monitor*.

The *Monitor*, "conservative" by most standards, clearly benefitted from a moderate position. By criticizing McCarthy's actions, but not name-calling, and by thoughtful reporting and analysis based on logic, not sensationalized responses to McCarthy, it set the tone for dealing with internal crises at the newspaper in the same manner. Suspicions by management were raised at times, but fears were dealt with in a more reasonable fashion than at other newspapers. Mrs. Eddy's admonition to the newspaper "to injure no man, but to bless all mankind" provided words of wisdom to live by for the Mother Church Board of Directors, the Christian Science Publishing Society Board of Trustees, and editors, columnists, and reporters for the *Christian Science Monitor*. That wisdom served the *Monitor* well during the McCarthy era.

NOTES

1. Edwin R. Bayley, *Joe McCarthy and the Press* (Madison, Wisc.: University of Wisconsin Press, 1981), 219–220.

2. Ibid., 220.

3. Ibid., 219.

4. Joseph C. Harsch, "State of the Nations: Moment of Decision," *Christian Science Monitor*, 12 March 1954, 1.

5. James Reston, *Deadline: A Memoir* (New York: Random House, 1991), 216.

6. William F. Buckley, Jr. "On the Right: Ed Murrow vs. Joe McCarthy," *National Review*, v. 46, 11 July 1994, 70.

7. Of course, this does not count reporters and columnists from the *Monitor* writing for other publications. As noted earlier, Strout often compared McCarthy to Hitler and others in his TRB column in the *New Republic*.

8. Turner Catledge, *My Life and* The Times (New York, Evanston and London: Harper & Row Publishers, 1971), 233.

SELECTED BIBLIOGRAPHY

BOOKS

Anderson, Jack, and Ronald W. May. *McCarthy: The Man, the Senator, the ISM*. London: Victor Gollancz Ltd., 1953.
Aronson, James. *The Press and the Cold War*. Indianapolis and New York: Bobbs-Merrill Company, 1970.
Barth, Alan. *Government by Investigation*. New York: Viking Press, 1955.
Bayley, Edwin R. *Joe McCarthy and the Press*. Madison, Wisc.: University of Wisconsin Press, 1981.
Blumberg, Nathan B. *One Party Press? Coverage of the 1952 Presidential Campaign in 35 Newspapers*. Lincoln, Nebr.: University of Nebraska Press, 1954.
Brock, Clifton. *Americans for Democratic Action: Its Role in National Politics*. Westport, Conn.: Greenwood Press, 1985.
Buckley, William F., and Brent L. Bozell. *McCarthy and His Enemies: The Record and Its Meaning*. Chicago: Henry Regnery Company, 1954.
Canham, Erwin D. *Commitment to Freedom: The Story of the Christian Science Monitor*. Cambridge, Mass.: Houghton Mifflin Company, 1958.
Caswell, Lucy Shelton, ed. *Guide to Sources in American Journalism History*. New York and Westport, Conn.: Greenwood Press, 1989.
Cater, Douglass. *The Fourth Branch of Government*. Houghton Mifflin Company, 1959.
Catledge, Turner. *My Life and* The Times. New York, Evanston and London: Harper & Row, 1971.
Caute, David. *The Great Fear: The Anti-Communist Purge under Truman and Eisenhower*. New York: Simon & Schuster, 1978.

Cloud, Stanley, and Lynne Olson. *The Murrow Boys: Pioneers on the Front Line of Broadcast Journalism*. Boston and New York: Houghton Mifflin Company, 1996.
Cook, Fred J. *The Nightmare Decade: The Life and Times of Senator Joe McCarthy*. New York: Random House, 1971.
Crosby, Donald F. (S.J.). *God, Church, and Flag: Senator Joseph R. McCarthy and the Catholic Church, 1950–1957*. Chapel Hill, N.C.: University of North Carolina Press, 1978.
Davis, Elmer. *But We Were Born Free*. Indianapolis and New York: Bobbs-Merrill Company, 1954.
De Antonio, Emile, and Daniel Talbot. *Point of Order: A Documentary of the Army-McCarthy Hearings*. New York: W. W. Norton and Company, 1964.
Diggins, John P. *Up from Communism*. New York: Harper & Row, 1975.
Donner, Frank. *The Un-Americans*. New York: Ballantine Books, 1961.
Donovan, Robert J., and Ray Sherer. *Unsilent Revolution: TV News and American Public Life, 1948–1991*. Cambridge, England: University Press, 1992.
Emery, Edwin. *The Press and America: An Interpretative History of the Mass Media*. 3d ed. Englewood Cliffs, N.J.: Prentice-Hall, 1972.
Folkerts, Jean, and Dwight L. Teeter, Jr. *Voices of a Nation*. New York: Macmillan, 1989.
Fried, Richard M. *Men against McCarthy*. New York: Columbia University Press, 1976.
Fried, Richard M. *Nightmare in Red: The McCarthy Era in Perspective*. New York: Oxford University Press, 1990.
Gillon, Steven M. *Politics and Vision: The ADA and American Liberalism, 1947–1985*. New York and Oxford: Oxford University Press, 1987.
Gitlin, Todd. *The Whole World Is Watching; Mass Media in the Making and Unmaking of the New Left*. Berkeley, Los Angeles, London: University of California Press, 1980.
Goldman, Eric F. *The Crucial Decade—And After: America, 1945–1960*. New York: Random House, 1956.
Griffith, Robert. *The Politics of Fear: Joseph R. McCarthy and the Senate*. 2d ed. Amherst, Mass.: University of Massachusetts Press, 1987.
Harsch, Joseph C. *At the Hinge of History: A Reporter's Story*. Athens, Ga.: University of Georgia Press, 1993.
Klehr, Harvey, John Earl Haynes, and Frididrikh Igorevich Firsov. *The Secret World of American Communism*. New Haven and London: Yale University Press, 1995.
Kluger, Richard. *The Paper: The Life and Death of the NewYork Herald Tribune*. New York: Alfred A. Knopf, 1986.
Krieghbaum, Hillier. *Facts in Perspective: The Editorial Page and News Interpretation*. Englewood Cliffs, N.J.: Prentice-Hall, 1956.
Landis, Mark. *Joseph McCarthy: The Politics of Chaos*. London and Toronto: Associated University Press, 1987.
Latham, Earl, ed. *The Communist Controversy in Washington: From the New Deal to McCarthy*. Cambridge, Mass.: Harvard University Press, 1966.
Liebovich, Louis. *The Press and the Origins of the Cold War, 1944–47*. New York and Westport, Conn.: Praeger, 1988.

Selected Bibliography

Luthin, Richard H. *American Demagogues: Twentieth Century*. Boston: Beacon Press, 1954.
Lyons, Louis M., ed. *Reporting the News*. Cambridge, Mass.: The Belknap Press of Harvard University, 1965.
Lyons, Louis M., ed. "Nieman Reports and Nieman Fellowships." *Reporting the News: Selection from* Nieman Reports. New York: Atheneum, 1968.
Matthews, Christopher. *The Rivalry that Shaped Postwar America: Kennedy and Nixon*. New York: Simon & Schuster, 1996.
McCarthy, Joseph. *McCarthyism: The Fight for America*. New York: National Weekly, 1952.
McKerns, Joseph P., ed. *Biographical Dictionary of American Journalists*. New York: Greenwood Press, 1989.
Navasky, Victor S. *Naming Names*. New York: Viking Press, 1980.
Neville, John F. *The Press, The Rosenbergs, and the Cold War*. Westport, Conn.: Praeger, 1995.
Newman, Robert P. *Owen Lattimore and the "Loss" of China*. Berkeley: University of California Press, 1992.
Oshinsky, David M. *A Conspiracy So Immense: The World of Joe McCarthy*. New York: The Free Press, 1983.
Potter, Charles E. *Days of Shame*. New York: Coward-McCann, 1965.
Ralston, Richard E., ed. *Communism: Its Rise and Fall in the 20th Century; From the Pages of the* Christian Science Monitor. Boston: Christian Science Publishing Society, 1991.
Reeves, Thomas C. *The Life and Times of Joe McCarthy*. New York: Stein & Day, 1982.
Reston, James. *The Artillery of the Press*. New York: Harper & Row, 1967.
Reston, James. *Deadline: A Memoir*. New York: Random House, 1991.
Riley, Sam G., ed. *Biographical Dictionary of American Newspaper Columnists*. Westport, Conn. and London: Greenwood Press, 1985.
Rogin, Michael Paul. *The Intellectuals and McCarthy: The Radical Specter*. Cambridge, Mass. and London: The MIT Press, 1967.
Rosteck, Thomas. See It Now *Confronts McCarthyism: Television Documentary and the Politics of Representation*. Tuscaloosa, Ala. and London: University of Alabama Press, 1994.
Rosten, Leo C. *The Washington Correspondents*. New York: Harcourt Brace and Company, 1937.
Rovere, Richard H. *Senator Joe McCarthy*. New York: Harcourt Brace Jovanovich, 1959.
Schrecker, Ellen. *The Age of McCarthyism: A Brief History with Documents*. Boston and New York: Bedford Books of St. Martin Press, 1994.
Strout, Richard L. *TRB: Views and Perspectives on the Presidency*. New York: Macmillan, 1979.
Tuck, Jim. *McCarthyism and New York's Hearst Press: A Study of Roles in the Witch Hunt*. Lanham, N.Y. and London: University Press of America, Inc., 1995.
Wechsler, James A. *The Age of Suspicion*. New York: Random House, 1953.

MAGAZINES AND NEWSPAPER ARTICLES

"Agency Heads Accused of Favoring Catholics." *Church and State: A Monthly Review*, December 1953, 2.
"Are Our Headlines Fair?" *Bulletin of the American Society of Newspaper Editors*, 1 May 1950, 8.
"Army-McCarthy: Clouded Verdict." *Newsweek*, 28 June 1954, 20.
"Barth Asserts Press Is Used for 'Dirty Work.' " *Editor and Publisher*, 10 May 1952, 20.
Bernays, Edward L. "Press and Public Agreed on Deviation from Ideals. Appraisal is made on the basis of Pulitzer-Ouchs-Gibson standards." *Editor and Publisher*, 17 May 1952, 11, 59.
Boylan, James. "Declarations of Independence: A historian reflects on an era in which reporters rose up to challenge—and change—the rules of the game." *Columbia Journalism Review*, November/December 1986, 30–39.
Brown, Robert U. "Editors See No Threat in Communist Indictments." *Editor and Publisher*, 1 September 1951, 7.
Brown, Robert U. "Shop Talk at Thirty." *Editor and Publisher*, 18 November 1950, 72.
Brown, Robert U. "Shop Talk at Thirty." *Editor and Publisher*, 16 February 1952, 72.
Brown, Robert U. "Shop Talk at Thirty." *Editor and Publisher*, 3 April 1954, 64.
Buckley, William F., Jr. "On the Right: Ed Murrow vs. Joe McCarthy." *National Review*, 11 July 1994, 70.
"Canham Attacks Move to Bar Reds from News." *Editor and Publisher*, 19 March 1949, 45.
Chicago Tribune, 1 February 1950–31 December 1954.
Christian Science Monitor, 1 February 1950–31 December 1954.
Davis, Elmer. "News and the Whole Truth." *Atlantic Monthly*, August 1952, 32–38.
"Dick Strout's Two Lives." *New York Times*, 22 April 1990, A24.
Dilliard, Irving."The Press and the Bill of Rights: The Challenge of the Second Lovejoy Lecture." Speech reprinted in *Nieman Reports*, January 1954.
Editorial. "The *Monitor* Bomb." *The Christian Century*, 25 November 1954, 1350–1351.
Editorial. "Dirty Work." *Editor and Publisher*, 17 May 1952, 38.
Editorial. "Disgraceful." *Editor and Publisher*, 29 May 1954, 30.
Editorial. "In The Middle." *Editor and Publisher*, 8 May 1954, 42.
Editorial. "Intimidation." *Editor and Publisher*, 2 February 1952, 28.
Editorial. "Wechsler vs. McCarthy." *Editor and Publisher*, 16 May 1953, 38.
Editorial. "Revival of Bigotry." *The Tablet*, 5 December 1953.
Estabrook, Robert H. "Press Performance in the Campaign." *Nieman Reports*, January 1953, 12.
Estabrook, Robert H. Speech "The Free Man's Color." Reprinted in *Nieman Reports*, April 1951, 24.
"The Fetish of Objectivity." *Time*, 4 May 1953, 49.
"Five Men Do 13-Part Profile on McCarthy." *Editor and Publisher*, 3 April 1954, 8.
Foell, Earl W. "Harding to Reagan with Dick Strout." *Christian Science Monitor*, 22 August 1990, 19.

Selected Bibliography 161

Friendly, Alfred. "McCarthy Revisited: The Role of the Press in a Dark Hour." *Washington Post*, 13 February 1977, C1–C5.
Gilbert, J. J. *"Christian Science Monitor* Charges Exploded by Investigation." *The Pilot*, 9 January 1954, 1–6.
Gould, Louis L. Review of *The Paper's Papers: A Reporter's Journey Through*, by Richard F. Shepard. *Quill*, September 1996, 33.
Hayne, F. Bourn. "What Do Readers Think of the Press?" *Nieman Reports*, October 1952, 20.
"The Hazen Report." *The APME Red Book 1950*, 65, 69–70.
Heath, William H. "Unfair Headline and Story Emphasis." *Bulletin of the American Society of Newspaper Editors*, 1 September 1953, 3.
Hertzberg, Hendrik. "Columnist with a Conscience: Richard L. Strout the Journalist Who Found the Heart of History." *Washington Post*, 21 August 1990, 1 & C1.
Hoyt, E. C. "Unfair Headline and Story Emphasis." *Bulletin of the American Society of Newspaper Editors*, 1 September 1953, 2.
"Hoyt Insists on 'Fair Play' in Staff Memo." *Editor and Publisher*, 28 February 1953, 12.
"INS Editors and Publishers Compile 'Big 10' Stories of '50." *Editor and Publisher*, 6 January 1951, 60.
Kilpatrick, Carroll. "Our Own Grey Eminence: TRB at Eighty." *New Republic*, 18 March 1978, 16, 17.
Lyons, Louis. "Proceedings: 20th Annual Convention of the American Newspaper Guild." 29 June–3 July 1953, 73.
Marvin, John E. "Expressed Editorially: Not Conclusive but Cause for Concern." *Michigan Christian Advocate*, 10 December 1953, 4–5.
"McCarthy." *The AMPE Red Book 1953*, 49–59.
"McCarthy Again." *Newsweek*, 7 January 1952, 16.
"McCarthy Charged with Abusing Press." *Editor and Publisher*, 18 September 1954, 8.
"The McCarthy Headlines." *Bulletin of the American Society of Newspaper Editors*, 1 June 1950, 3.
McCarthy, Mary. "The Menace to Free Journalism in America." *Nieman Reports*, October 1953, 46.
"McCarthy Revisited: The Role of the Press in a Dark Hour." *Washington Post*, 13 February 1977, C1–C5.
"McCarthy Studies Press 'Infiltration.'" *Editor and Publisher*, 27 March 1954, 13.
"McCarthy Tones Down Attack on *New York Post.*" *Editor and Publisher*, 29 May 1954, 13.
"McCarthy and TV." *Editor and Publisher*, 14 August 1954, 38.
Mencher, Melvin. Review of *McCarthy: The Man, the Senator, the ISM*, by Jack Anderson and Ronald W. May. *Nieman Reports*, January 1953, 47.
Milwaukee Journal, 1 February 1950–31 December 1954.
Mitgang, Herbert. Review of *TRB on the Presidency*, by Richard L. Strout. *New York Times Magazine*. 21 October 1979, 63.
New York Times, 1 February 1950–31 December 1954.

"Newspaperman's Newspaper." *Time*, 27 January 1958, 42, 44.
Oakes, John B. "The Dangerous Obligations of a Newspaperman." *Nieman Reports*, October 1953, 6.
"Proceedings." *20th Annual Convention of the American Newspaper Guild*, 29 June–3 July 1953, 73.
"Rating McCarthy." *Newsweek*, 22 March 1954, 26.
"The Real TRB." *Newsweek*, 29 July 1968, 66.
"Richard L. Strout, RIP." *National Review*, 17 September 1990, 18.
Sabine, Gordon A. "McCarthy Abuse Is Text for Dean's Advice." *Editor and Publisher*, 6 June 1953, 59.
San Francisco Examiner, 1 February 1950–31 December 1954.
Scherer, Ron. "Book Links Winner of 1950 Pulitzer Prize to Communist Party." *Christian Science Monitor*, 11 April 1995, 3.
Scherer, Ron. "Soviet Archives Detail How U.S. Communists Aided USSR." *Christian Science Monitor*, 11 April 1995, 1.
Stevens, Edmund, Jr. to editor "In Defense of My Father's Political Ties." *Christian Science Monitor*, 28 April 1995, 19.
"The Stevenson Story." *Newsweek*, 3 November 1952, 30.
Tebbel, John. "Rating the American Newspapers—Part I," *Saturday Review*, 13 May 1961, 59–62.
"TRB Remembered." *New Republic*, 10 December 1984, 64, 65.
"TV, or Not." *Editor and Publisher*, 11 September 1954, 40.
"U.P. Editors List Ten Biggest Stories." *Editor and Publisher*, 20 December 1952, 9.
"War, Assassination Attempt to '50 List." *Editor and Publisher*, 16 December 1950, 10.
"Wechsler Implores ASNE to Speak Out Eloquently." *Editor and Publisher*, 9 May 1953, 7–8.
White, David Manning. "The Cult of Incredibility." *Nieman Reports*, April 1952, 10.
"The Woolard Resolution." *The APME Redbook 1952*, 12–15 November 1952, 227–229.

SCHOLARLY ARTICLES

Aucoin, James J. "The Re-emergence of American Investigative Journalism." *Journalism History*, 21:1 (Spring 1995): 3–15.
Elliot, P., and P. Schlesinger. "Some Aspects of Communism as a Cultural Category." *Media, Culture and Society*, 1:2 (1979): 195–210.
Hulten, Charles M. "The Impact of Senator Joseph McCarthy on the Press in the United States." *Gazette: International Journal of Science of the Press*, 4/1 (January 1958).
Miller Karen S. " 'Typical Slime by Joe McCarthy': Ralph McGill and the Anti-McCarthyism of the South." *American Journalism*, 13:3 (Summer 1996): 319–332.
Pauly, John J. "A Beginner's Guide to Doing Qualitative Research in Mass Communication." *Journalism Monographs*, 125 (February 1991): 1–29.
Pfaff, D. W. "The *St. Louis Post-Dispatch* Debate over Communism: 1940–1955." *Mass Communication Review*, 16(1/2)(1989): 52–62.

Rossi, John P. "The British Reaction to McCarthyism, 1950–54." *Mid-America: An Historical Review*, 70:1 (January 1988): 5–18.
Zelizer, Barbie. "Journalists as Interpretive Communities." *Critical Studies in Mass Communication*, 10 (1993): 219–237.

DISSERTATIONS AND MASTER'S THESES

Cade, Dozier C. "A Critical Analysis of the Role of American Daily Newspapers in the Current Encroachment by Government and Society on Freedom of Expression in the United States." Ph.D. diss., University of Iowa, 1954.
Deaver, Jean Franklin. "A Study of Senator Joseph R. McCarthy and 'McCarthyism' as Influences upon the News Media and the Evolution of Reportorial Method." Ph.D. diss., University of Texas, 1969.
Keuhl, Marshall Reed. "Philip C. Jessup: From America First to Cold War Interventionist." Ph.D. diss., Kent State University, 1985. Abstract in *Dissertation Abstracts International* 47(1986): 290A.
Morrison, Dennis Lewis. "Leadership in the Senate: A Study of Margaret Chase Smith's 1950 Declaration of Conscience Speech." Ph.D. diss., University of Houston, 1993. Abstract in *Dissertation Abstracts International* 54(1994): 2831A.
O'Brien, Michael James. "Senator Joseph McCarthy and Wisconsin: 1946–1957." Ph.D. diss., University of Wisconsin–Madison, 1971. Abstract in *Dissertation Abstracts International* 32 (1971): 1451A.
Selcraig, James Truett. "The Red Scare in the Midwest, 1945 to 1955: A State and Local Study." Ph.D. diss., University of Illinois Urbana–Champaign, 1981. Abstract in *Dissertation Abstracts International* 42 (1981): 2824A.
Weintraub, Rebecca. "Joseph McCarthy as Leader: An Image Analysis." Ph.D. diss., University of Southern California, 1983. Abstract in *Dissertation Abstracts International* 44 (1983): 1243A.

UNPUBLISHED LETTERS, MEMORANDUMS, AND PERSONAL COMMUNICATIONS

Canham, Erwin D., letter to Richard L. Strout, 18 August 1950. Richard L. Strout Papers, Weston, Mass.
Canham, Erwin D., memorandum to staff, September 1950. Richard L. Strout Papers, Weston, Mass.
Canham, Erwin D., letter to Richard L. Strout, 15 September 1950. Richard L. Strout Papers, Weston, Mass.
Canham, [Erwin] Mr., communication to Christian Science Board of Directors, 6 August 1952, 1–3. Church History Department, The First Church of Christ, Scientist, Boston, Mass.
Canham, Mr., memorandum to Mr. Davis, 27 January 1953. Richard L. Strout Papers, Weston, Mass.
[Canham, Erwin D.] E.D.C. memorandum to Mr. [Saville] Davis and Mr. [Don] Richardson, 12 June 1953. Richard L. Strout Papers, Weston, Mass.

Christian Science Board of Directors communication to Mr. Erwin D. Canham, 16 November 1950, 1–4. Church History Department, The First Church of Christ, Scientist, Boston, Mass.

Christian Science Board of Trustees communication to Christian Science Board of Directors, 22 April 1953. Church History Department, The First Church of Christ, Scientist, Boston, Mass.

Christian Science Board of Directors communication to Christian Science Publishing Society, 5 June 1953. Church History Department, The First Church of Christ, Scientist, Boston, Mass.

[Davis], Saville, confidential letter to Roscoe [Drummond], undated. Richard L. Strout Papers, Weston, Mass.

[Davis], Saville, personal note to RLS [Richard L. Strout], 16 September 1952. Richard L. Strout Papers, Weston, Mass.

[Davis, Saville R.] S.R.D. memorandum to American News Department and Roscoe Drummond, 15 June 1953. Richard L. Strout Papers, Weston, Mass.

[Davis, Saville R.] S.R.D. memorandum to American News Department and Roscoe Drummond, 17 June 1953. Richard L. Strout Papers, Weston, Mass.

[Davis] Saville, confidential memorandum to [Stringer, William H.] Bill, 24 February 1954. Richard L. Strout Papers, Weston, Mass.

[Davis], Saville, to Dick [Strout], 27 April 1954. Richard L. Strout Papers, Weston, Mass.

Davis, Saville, memorandum to Dick [Strout], 31 July 1958. Richard L. Strout Papers, Weston, Mass.

Drummond, Roscoe, confidential to Saville [Davis], 12 February 1953. Richard L. Strout Papers, Weston, Mass.

Gale, Bernays, Falk, and Eisner, to Richard L. Strout, 15 August 1950. Richard L. Strout Papers, Weston, Mass.

[Harsch, Joseph C.] JCH to Davis [Saville], 7 January 1954, Church History Department, The First Church of Christ, Scientist, Boston Mass.

[Harsch, Joseph C.] JCH to Saville [Davis], 21 June 1954, Church History Department, The First Church of Christ, Scientist, Boston, Mass.

Harsch, Joseph C., telephone conversation with author, 20 August 1996.

Hayward, Henry, telephone conversation with Professor John Williams, Principia College, Elsah, Ill., 3 July 1989, provided to author by Williams.

Oxnam, G. Bromley, to Mr. Joseph C. Harsch, 22 March 1954, Richard L. Strout Papers, Weston, Mass.

Sperling, Godfrey, Jr., telephone conversation with author, 29 April 1994.

Spike to Roscoe [Drummond], 3 November 1952. Richard L. Strout Papers, Weston, Mass.

Strout, Richard L., to Mother, Alan, Phyliss, and Nancy, 23 April 1950. Richard L. Strout Papers, Weston, Mass.

Strout, Richard L., to Erwin D. Canham, 4 September 1950. Richard L. Strout Papers, Weston, Mass.

Selected Bibliography

Strout, Richard L., notes on confirmation of Jessup-Stassen, 2 Oct.–9 Nov. 1951. Richard L. Strout. Weston, Mass.
[Strout, Richard L.] RLS to Dear Family, 1 April 1952. Richard L. Strout Papers, Weston, Mass.
Strout, Richard L., personal note to Saville [Davis], 16 September 1952. Richard L. Strout Papers, Weston, Mass.
[Strout, Richard L.] r to Dear Family, 29 September 1952. Richard L. Strout Papers, Weston, Mass.
Strout, Richard L., to Hon. George M. Humphrey, 3 February 1953. Richard L. Strout Papers, Weston, Mass.
Strout, Richard L., to Roscoe Drummond, 6 February 1953. Richard L. Strout Papers, Weston, Mass.
[Strout, Richard L.,] Dick, to Bill [Stringer] and Saville [Davis] (not confidential), on or about 24 February 1953. Richard L. Strout Papers, Weston, Mass.
Strout, Richard L., log Presidential Press Conference, 25 February 1953. Richard L. Strout Papers, Weston, Mass.
[Strout, Richard L.] Dick, personal note to Bert [Person Unknown], 5 August 1953, Richard L. Strout Papers, Weston, Mass.
Strout, [Richard L.] personal note to Self, 26 April 1954. Richard L. Strout Papers, Weston, Mass.
[Strout, Richard L.] r to Family, 29 April 1954. Richard L. Strout Papers, Weston, Mass.
[Strout], Dick, to Saville [Davis], (not sent—revised), 30 April 1954. Richard L. Strout Papers, Weston, Mass.
[Strout], Dick, to Saville [Davis] (not sent), 10 May 1954, Richard L. Strout Papers, Weston, Mass.
[Strout], Dick, to Saville [Davis], 17 May 1954, Richard L. Strout Papers, Weston, Mass.
[Strout, Richard L.] r to Susie, 9 November 1954. Richard L. Strout Papers, Weston, Mass.
[Strout, Richard L.] r to Folks, 3 December 1954. Richard L. Strout Papers, Weston, Mass.
[Strout], Dick, to Saville [Davis], 28 July 1958, Richard L. Strout Papers, Weston, Mass.
Tally Sheet about Number of Letters For and Against Joseph C. Harsch "Religious Controversy" Column, 26 January 1954, Church History Department, The First Church of Christ, Scientist, Boston, Mass.

INDEX

Acheson, Dean: McCarthy criticism, 1951, 42–43; National Press Club speech, 6
Amerasia: *Monitor* controversy, 20–22; OSS raid, 5, 20–22; Tydings investigation, 9–10
Americans for Democratic Action (ADA): accusations against, 3–4; McCarthy's Stevenson speech, 64–65
Army-McCarthy hearings, 125–31
Aronson, James, 46
ASNE (American Society of Newspaper Editors): Canham as president of, 6; freedom of the press, 47; Wechsler case, 93–96

Bayley, Edwin R., *Monitor* criticism, xi–xii, 148
Benton, William: Benton resolution, 38–40, 72–75; Hennings subcommittee investigation, 40
Blacklist: American Business Consultants, 2; "Red Channels," 2
Bohlen, Charles "Chip," 104–6

Bookburning, 96–101
Buckley, William F.: McCarthy February 20 speech, 8; McCarthy legacy today, 154
Budenz, Louis F., 13–14

Canham, Erwin D.: *Amerasia* controversy, 21; Army-McCarthy ABC broadcast, 128–29; ASNE president, 6; Eisenhower cabinet, 87–88; Eisenhower endorsement, 67; freedom of the press threat, 47–48, 77; Harsch–Catholic Church controversy, 109; McCarthyism term, 92; *Monitor*'s uniqueness, 22; Mother Church/Publishing Society dispute, xiv; staff credo, xv; Stevens not communist, 138; Strout not communist, 58–59; tenure at *Monitor*, xv
Censure: motion, 131–35; postcensure, 135–36; vote, 134
Chicago Tribune: Army-McCarthy hearings, 130; Benton resolution, 39–40, 74–75; censure vote, 135; Jes-

sup UN nomination, 45; Lattimore loyalty probe, 54–57; Lincoln Day speech, 7; Marshall controversy, 42; McCarthy death, 136–37; McCarthy primary victory, 1952, 62–63; McCarthy election victory 1952, 71; McCarthy/Stevenson speech, 66; midterm election 1950, 24–25; Murrow/McCarthy broadcast, 123–24; Rosenberg case, 46, 107; Tydings report, 19; Wechsler case, 130

Christian Science Monitor: Amerasia case, 21; Army-McCarthy hearings, 125–31; Bayley criticism, xi; Benton lawsuit, 75; Benton resolution, 39–40, 73–75; Bohlen nomination, 104–6; bookburning, 98–101; censure, 131–35; circulation, xi, xiv; Communist at *Monitor*, 137–40; Communist Party numbers, 25–26; conclusion, 155–56; creation, xii–xiv; *Denver Post*, 110; Dulles, 101–4; Eisenhower election endorsement, 66–69; Eisenhower election victory, 69–70; Eisenhower support of, 102–3; Gillette subcommittee investigation and report, 37–38, 50; Greek ships, 101; Harsch versus Catholic Church, 107–9; history, xiii–xvii; Jessup nomination, 44–45; Lattimore coverage letters, 54; Lattimore loyalty probe, 53–57, 151; letters to *Monitor*, 75–77; Lincoln Day speech, 7; MacArthur controversy, 40–41; Marshall controversy, 41–42; McCarthy death, 136–37; McCarthy election victory, 1952, 63–72; McCarthy early coverage, 11–15; McCarthy initial editorial, 10; McCarthy initial editorial cartoons, 11; McCarthy primary election victory 1952, 59–63; McCarthy/Stevenson speech, 63–67; McCarthy strategy 1953, 77; McCarthy viewed abroad, 14–15; McCarthyism term, 92; *McCarthyism: The Fight for America*, 57–59; midterm election 1950, 23–24; Murrow/McCarthy broadcast, 124–25; Nimitz Commission, 36; Peress case, 121–25; post-censure perspective, 135–36; pre-McCarthy Cold War coverage, 5–6; Republican Party Plans, 1952, 46; Rosenberg case, 46, 106–7, 153–54; Senate immunity, 12–13, 16–17, 42, 148; Smith's declaration of conscience speech, 17–18; status, xi, xvi–xvii, 96–97; Strout not communist, 58–59; summary of McCarthy coverage, 147–55; Tydings subcommittee investigation and report, 19, 150–51, 153; USIS, 98–101; VOA, 96–98, 149; Wechsler case, 93–96; Zwicker case, 122–23

Christian Science Publishing Society: creation, xiii; Mother Church dispute, xiv

Communism: hysteria, 1–5; internal threat, 14–15; party numbers, 3, 25–26, 35, 152

Daily Worker, 2, 4, 13, 35, 57–59

Davis, Saville R.: Eisenhower's cabinet and Strout, 87–88; Harsch Catholic Church controversy, 109; McCarthyism term, 92; Stevenson endorsement, 66–67; Strout's ban, 88–92; tenure at *Monitor*, xvi

Drummond, Roscoe: Bohlen nomination, 105; internal communism, 14–15; Jessup nomination, 43; Lattimore loyalty probe, 56; McCarthy viewed abroad, 14–15; Strout's ban, 88–92; tenure at *Monitor*, xv; Washington bureau chief, 43; Wechsler case, 93–94

Dulles, John Foster, 101–4

Eddy, Mary Baker: death, xiv; *Monitor* coverage and credo, xiii–xiv, 18, 148–55; *Monitor* founder, xiii

Index

Editor and Publisher: censure hearings close, 132–33; freedom of the press boycott, 78; McCarthyism, criticism of, 129; objectivity, 79; top newspapers, 27; Wechsler case, 93–94; 1951 poll, 47; 1952 poll, 61, 80; 1953 poll, 112
Elections, 1952, 59–72

First Church of Christ, Scientist: Board of Directors, xiv; Canham's "injure no man" memo, 22; founding, xiii; leader, xiii
Flanders, Ralph: censure motion, 131–32; Republican Party split, 123–24
Fried, Richard M., 66, 109

Gillette, Guy M.: subcommittee formation, 36; subcommittee hearings, 36–38; subcommittee report, 37
Gilstrap, Max K.: McCarthy background, 13; McCarthy election victory, 1952, 60–72
Greek shipping controversy, 101
Griffith, Robert, 135–36

Harsch, Joseph C.: Acheson, 43; Army-McCarthy hearings, 126–27, 130; Benton resolution, 38–39; Catholic Church controversy, 107–9, 154; Dulles, 103–4; Eisenhower and Republican Party, 136, 151; Gillette subcommittee, 150; Lattimore loyalty probe, 56; McCarthy death, 137; MacArthur controversy, 40–41, midterm election, 1950, 23–24; *Monitor* status, xvii; Republican Party plans, 1952, 45; Rosenberg case, 106; State Department, 56–57; tenure at *Monitor*, xvi; Tydings investigation and report, 10, 18–19, 150; VOA, 98
House Un-American Activities Committee (HUAC), 1, 4

Jessup, Phillip C., 43–45

Lattimore, Dr. Owen: loyalty probe and indictment, 53–57; McCarthy charges and rebuttal, 12–16

MacArthur, Douglas, 40–41
Marshall, George Catlett, 41–42
McCarran, Pat: Lattimore loyalty probe, 53–57, recommendations, 55–56
McCarthy, Joseph R.: Acheson, conflict with, 1951, 42–43; Benton resolution, 38–40; Bohlen nomination, 104–6; censure, 131–35; death, 136–37; Dulles, 101–4; election, xiii; Gillette subcommittee, 38; Greek ships, 101; Jessup nomination challenge, 43–45; Lattimore attacks, 12, 53–57; Lincoln Day speech, 7; Malmedy, 4; Marshall speech, 41–42; Murrow broadcast, 123–25; mythology, 4–5; primary victory, 1952, 62; Smith's declaration of conscience speech, 17–18; State Department investigation, 10–11; State Department speech, 8; Stevenson speech, 63–67; strategy 1953, 77; suing Benton, 72–73; Tydings defeat role, 25; Tydings defeat investigation, 36–38; VOA/USIS, 96–101; Wechsler case, 92–96; Zwicker attack, 121–23
McCarthyism: definition, xii–xiii; *Denver Post*, 110; events leading to, 1–5; *McCarthyism: The Fight for America*, 57–59; *Monitor* use of term, 92; Wechsler case, 94
Media Self-Critique: 1950, 26–27; 1951, 46–48; 1952, 77–80; 1953, 109–12
Midterm elections, 1950, 22–25
Milwaukee Journal: Army-McCarthy hearings, 128; Benton resolution, 74; Bohlen nomination, 104–5; censure vote, 135; Gillette subcommittee report, 38; Jessup nomination,

44; Marshall controversy, 42; McCarthy primary victory, 1952, 61–62; McCarthy/Stevenson speech, 66; Murrow/McCarthy broadcast, 124; Smith's declaration of conscience speech, 18; Tydings report, 19; VOA/USIS, 97, 99; Wechsler case, 94–95; Zwicker case, 123

Murrow, Edward R.: McCarthy show, xi, 123–25; Shirer firing, xvi

Navasky, Victor S., 96

New York Post, 92–96

New York Times: Army-McCarthy hearings, 130; Benton resolution, 39, 75; Bohlen nomination, 105; censure, 132, 134–35; Gillette subcommittee report, 38; Lattimore loyalty probe, 55–57; Lincoln Day speech, 7, 10; MacArthur controversy, 41; McCarthy death, 137; McCarthy effect, 147, 155; McCarthy election victory, 1952, 70–71; McCarthy initial editorial, 10; McCarthy primary victory, 1952, 62–63; McCarthy/Stevenson speech, 65–66; midterm election 1950, 24, 153; Rosenberg case, 106; Smith's declaration of conscience speech, 18; Tydings investigation and report, 13, 19; VOA/USIS, 99–100; Wechsler case, 95; Welch versus McCarthy, 130

Oshinsky, David M.: Bohlen nomination, 105–6; postcensure, 135–36

Peress, Dr. Irving, 121–23

"Red Channels," 2

Reeves, Thomas C.: Catholic press, 107; McCarthy February 20 speech, 8

Rosenberg case, 46, 106–7

Rovere, Richard H.: McCarthy Feb. 20 speech, 8; McCarthy/Stevenson speech, 66; postcensure, 135–36

San Francisco Examiner: Bohlen nomination, 105; censure, 132, 135; Gillette subcommittee, 36, 38; Lattimore loyalty probe, 55–57; MacArthur controversy, 41; Marshall controversy, 41–42; McCarthy death, 137; McCarthy election victory, 1952, 62, 71; McCarthy/Stevenson speech, 66; midterm election, 1950, 25; Tydings report, 19; VOA/USIS, 97, 100; Welch versus McCarthy, 130

Sawyer, Roland: bookburning, 100; Lattimore loyalty probe; 54–57; Welch versus McCarthy, 129–30

Secret World of American Communism, 138–39

Smith Act, 1

Smith, Margaret Chase: declaration of conscience speech, 17–18; denounces Republican Party plans, 45; 1952 McCarthy criticism, 73–74

Stanford, Neal: Benton resolution, 75, 90; Bohlen nomination, 104; Lattimore loyalty probe, 55; McCarthy 1953 strategy, 77

Stringer, William H.: Army-McCarthy hearings, 125; censure, 132; McCarthy death, 136–37; Murrow/McCarthy broadcast, 124; Strout ban, 89–91; tenure at *Monitor*, xv–xvi

Strout, Richard L.: Acheson, 42–43; *Amerasia* case, 20–21; Army-McCarthy hearings, 126–31; awards, xvii; ban from covering McCarthy, 88–92, 154–55; Bayley book quote, xii; Benton resolution, 72–73; Bohlen nomination, 104; Budenz testimony, 14; career summary, xvii–xviii; censure, 132, 134; Dulles, 102; Eisenhower's cabinet,

Index

87–88; election, 1952, 60; *Farewell to the Model T*, xvii; Gillette subcommittee, 37, 150; HUAC, 6; Jessup nomination, 43–44; Lattimore loyalty probe, 37, 53–54, 151; Maud, xvii; McCarthy election victory, 1952, 71; McCarthy finances, 74–75; McCarthy, personal opinion of, 15; McCarthy State Department communist numbers, 16; McCarthy/Stevenson speech, 63–65; McCarthy viewed abroad, 15; *McCarthyism: The Fight for America*, 57–58, 153; midterm election 1950, 22–24; Nimitz Commission, 36; Objectivity, 17, 152; Republican Party plans, 1952, 45–46; Smith declaration of conscience speech, 73–74; Stevenson for President, 66–67; Stevenson versus Eisenhower press, 68–69; *TRB: Views and Perspectives on the Presidency*, xvii; Tydings report, 18–19, 150; Tydings subcommittee, 9–18; Zwicker case, 122

Taft, Robert A., 45–46
Truman, Harry S.: Jessup UN nomination, 43–45; Loyalty Review Board, 2; McCarthy controversy, 40–41; Nimitz Commission, 35–36; Truman Doctrine, 1–2; Executive Order 9835, 2
Tydings, Millard: election loss to Butler, 25; Gillette subcommittee investigation, 36–38; Tydings subcommittee, 8–9, Tydings subcommittee report, 18–19

United States Information Service (USIS), 98–101

Voice of America (VOA), 96–98

Wechsler, James A., 92–96, 112
Welch, Joseph N., 126, 129–31

Zwicker, Ralph W., 121–23

About the Author

LAWRENCE N. STROUT is Gibbons Distinguished Professor of Journalism at Mississippi University for Women. Professor Strout was a broadcast journalist from 1975 to 1989, prior to his career as a teacher and researcher concentrating on broadcast and print journalism. His essays on American journalism history have appeared as book chapters as well as articles in *Journal of American Culture* and *Media History Digest*.